The Cult of the Dead in
a Chinese Village

EMILY M. AHERN

The Cult of the Dead in
a Chinese Village

STANFORD UNIVERSITY PRESS
Stanford, California   1973

Stanford University Press
Stanford, California
© 1973 by the Board of Trustees of the
Leland Stanford Junior University
Printed in the United States of America
ISBN 0-8047-0835-5
LC 72-97202
Published with the assistance of
the Andrew W. Mellon Foundation

To my parents, Henry and Zoë Godshalk

Preface

WHEN I went to Taiwan in 1969 to study ancestor worship and lineage organization in a Chinese village, I decided on Ch'inan, a village in northern Taiwan, as an excellent location for research: with four large ancestral halls, it seemed likely that ancestor worship and lineages would be important and elaborate there. No other village in the area gives the casual onlooker such obvious evidence of the strength of an ancestral cult. After my husband and I were introduced in the community by a man who was born there but had found more lucrative employment in the nearby market town of Sanhsia, the problem of where to live solved itself. When a collateral relative of his, a lonely old lady, heard we needed a place to live, she virtually demanded that we move in with her. Most of her family had left home—only one of her sons was home regularly—and so she was able to give us a bedroom and to let us share kitchen, dining, and entertaining facilities. Our cook occupied a section of another room.

We remained in this house for the duration of our stay. People in Ch'inan seemed receptive enough to our presence, not least because the accessibility of our household meant they could satisfy their curiosity about us. They had little trouble understanding why my husband was there. He commuted to Taipei to study Chinese philosophy, and though at twenty-five he seemed an unbelievably old student, his role was still clear and acceptable. But they had considerably more difficulty with my activities. My stock reply in response to questions about what I was doing was "studying old customs and practices." This conveyed the idea that my doings were harmless, and, more important, not connected with the government. But it failed to explain how an adult could spend so much time at something that is sheer leisure for the villagers—talking to people—and a standard greeting when I appeared came to be, "Oh, you've come to play again." Any ease with which I was received was largely due to the presence of the nineteen-year-old unmarried woman who served as my assistant during most of my stay. Her father owned a sawmill in one section of the village, and as far as I was able to determine, was highly respected by most of the villagers. She acted at first as my language interpreter from Mandarin to Taiwanese, and then when my Taiwanese improved, as interpreter of social situations, saving me from making blunders and unwittingly asking embarrassing questions.

After the initial stir over my arrival in the community, my assistant and I, largely because of our sex and age, made a relatively inconspicuous pair. We were often able to attend major functions in Ch'inan such as weddings and funerals without being treated as honored guests. This meant that I could concentrate on observing ritual minutiae rather than sitting with other guests out of sight of most of what was happening. Males in Chinese society are exceedingly concerned with extending formal politeness on ceremonial occasions, especially to other men, so that when my husband accompanied me anywhere, people felt more called on to extend the courtesies due a guest. The reception given my questioning and observing varied greatly. Some people were hostile and suspicious from the start and remained so until the end. Others overcame their initial doubt and at least tolerated my curious activities. Still others seemed genuinely to enjoy conversations about Chinese customs and would freely contribute their insights to problems and puzzles I encountered. Virtually all the material in this book, and the inspiration for many of the ideas, I owe to the kindness and thoughtfulness of the people of Ch'inan. I wish to thank in particular our landlady for her hospitality, tolerance, and good humor, and my assistant for her perseverance and unfailing loyalty.

I owe many debts as well to those who helped me transform raw data into the doctoral dissertation on which this book is based.

To Professor Robert J. Smith I extend my thanks for his generous help and careful supervision of my dissertation at Cornell University. To Professor Arthur Wolf, of Stanford University, I am indebted for help in choosing a field site and for granting me access to government records that he obtained only with considerable personal effort. In addition, I am grateful for his perceptive comments on the manuscript and for his consistent aid and support throughout the period of research. To Professor Maurice Freedman I owe a special debt; it was largely the ideas he presented in his own analysis of Chinese ancestor worship that led me to study this subject. That I have been critical of some of his ideas should be taken as an indication of their ability to stimulate and provoke thought. I am grateful also for his criticisms of an earlier draft of this book. Still others read and commented on portions of the manuscript, and I here thank each of them: Professors Don De-Glopper and John McCoy; Steven Harrell; Bruce Holbrook; and Margery Wolf. I would also like to thank Professor Chang Kwang-chih of Yale University, who wrote the characters in the Character List; and my father, Henry Godshalk, who developed some of the prints in the picture section. Above all, my thanks go to Dennis Ahern for his patience and understanding and for the help he gave both in the field and during the preparation of the manuscript.

Financial support for research from September 1969 to September 1970 was provided by a Fulbright-Hays Fellowship and a grant from the China Program of Cornell University; a Predoctoral Fellowship from the American Association of University Women guaranteed the leisure to write the manuscript the following year; and costs of preparing the manuscript for publication were defrayed by a grant from the Concilium on International and Area Studies of Yale University. I am most grateful to all these agencies for the support I received.

E.M.A.

Contents

Eight pages of pictures follow page 130

Introduction

TAIWAN IS a country of great ethnic diversity; Chinese society is a subject of great complexity. This study deals primarily with Ch'inan, a village in northern Taiwan whose residents belong to one ethnic group: Hokkien-speaking Chinese whose ancestors made the journey from the southeast coast of mainland China over 200 years ago. And it deals almost exclusively with one aspect of life in that village: the related complex of institutions associated with the care and management of the dead. That is, I have not attempted anything like a complete, well-rounded ethnography, but have tried to concentrate on those aspects of community organization that most influence the form of the ancestral cult: the internal organization of the lineage communities in the village and their relationship to each other in the larger community of Ch'inan.

In Part 1 I describe the history of Ch'inan and how the village is organized today, providing necessary background for understanding the way the form of the community affects the cult of the dead. To this end, several kinds of material are presented. I have used historical records, both those kept by the villagers and those written by outsiders, and including not only records intended for posterity, like lineage genealogies, but also such things as lists of contributors to community projects posted on the walls of temples and ancestral halls, which reflect the life of the time. To these I add my own observations of incidents that involved part or all of the community and the dynamics that they revealed. Finally, I give the villagers' view of the community and how it came to be as it is.

In the first four chapters of Part 2, I look at the sociological correlates of ancestor worship in ancestral halls or before domestic altars. This is where the influence of the shape of the community on the form of the cult can be most clearly seen. In addition, some aspects of worshiping ancestral tablets lead into a different area of concern: the villagers' conception of the reciprocal obligations and duties of the living and the dead and what effect their expectations have on the way the ancestors are worshiped.

In Chapters 10–13 I turn to the darker side of ancestor worship, in which the dead stand out as dangerous creatures capable of harming and frightening the living. An attempt is made to account for the malevolent character of the ancestors in a cross-cultural context, and by means of a local myth, to present the villagers' own view of the nature of the ancestors. Finally, I try to show in the most graphic way possible how people think of the dead in the underworld by recounting at length one man's visit to his ancestors there under trance.

In the concluding chapter the Ch'inan case is subordinated and placed in a wider perspective. First, it is compared to a nearby community with a quite different historical development. Here it is possible to see how ritual acts and objects take slightly different forms under different conditions. Then, taking Ch'inan as but one particular case among many, often very different, cases in mainland China and other parts of Taiwan, I seek answers in other Chinese communities to some of the major questions I raised for Ch'inan: how the form of the community affects the cult of the ancestors; how different reciprocal obligations between the living and the dead affect ancestor worship; what determines the malevolence or benevolence of the ancestors; in what ways people react to the obligations of ancestor worship. In this undertaking, my purpose is to suggest tentatively what conditions would lead to different answers to these questions and what series of related traits would be most likely to be found together in a single Chinese community.

PART ONE

The Setting

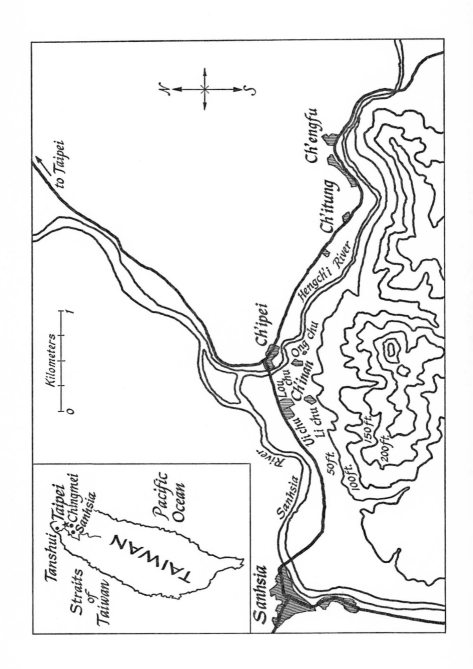

Straits of Taiwan

Tanshui
Taipei
Chingmei
Sanhsia

TAIWAN

Pacific Ocean

to Taipei

Kilometers
0   1

Ch'ipei

Hengch'i River

Ch'itung

Ch'engfu

Ong chu
Ui chu Lou chu
Li chu Ch'inan

Sanhsia River

50 ft.
100 ft.
150 ft.
200 ft.

Sanhsia

CHAPTER 1

The Village in Space and Time

Near the southern edge of the Taipei basin in northern Taiwan lies the village of Ch'inan, a cluster of four roughly compact settlements. In front of them stretches an expanse of rice fields, green or golden as the seasons change. Behind them rise the jagged peaks of the central mountain range, covered with tangled, teeming vegetation. The shape of the district is roughly triangular, with the mountains forming a wide base. The two sides are formed by the Sanhsia River on the west and the Hengch'i River on the east. The Hokkien-speaking Chinese who crossed to Taiwan from the mainland in the early eighteenth century chose the area for a permanent settlement because of its proximity to both water and mountains.

Today the residents of Ch'inan live in four settlements, called *chu* in Taiwanese. Each is dominated politically by the members of a distinct patrilineal lineage bearing a different surname.* But at the same time, each is a territorial unit as well; all residents of the area surrounding the houses of the Ong lineage members, for example, are said to be residents of Ong *chu*, whether or not they are related to the Ong lineage. The other three *chu* are known as Li *chu*, Lou *chu*, and Ui *chu*. In the center of each of these settle-

---

* For romanizing Hokkien words and names I follow the system outlined in Nicholas C. Bodman, *Spoken Amoy Hokkien* (Kuala Lumpur: 1955). Tone marks have been omitted in the text but are added in the Character List, p. 273. All the persons mentioned in the text have been given pseudonyms, and these pseudonyms have been substituted where necessary (in brackets) in quoted material. I have romanized names of places and administrative units in Mandarin, using standard post-office spelling for well-known places and the Wade-Giles system for the rest.

ments, and in some cases towering over them, is an ancestral hall that houses the tablets for the deceased members of the lineage.

In the first few weeks after I moved into the Ong settlement in Ch'inan, several people gave me unsolicited sketches of their social world. A common description was: "All the people living around here are Ongs, so we call this place Ong *chu*. There are also Lis, Lous, and Uis, who live in Li *chu*, Lou *chu*, and Ui *chu*. These four *chu* together make up Ch'inan *li* [an administrative unit usually corresponding to a village]. Across the stream are Ch'ipei *li* and Ch'itung *li*. These two *li*, together with Ch'inan, are called Hengch'i." The most immediate links Ch'inan has with the world outside the village are through these two neighboring *li*, Ch'ipei and Ch'itung. Ch'ipei, only a five-minute walk away, is the local market center for both Ch'inan and Ch'itung. Here women shop daily for vegetables and inexpensive household goods. In addition, Ch'ipei has served as a proving ground for some Ch'inan residents, who have attempted to set up snack shops, noodle factories, or other business enterprises there. If their businesses have prospered, these entrepreneurs may stand an economic and social notch above their relatives in the agricultural village across the stream.

Just as many residents of Ch'ipei consider Ch'inan their ancestral home, so do many people living in Ch'itung. Ch'inan's residents moved to Ch'itung not to open businesses but rather to clear usable land, either near the river for rice paddy or in the mountains for tea plants. Even Ch'inan residents who have no relatives in Ch'itung often go there: an elementary school serves the children in all three *li*, and a coal mine provides wage labor for many of the young men of the three communities.

Ch'inan, Ch'ipei, and Ch'itung, together known as Hengch'i, thus have both economic and social ties. Beyond this they take part in a rotating ritual cycle that is both an expression of their other connections and, ordinarily, a reinforcement of them. This ritual cycle involves a worship pageant for two gods, one a warrior, the other a physician, known jointly as the Ang-kong. Together these gods are brought once a year to Hengch'i from their temple in Chingmei, a town located northeast of Hengch'i on the other side of a low range of hills. My informants in Ch'inan knew little of the history of their connection with the temple, almost ten miles away by the direct, transmontane route. The temple manager could tell me only that the Ang-kong were the primary gods in the district of Anch'i on the mainland, where the ancestors of most Hengch'i residents originated. Whatever the historical facts, residents of Ch'inan say they continue to worship the Ang-kong because they are powerful gods who saved the people of Hengch'i from disaster twice in the past. According to one story, a plague of locusts had descended on the crops in the area and threatened to destroy everything in sight. After the images of the Ang-kong were brought from Chingmei and the gods beseeched to dispel the insects, a huge flock of black crows arrived, devoured all the insects, and flew away. According to another story, a group of Hengch'i residents engaged in battle with the aborigines were badly outnumbered and faced imminent defeat. But suddenly, terrified looks came over the aborigines' faces, and they fled to the mountains in rout. Later the Hengch'i people heard that the aborigines had seen two gigantic figures on horseback waving yellow flags and charging down on them. Since the Ang-kong characteristically carry yellow flags, the villagers knew that the gods had appeared to save them from destruction.

In gratitude for the debt they owe the Ang-kong, the people present an opera and food offerings to the gods once a year. Responsibility for this worship (*pai-pai*) rotates among the three communities, Ch'inan, Ch'ipei, and Ch'itung, each carrying out the festivities for one year. When Ch'inan's time comes, the responsibility is in turn rotated among the four settlements. So, if the *pai-pai* is held by Ch'itung one year, it will be held by Ch'ipei the next year, and by the Ong settlement in Ch'inan the third year. Then, three years later, when it is Ch'inan's turn again, the Li settlement will hold the *pai-pai*, and so on. For three or four days beginning on the twenty-sixth of the eighth lunar month, the settlement in charge must provide opera performances or puppet

shows for the entertainment of the gods and the residents of
Hengch'i.* The year I lived in Ch'inan, the opera was held in
Ch'ipei. At night loudspeakers amplified the voices of the actors
and the music of the accompanying instruments so loudly that
the opera was perfectly audible on the other side of the river.
Nonetheless, nearly all the residents of Ch'inan (and Ch'itung)
spent at least part of every evening in Ch'ipei, enjoying the same
kind of entertainment that they themselves might have to finance
in one or two years. The rotating Ang-kong *pai-pai* marks out in
space the three socially and economically linked *li* and delineates
important spatial subdivisions within them.

Discussion of the Ang-kong *pai-pai* leads naturally into discussion of another ritual cycle. We noted that when responsibility for
the Ang-kong *pai-pai* devolves on Ch'inan, the responsibility in
turn rotates to one of the four *chu*. This subdivision in space is
marked again in another ritual cycle, this one for the benefit of
Tho-te-kong, the earth god. Unlike the Ang-kong, Tho-te-kong is
not a powerful being, able to appear at a moment of crisis and
save his patrons from danger. Both in his images and in his char-
acterization by actors, he is depicted as a jolly old man with white
whiskers and rosy cheeks. When he is impersonated at funeral ceremonies, he hobbles around to the accompaniment of jaunty music,
scaring and delighting the children by poking his cane at them
or trying to pinch them. He has a lively sense of humor and
makes jokes at the expense of everyone, especially the anthro-
pologist. Ordinarily his antics are only a prelude to his demand
for money, which he requires before he will fulfill his service of
guiding the soul of the dead over a narrow bridge into the underworld. But even his demand for payment is filled with good-
natured humor. In a typical routine the actor impersonating the
god claims that he must have a little more money because he has
a cold and needs expensive medicine, at which point he sneezes
convincingly. Tho-te-kong must also be paid before he will render

* Both a lunar and a solar calendar are used in Taiwan. Dates for *pai-pais*
are usually in terms of the lunar calendar, which places the first of the year
in the month of February.

other services—as a frequent analogy has it, "like a local policeman who wants some money on the side before he will help you out."

Since Tho-te-kong's primary jurisdiction is over the land and its products, he is worshiped before each of the two yearly rice crops is gathered in the hope of increasing the yield. On these occasions he is worshiped separately by land-owning units, usually single households. Seen as the protector of the earth, the crops that it yields, and the people who live on it, he is also worshiped by socially defined groups living on sections of land whose boundaries are defined by social ties. Thus each *li* in Hengch'i presents its own community-organized *pai-pai* to Tho-te-kong once a year. In Ch'inan responsibility for this *pai-pai* rotates among the four settlements, just as the Ang-kong *pai-pai* does, but in this case Ch'ipei and Ch'itung are not part of the rotation system; each has its own separate organization. The Ch'inan settlement responsible for the *pai-pai* presents an opera, which is usually held in the open area in front of the ancestral hall. But despite the opera's location within one settlement, it is said to be for the benefit of the Tho-te-kong in the centrally located Tho-te-kong temple, which belongs to the whole *li*. In addition, whether or not the Ong settlement has the responsibility for the rotating *pai-pai*, its residents present an opera for the benefit of the Tho-te-kong image located in their own temple. The relationship between these two Tho-te-kong temples will be discussed in detail later; we will see that, much as the rotating Tho-te-kong *pai-pai* delineates relevant territorial distinctions among the four *chu*, the two temples also mark a significant spatial division.

The importance of the division of the *li* into four *chu* is apparent from the extent of the ritual emphasis that division receives: yet another *pai-pai* cycle rotates among the four *chu*. Co-su-kong, the god who is the beneficiary of this cycle, has his headquarters in a large temple in Sanhsia, the market town located a few miles west of Ch'inan. Like the Ang-kong, he is said to have been brought to Sanhsia from Anch'i on the mainland; but unlike them, Co-su-kong is primarily thought of as a skillful physician, though tales are told of his prowess in battle and his ability to protect soldiers in combat. Many times while I was in the village, an image of Co-su-kong was brought from the temple to diagnose illnesses and prescribe treatment. Most often Co-su-kong would communicate his will by possessing the body of one or more of the villagers, who would, in trance, speak the words of the god or write them on a table covered with sand. These sessions were usually organized by a small group, perhaps the immediate relatives of the sick person. The rotating *pai-pai* for Co-su-kong operates in exactly the same way as the Tho-te-kong cycle, the responsibility passing annually to each Ch'inan settlement in turn. For this *pai-pai*, too, Ch'ipei and Ch'itung have their own organizations. But in every case it is quite definitely conceived as a community activity. I was told that all residents of the Ch'inan community responsible for the *pai-pai* could participate, regardless of their surname. In this way the rotating *pai-pai* for Co-su-kong reiterates the spatial division of the *li* into four *chu*.

Co-su-kong is also the recipient of an extremely elaborate *pai-pai* organized by the managers of the Sanhsia temple. Every year each family bearing the chosen surname out of a list of seven major surnames in the area is responsible for killing a pig and presenting it with many other offerings to Co-su-kong. Since each of the Ch'inan settlements is occupied in the main by families with one surname, when the killing of the pigs is assigned to one of the surnames represented in Ch'inan, it tends to involve a majority of residents in one of the settlements. Yet this *pai-pai* is not conceived, nor does it operate, as a community activity. Bearers of the chosen surname, for example, Ong, participate whatever their residence; residents of an area in which most people bear the chosen surname, Ong, do not participate unless they are Ongs. Participation in this *pai-pai* tends to be restricted to those whose ancestors were indigenous to the area around Sanhsia. The members of one family that moved to Ch'inan from southern Taiwan told me they did not offer a pig to Co-su-kong because "only the people of Sanhsia and thereabouts have that custom."

Taken together, the ritual cycles for Tho-te-kong, Co-su-kong, and the Ang-kong show the most important connections between Ch'inan and other areas and the primary spatial divisions within the village. The rotation of the Ang-kong *pai-pai* among Ch'inan, Ch'ipei, and Ch'itung adds a ritual tie to the social and economic bonds within Hengch'i. The rotation of the Tho-te-kong and Co-su-kong *pai-pais* within Ch'inan delineates clearly the four separate *chu* and, at the same time, shows their interconnection as parts of Ch'inan. The most far-reaching ritual connection between Ch'inan and the outside world is in the killing of the pigs for Co-su-kong. Participation in this ritual ties Ch'inan's residents to a wide area: the residents of Sanhsia *chen* (an administrative division roughly corresponding to a township) and several *chen* adjacent to Sanhsia are all included in the *pai-pai*. Every year, when the residents of this area make offerings to Co-su-kong, they express both their common residence in contiguous *chen* and their common origin from the same area of the mainland. It is said that the ancestors of those who worship Co-su-kong today originally lived and worshiped him in the county of Anch'i in Fukien province on the mainland.

The four rotating *pai-pais* for the gods locate Ch'inan and its subdivisions in space. Other, more commonplace rituals locate the residents of Ch'inan in time. Many times each year every family must pay homage to its ancestors, including all direct ascendants back to the founding ancestors of the lineage. This means that people must keep track of at least five generations of ascendants between those now living and the ancestors who first settled in Ch'inan. On the death-day anniversary of each of these forebears, the living descendants must prepare a rich feast. Chickens are slaughtered and expensive foods such as pork liver or pig's feet are purchased. In addition, the women may make a kind of sticky cake of glutinous rice. After these delicacies are presented to the ancestor being worshiped, they are consumed by the family and probably some guests from the neighborhood as well. In this way the family reaffirms its ties to the past through its continuity with a line of deceased members stretching back to the days of the settlement of Ch'inan.

The people of Ch'inan are firmly rooted in the past; their history and origins are important to them. Virtually everyone in the four Ch'inan lineages knows that the ancestors of all four lineages lived near the coast of the Chinese mainland, in Anch'i *hsien* (county), Fukien province, before coming to Taiwan. The places of origin listed in the four lineage genealogies indicate that each family lived in a different place in Anch'i *hsien*. The Lis and Ongs lived closest to each other, occupying two different settlements, or *chu*, in the same *li*.

According to oral tradition, the founding ancestors of the four Ch'inan lineages left Anch'i about 200 years ago. After crossing the Taiwan straits, they landed at the mouth of the Tanshui River, about 20 miles northwest of Ch'inan. From there they traveled inland, and most of them finally settled in Ch'inan, where the earth was good for rice, water was plentiful, and mountain land was available for planting tea. The Uis have a slightly different history; they settled first in a nearby area and only later moved to Ch'inan to live with their acquaintances from the mainland, the Lous. All four groups agree that the Uis settled in Ch'inan last; and all also agree that the Lis must have arrived sometime before the Lous, because the wife of the first Lou settler was the daughter of the first Li settler. As for the question of who came into the area earlier, the Lis or the Ongs, opinions differ: the Lis claim that they were first, and that the Ongs came afterward; the Ongs say it was the other way around.

The fact is, so few documents are available on the settlement of the area that a historically accurate reconstruction cannot be made. The *Taipei Hsien Gazetteer* states: "Ch'inan was settled at the beginning of the Ch'ien-lung period [1736–95] by Ch'uan-chou people named [Li]" (p. 9). Comparing that statement with information given in the lineage genealogies, we find that the first Li settler lived too late (1746–1822) to have arrived as a young man at the time cited by the *Gazetteer*. The same is true of the first Lou settler, who lived even later (1764–1827). As we have seen, the Uis came later still.

The Ongs, however, have an oral tradition that four Ong brothers settled in Ch'inan considerably earlier than the two brothers who are now the focal ancestors of the Ch'inan Ong lineage. In fact, the genealogy ([Wang] P'an Shih 1956) lists a set of four siblings two generations above the two focal ancestors, and says of one of them, the grandfather of the two focal ancestors: "With great effort, he crossed to Taiwan and began to settle and cultivate the earth. Because he was raising descendants, he settled in Hengch'i and built a house. At this time the aborigines in the mountains were uncivilized. Because they were very fierce, extreme strength was needed to protect any enterprise. When he grew old, he returned to the mainland, fell sick, and died." There is supporting evidence for the Ong tradition—an old grave for the wife of this man lies just behind the Ong settlement. Moreover, the life-spans of the man (1705–77) and his wife (1706–67) are exactly right for them to have settled in the area as young adults at the time cited by the *Gazetteer*. If the evidence of the date given in the *Gazetteer*, the information in the Ong genealogy, and the gravestone are taken together, it would appear that the Ongs settled in the area first, perhaps a full 20 years before the Lis.

Once the original settlers chose Ch'inan as their home, the first order of business was doubtless to clear the land and construct flat paddy fields with an irrigation system to flood them. It is likely that the Ongs constructed their system separately, using two streams that flow from the mountains behind them. These probably provided enough water to irrigate the Ong land both in back and in front of their settlement. The Lis, located near the mountains, would have had first use of water from a large stream emerging behind them. Its waters are used today to irrigate some land belonging to the Lous in front of their settlement. The Lis and the Lous probably worked together to construct a system that watered first the Li land near the mountains and then the Lou land near the road. Likewise, the Uis, who own large amounts of land between the highway and the Sanhsia River, would have had first use of a stream that comes out of the mountains to the west of their settlement. Its waters were once used as well to irrigate fields farther downstream belonging to the Lous. The Lous must also have cooperated with the Uis to provide for irrigation of their land across the road.

Although it seems certain there was considerable cooperation among surname groups to construct the irrigation network in the beginning, it also seems likely that minimal cooperation was necessary to regulate the system once it began operating, for the area's rainfall is not only plentiful, averaging 83 inches a year, but also fairly evenly distributed throughout the year, with about 60 per cent falling during the five months May through September (Hsieh 1964: 53). In addition, access to water is well distributed. Besides the two substantial water courses that bound the area, there are four smaller streams originating in the mountains behind the village and flowing through the settlements. During the year I was there, I discovered no evidence of quarreling over water rights; the rivers and streams did not dry up, and farmers claimed they virtually always had all the water they needed. The initial building of an irrigation network was probably one of the first instances of cooperation among the settlements. Once completed, however, it seems to have provoked neither continuing conflict nor further cooperative effort.*

As hinted by the section of the Ong genealogy quoted above, another important concern of the first settlers was to defend themselves against the attacks of the aborigines who had been ousted from their lands. The *Gazetteer* states (p. 9), "At the time of settlement, because untamed aborigines were causing trouble, people named [Ong], [Lou], and [Ui] came to cooperate with the [Lis] in resisting them and to begin developing the land." From the start, then, the four groups were thrown together, not only in the same geographical area but also in a cooperative struggle to ward

* In contrast, in an area of southern Taiwan described by Burton Pasternak (1972a: 26–31; 1972b: 193–213) rainfall is more unevenly distributed so that about 80 per cent falls between May and September, and water is thus often insufficient for rice cultivation. Consequently, elaborate systems of cooperation to maintain irrigation networks have developed.

off attacks from hostile strangers. Their location on the same side
of the river, on a section of land enclosed by a mountain range,
made their settlements accessible to one another and made them
natural allies against their enemies. The amphitheater-like nature
of the area between the mountains and the two rivers, together
with the fact that bamboo was traditionally grown along the banks
of the two rivers, perhaps led to the first Chinese name for this
area: Within the Circle of Bamboo. Although most of the bamboo
is gone now, Ch'inan is still referred to by that name.

The early settlers at first had to rely on cooperation with the
other settlers "Within the Circle of Bamboo" in their struggle
against the aborigines, but eventually they had the help of an
organized guard line, which was established by the Chinese government during the reign of Ch'ien-lung (1736–95) and maintained after the Japanese occupation in 1895. At the farthest reach
of mountain territory then occupied by Chinese, a wide swath was
cut in the forest, guardhouses were set up on stilts, and guards
were posted to prevent or at least warn of attacks from aborigines.
That this line was still maintained in the mountains behind Ch'i-
nan in the Japanese period means that for over 100 years the residents of Ch'inan were subject to attack from unpacified aborigines
(*Report* 1911: 11–13).

These attacks were deadly and vicious in nature. As late as 1903
James W. Davidson, a war correspondent who accompanied the
Japanese expedition to occupy Taiwan, could write of an area
near Ch'inan, "On several occasions the savages had swooped down
upon the little Chinese villages, killing a dozen or so of the peas-
ants and flying back to their forest home with the heads" (pp. 253–
54). But the violence was not all one-sided, as Davidson makes clear
(pp. 254–55):

One horrible feature of the campaign against the savages was the sale by
the Chinese in open market of savage flesh. . . . After killing a savage, . . .
the body was then either divided among its captors and eaten, or sold to
wealthy Chinese and even to high officials, who disposed of it in a like
manner. The kidney, liver, heart, and soles of the feet were considered
the most desirable portions, and were ordinarily cut up into very small
pieces, boiled, and eaten somewhat in the form of soup. . . . During the

outbreak of 1891, savage flesh was brought in—in baskets—the same as pork, and sold like pork in the open markets of Tokoham [Tach'i, a town south of Sanhsia] before the eyes of all.

In corroboration of this account, some of the Ch'inan villagers told me they had heard tales of eating aborigines' flesh from their ancestors. The meat was said to have been the sweetest and most delicious of all delicacies.

Beyond the settlers' efforts to clear the land and ward off the attacks of the aborigines, we know little of the early history of the area. But in accounts of the Japanese occupation, the people of Sanhsia are again mentioned in connection with violent resistance, this time against the invading Japanese. Davidson details a battle fought in and near Sanhsia in July 1895. A large force of Japanese soldiers had been stranded near Tach'i by attacks from the Taiwanese. To free the embattled force and crush the stubborn Taiwanese insurgents in the area, two detachments of Japanese set out from Taipei. At the same time the force at Tach'i marched north. The three units were to converge at Sanhsia, where a large group of insurgent Taiwanese was reportedly gathering. Davidson's description (p. 330) indicates the violence of the ensuing battle and the fierce determination of invader and resister alike:

The main column, under the personal command of Major-General Yamane, advanced, on the morning of the 22nd, from Tokoham [Tach'i] to the vicinity of a village about five miles from Sankakeng [Sanhsia]. Here they encountered and repulsed a body of some five or six hundred insurgents posted on an eminence, inflicting a loss on them of some thirty-five killed, and suffering themselves a loss of three wounded. Such houses in the vicinity as had harbored the insurgents were burned to the ground. The enemy were found next morning (23rd) re-assembled on the high hills surrounding the Japanese position. The precipitous sides of the mountains, combined with the opposition of the insurgents, made the task one of considerable difficulty. But artillery fire, supported by an infantry charge, was at length too much for the Chinese, who retreated with a loss of forty. It was not an easy victory, however, the Japanese meeting with a loss of twenty-four, including two killed.

The members of one of the lineages in Ch'inan, the Uis, say that their forebears were part of the resistance organization against the

Japanese, and that they fought in battles like the one Davidson describes. Their ancestral hall, like that of the Lous, was burned to the ground, exactly as Davidson says. The other Ch'inan lineages were apparently somewhat less determined about resisting. Later on, we will see what effects this difference in resisting the Japanese had on relationships among the four lineages.

During the Japanese period, Ch'inan and the surrounding area were not as oriented toward the outside world as they are today. At that time a lucrative resource was still to be found in the mountains in the form of the camphor tree. Ch'engfu, the next small town past Ch'itung, was a center for the distillation of the precious camphor oil. From there it was transported by cart and boat down the valley to the Sanhsia River and on out to ports to be exported. The profit to be made from camphor was probably incentive for the people to remain in the area and not seek employment outside. In addition, tea, which is still grown on the hills in the region, is said to have been much more profitable in the early part of the century. The presence of these sources of income in the area may have accounted in part for its fairly late connection with other regions.

Even when the first railway was built in the area it did not pass through Sanhsia or Ch'inan. To reach it one had to travel all the way to Sanhsia, cross the river, and then travel several miles farther, to Yingke or Shulin. The first fast means of transportation out of Ch'inan was a narrow gauge railway built in 1930; but even then, it was meant only to transport coal from the mountains behind Ch'inan and service stopped short of the outskirts of Taipei. Other means of transportation were poor; until the late 1930's the road toward Taipei on the Ch'inan side of the river was a muddy, rutted trail. The road was paved by 1940, but there was no kind of public transportation along it until 1950, when service by highway buses was initiated between Sanhsia and Taipei.

As a result of this fairly late development, the area is not as urbanized as one might expect of a district so close to the expanding urban center of Taipei. Today, with factories being built outward from Taipei toward Sanhsia at a great pace, and with people turning more and more to the city for employment, one wonders how long Ch'inan will stay a green, wooded village. Yet, the rapid, convenient transportation to and from Taipei that now makes the city so accessible may help to preserve, if not the traditional green-ness of the area, at least some aspects of its traditional pattern of life; for where it is possible to have both the benefits of city wages and the freshness of country air, many people prefer this arrange-ment. Not a few successful Taipei businessmen continue to com-mute to and from their homes in Ch'inan; and not a few newly-weds settle into their parents' houses there, content to ride the bus to their jobs in the city. For the moment, many aspects of village life in Ch'inan continue on as they have for over 200 years.

The traditional and even old-fashioned character of the village is recognized throughout the area. On bus rides between Sanhsia and Taipei I was often approached by strangers wanting to know why I was living in Ch'inan. Many people, once they understood that I was interested in "studying old customs and practices," re-plied in this vein: "Ch'inan is a good place for that. People in Hengch'i are really old-fashioned. They have preserved all the oldest traditions and customs and have not let them weaken." In this village, known in the area for its maintenance of traditional customs, I was to find not only a high level of interest in customs associated with community organization and the cult of the dead, but also, happily, innumerable opportunities to observe those customs in practice.

CHAPTER 2

The Ong Settlement

BEFORE ANALYZING the relationship between the cult of the dead and community organization, I will discuss in some detail the political and economic character of the community. In this chapter and the next I describe the four settlements that make up the community, developing a kind of character sketch for each of them. As I go along I also present correlative data for each settlement wherever possible; that is, information on the management of corporate property, leadership, corporate activity, and other crucial topics is included for all four lineages. Returning to these data in a later chapter, I will attempt to determine some causal links between the variables that characterize a Chinese lineage community.

The Ong settlement is located on the south bank of the Hengch'i River. The narrow piece of land that begins at the highway and stretches southward into the valley until it ends in steep mountains about two miles from the road belongs mainly to residents of the Ong settlement. This territorial unit is organized much more complexly than the other three settlements in the *li*. It embraces more different surnames and more clusters of houses than any of the others. Yet all the disparate groups of residents hold themselves, and are held by others, to be part of the Ong settlement. A few yards after turning off the highway onto the Ch'inan road, one must decide whether to take the left branch of the fork in the road, which leads to the Ong settlement, or the right branch, which leads eventually to each of the other settlements. The left branch first winds for a short way through rice paddy, then swings

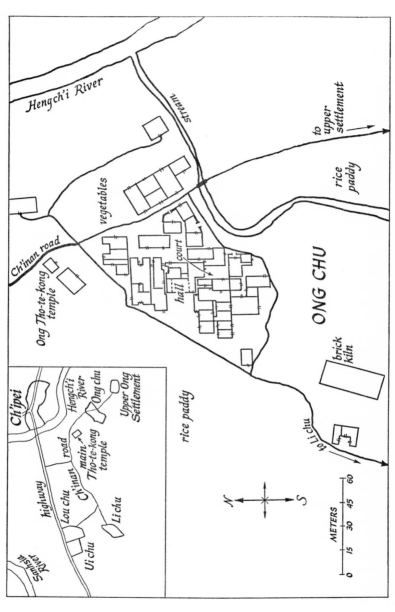

On this map and on the maps of the other settlements, lines have been drawn between rooms occupied by different households. In some cases, however, members of the same household live in rooms that are not adjacent, so that the number of separate living units shown exceeds the number of households in the settlement.

around the back of the main earth-god temple of the *li*, and finally begins to follow the bank of the Hengch'i River. A few yards on, the road passes another earth-god temple. The god inside faces the same direction as the road, confronting a large cluster of brick farmhouses. These houses, mostly oriented in the same direction as the ancestral hall, which is roughly in their center, form the main Ong settlement, the center of most group activity and conflict in this settlement.

This part of the settlement has a population of 314, divided among 40 households, each with a separate household economy. Of these, one family moved to Ch'inan from another area because the head of the household wanted to work in a nearby coal mine. Its members have no agnatic connection to the Ong lineage. In addition, there are four households composed entirely of people with surnames other than Ong. Each was established as the result of a uxorilocal marriage. This means that a man with a different surname married an Ong woman and moved into her father's household, helping to support her and her parents. In each union, some of the children were named Ong, and some were named after their fathers. In four instances, the children named after their fathers eventually set up their own households in the Ong settlement. Nine other households include uxorilocally married men, some of whose children have taken their fathers' names and thus are not named Ong. But in these cases the children have not set up their own permanent residences in the settlement. In all but two of the nine cases, the head of the household is the Ong father of a uxorilocally married daughter. In the other two, the uxorilocally married woman herself is considered the household head. Thus, 35 of the 40 household heads, or about 88 per cent, are unambiguously members of the Ong lineage (see Table 1).

If one follows the Ch'inan road through the main Ong settlement and out the other side, one passes through another section of paddy fields and arrives in a few minutes at a second cluster of houses. This area, located upstream from the main Ong settlement, is known as the "upper settlement" (*tieng-chu*). Here the

TABLE 1

Number of Residents and Households in Ch'inan, 1970

Settlement	Lineage population	Total population	Lineage households	Total households
Lower Ong	287	314	35	40
Upper Ong	116	214	17	31
Li	163	226	22	32
Lou	208	269	27	37
Ui	241	253	29	31
TOTAL	1,015	1,276	130	171

lineage Ongs form a less substantial portion of the population. In the section nearest the main settlement there are 17 households of lineage Ongs with a total of 116 people. Descendants of a man who moved away from the main settlement four generations ago, all of these Ongs live clustered together in wings and offshoots of wings that were originally attached to a U-shaped compound. They refer to the main Ong settlement as the *"kong-chu,"* a term that translates literally as "common settlement," but which they say has the sense of "settlement of common origin."

Included also within the upper settlement are 98 residents who do not belong to the Ong lineage. Just past the *tieng-chu* lineage Ongs are five households of Ongs who are not related to the lineage Ongs or to each other. Interspersed among them are five households of people with other surnames also unrelated to the Ong lineage. These residents do not live clustered closely together, but in separate houses, facing different directions, scattered on either side of a path. Beyond this area and separated from it by a short distance are three households of people surnamed Ui. They are members of the Ui lineage in Ch'inan and take part in all the major functions of that lineage. Much farther up the valley, half an hour's walk or so, are several widely scattered houses. None of their occupants belongs to the Ong lineage. The closest household is considered part of Ch'inan; the rest are not. Although regarded by the township government as part of Ch'inan *li*, they are not participants in its affairs. Because they live far up the valley, where the level land on either side of the river is narrow, they are actually physically closer to another village on the other side of the river than they are to the Ong settlement. Most of their social dealings take place across the river, which is often shallow enough to wade.

Here, then, in broad outline, are the largest social and residential components of the Ong settlement. By examining the way in which these components and the subgroups within them relate to one another during organized social activities, the nature of the lineage and its relationship to nonlineage co-residents will become clearer.

All activities involving the Ong lineage are profoundly affected by its division into two parts called the head and the tail (*thau* and *be*). The Ongs say that the *thau* and the *be* are descended, respectively, from the oldest and youngest brother of a set of six siblings, the grandchildren of one of the four Ong brothers who are said to have been the original settlers of Ch'inan. No one seemed sure what happened to either the sons of the four brothers or the middle four siblings of the *thau* and *be* ancestors. Some thought that they moved to the south of Taiwan, and others that they returned to the mainland. What everyone emphasized was that the Ongs are descended from two brothers; these two focal ancestors correspond to the lineage's division into two parts.

In describing the division within the lineage, the Ongs often begin by pointing out that the *thau* and the *be* are residentially distinct: everyone who lives to the right of the ancestral hall is *be*, and everyone who lives to the left is *thau*.* In fact, this is generally true. All those who live to the right of the hall are descended from the *be* ancestor, and all but six of the households living on the left side of the hall are descended from the *thau* ancestor. The six misplaced *be* families moved to the left side, they claim, because they needed to use some open land on the *thau* side of the hall to build new houses. Still, the oldest houses, the wings on the left side of the hall, are all occupied by *thau* Ongs. The Ong lineage members living in the upper settlement as well as others who

---

* I refer to left and right as one faces the hall. When I describe ancestral halls and altars below I adopt the same convention.

have moved out of Ch'inan are also descended from the *be* ancestor and are said to be members of the *be*. Hence the division is not strictly residential. Based on descent and exacerbated by residential separation, this division permeated every community activity I saw the Ongs attempt to organize.

Below the generation of the two brothers who are the focus of the *thau* and the *be*, there are no important genealogically based units. Although the majority of residents know that the eldest focal ancestor had four sons and the youngest had three, they do not regard these ancestors as the focus of sublineages below the founding ancestors. In fact, hardly any Ongs know from which son of the founding ancestors they are descended. Talk about branches, or *fang*, so common in other lineages, is nonexistent among the Ongs. For them the relevant distinction is between *thau* and *be*. Once a person is identified as belonging to one or the other of these segments, further identification is not needed.

The members of the two groups, *thau* and *be*, are fairly undifferentiated economically as well. Although some houses have been recently remodeled, in most cases the funds came from the wages of uxorilocally married men, not the endeavors of the Ong household head. The majority of houses are still mud-floored and without such modern improvements as plastered walls and screened windows. No one resident in the village is said to be very wealthy or even much wealthier than his neighbors. Most Ong household heads own and till a small amount of rice land (see Table 2) and depend on the earnings of their children in textile factories for cash. A sizable number of households depend on the earnings of one or more members in the coal mines. The only businesses in the settlement are a brick kiln, which is not yet making a profit, a small bakery that produces sweets for New Year, and a small store. Some Ongs who have moved out of the village have risen socially through election to political office, but economically their style of life is not much different from the villagers'. In general, the Ongs' standard of living is above subsistence but not high enough for many people to afford expensive luxuries such as motorcycles. No one is indigent, but neither is anyone very wealthy.

TABLE 2

Ownership of Corporate and Private Land in Ch'inan, 1970

(in *chia*)

Settlement	Corporate paddy land	Lineage members' privately owned land	
		Paddy land	Mountain land
Lower and upper Ong	—[a]	9.5	15.0
Li	.4	1.2	10.2
Lou	1.0	9.3	15.5
Ui	4.0	8.3	12.1
TOTAL	5.4	28.3	52.8

NOTE: My figures for ownership of land are only rough estimates, based on information obtained from an informal questionnaire. One *chia* is equivalent to 2.39 acres.

[a] The Ongs claim they own an extensive tract of corporate mountain land, but they could give me no estimate of its size in *chia*. None of the other lineages have corporate property of this kind.

Hence there are no economic cleavages of wealth and poverty within the lineage that correspond to or conflict with the political and genealogical division into *thau* and *be*.

The split between the two segments is related to a division in the leadership of the group. The most visible leader and organizer among the *thau* Ongs is an elected government official, the Ch'inan *li chang* (head of the *li*). The *li chang*, Pau-a, is a generous man, giving his time freely to those with questions or problems. Frequently, people engaged in some quarrel would end up in his house, choosing him willy-nilly as their arbiter and expecting him to restore equanimity between them. Nearly always, he was able to do so successfully. In terms of the life goals of most of those around him, Pau-a is a moderately successful man. Relations within his family are reasonably harmonious. He owns enough land to feed his family and enjoys besides the modest income that accompanies his position. In much of the community he is a respected arbiter and confidant. Further, he seems to enjoy his position of leadership. He is at ease and confident when delegating responsibility, making decisions, and sitting as an authority in matters at dispute.

The *be* segment's active leader in the settlement is a man named Hai-a. Since I lived in Hai-a's mother's house while he was in residence there, I came to know him very well. Sensitive about his failure as manager of a clock factory in Taipei, he had returned to the village a few years before I arrived to live in his mother's house. For a time he tried to make a living by running the brick kiln in the Ong settlement. But after his savings ran out, he was forced to tackle the outside economic world again by working part time in a clock repair shop near Taipei. Despite Hai-a's financial failures, his education is more extensive than most of his neighbors', as is his experience as a businessman in Taipei. Perhaps for these reasons others look to him for leadership, and he seems to feel it appropriate that he should provide it.

The history of the split in leadership between the *li chang* and Hai-a dates from the Japanese period. During the occupation the Japanese equivalent of the office of *li chang* was held by Hai-a's grandfather. After the Chinese resumed control, he retired and Pau-a was elected *li chang*. Pau-a has held the office virtually unchallenged, though not uncriticized, ever since. Until 1968, most affairs of the lineage and most community affairs of the *li* were instigated and organized by him. But about then, according to some of the Ongs, a feeling began to grow that Pau-a was neglecting many strictly lineage concerns, such as repairing the ancestral hall and collecting tax for some corporate mountain land, in favor of *li* concerns, such as paving the road that winds throughout the *li*. A group of *be* Ongs led by Hai-a thereupon prepared a plan of action and spelled it out in a remarkable brochure that was distributed to each member of the lineage. This document called for the convening of a grand meeting of the lineage and outlined in some detail a proposed "administrative organization" for the lineage. It envisioned both specific offices, including a business manager and a judicial chairman, and special committees for general affairs, receipts, and expenditures. The chief responsibility of the business manager would be overseeing the management of lineage property. The document stated, "The business manager should complete a property report, a statement of losses in property, an account of profits and losses, and a catalogue of property. After these are scrutinized by the judicial chairman, they must be submitted to the lineage members." If any losses were incurred as a result of mismanagement, the document stipulated that the business manager would have to reimburse the lineage. As an ultimate sanction, if the officers failed to carry out their duties properly, "the whole lineage must convene in a general meeting and must certainly remove them from office."

The preparation of this document by the *be* Ongs constituted an attempt to institute structure in the form of an organized leadership with specific duties to perform and subject to specific sanctions to ensure that these duties were carried out. Ostensibly the purpose was to preserve lineage property and buildings from extinction. As Hai-a put it, "The *li chang* never did anything about the lineage. The hall was falling apart from disrepair, and the government was threatening to reclaim our mountain land. We had to do something." Yet, in spite of Hai-a's high hopes, his effort did not entirely succeed. When the time came for the grand meeting of the lineage, "Only a few unimportant people showed up. All the capable men who know a lot about things stayed away." The outcome was that Hai-a was elected business manager by those present. After the meeting, he obtained the keys to the hall from Pau-a, who saved face by saying that the hall was not his responsibility anyway. I have no way of knowing whether tension was increased between Hai-a and the *li chang* during the period following the meeting. But certainly during the year 1969–70 when I lived in the settlement, the chasm between the *thau* and the *be,* headed by the *li chang* on one side and Hai-a on the other, seemed to be widening.

The *li chang,* in all contexts in which I observed him, seemed to attempt to build his influence by extending the activities he organized to all territorial residents of the settlement. I assume this was only a continuation of an earlier tendency, since it had been his ignoring of lineage matters in favor of community ones that had led to the general meeting organized by Hai-a. His orientation was apparent even from casual conversations. My questions about lineage matters, the ancestral hall, and the genealogy were met with plain indifference, shrugged shoulders, and claims of ignorance. Questions about community affairs, in contrast, brought unfeigned interest, detailed answers delivered with pride and excitement, and reams of charts and lists, which he produced from his desk drawer. A graphic illustration of the concerns of the *li chang*—and of the dichotomy within the community—is the wall alongside the door of the *li chang*'s house. It is covered with shreds of old name lists partly concealed by more recent ones: all are lists of *li* residents who contributed at some time or other to one of the various community-wide projects organized by the *li chang*. There were two lists visible at the time I was in the village. One named the people throughout the Ong settlement, of all areas and all surnames, who had donated to the repair of the road where it had been washed away by the river. The other, an older list, named the people throughout the *li* who had contributed to the original paving of the Ch'inan road. All other lists, which is to say those dealing with lineage matters and property, were pasted on the wall of the ancestral hall, symbol of the lineage.

Besides organizing occasional community projects to keep village roads in repair, the *li chang* manages three community ritual cycles within the Ong settlement: the rotating *pai-pais* for the Ang-kong, Tho-te-kong, and Co-su-kong. For each of these, the chief organizer is called the "pot master" (*lo-cu*). The *lo-cu* must engage an opera troupe, supervise the erection of a stage, see that images of the appropriate god are brought from the temple, and organize the selection of a new *lo-cu* to take charge when the responsibility falls once again to his settlement.

As soon as the *pai-pai* he is in charge of is over, the *lo-cu* arranges for the selection of his successor. He begins by obtaining a list of all those qualified for the position, theoretically all household heads resident in the settlement. Then, standing before the image of the god in question, he reads off the name of the first person on the list and throws two divining blocks, rounded on one side, flat on the other, on the floor before the god. If they both land flat side down, the god's response is "no"; if both land flat side up, the god is undecided or laughing at the questioner; if one lands up and one down, the god is answering "yes." The *lo-cu* throws several times for each name on the list, stopping as soon as he gets a no response. After each name he writes down the number of yes responses obtained. The person with the most yes answers will be the *lo-cu* the next time the *pai-pai* rotates back to this group. The runner-up will serve as the assistant *lo-cu*. Generally speaking, the *lo-cu* is not elevated to a position of great power by his election, though he may gain in prestige because it is thought that the god would not choose a man unless he has a "good heart." In the Ong settlement, the list of those eligible to be *lo-cu* is prepared by the *li chang* and presented to the *lo-cu* as an accomplished fact, so that the *lo-cu* does not have the power of exclusion implied in the act of drawing up a list. As we shall see, there is considerable variation among the settlements in the way the *lo-cu* is chosen and in who is allowed to participate.

Participation in the *lo-cu* election for each of the three community ritual cycles is in fact open to every resident of the Ong settlement, lineage member or not. Fortunately, I was able to locate the name list used in the last *lo-cu* election for the Co-su-kong *pai-pai*. It contains the name of every household head in the Ong settlement: those who live in the main settlement, those who live in the upper settlement, even those who live far up the valley near Ch'itung; Ongs, those connected to the Ongs through uxorilocal marriage, and those with other surnames. In fact the list is identical to one the *li chang* obtained from the government household registration office in Sanhsia containing the names of all persons registered as household heads in the official records. Hence the people living far up the valley, who are listed in the government records as residents of the *li*, are included on the list.

The *li chang* assured me that the same list is used for all three ritual cycle *pai-pais*; he gives the list to all the *lo-cus*. He seemed to feel very strongly that all the community *pai-pais* should be open to and contributed to by all residents of the area. For the Ong Tho-te-kong *pai-pai* and opera, too, which the *li chang* manages entirely on his own, all residents are urged to contribute. The *li chang* often said to me that the Tho-te-kong temple in the Ong settlement is "for everyone who lives here. We all live in the same place and worship at the same earth-god temple." Whether because of the concerns of his office, which make him responsible for all residents, or out of a desire to build up a political power base, the *li chang* views the settlement as a heterogeneous group of people with different surnames living together in one place. He sometimes said with a certain pride that there are a lot of different surnames in the Ong settlement.

This stands in considerable contrast to the views of Hai-a. According to him, "almost everyone who lives around here is an Ong," the Tho-te-kong temple in the settlement is an Ong temple, and the rotating *pai-pais* are Ong affairs. Though he admitted that residents with other surnames could participate in the *pai-pais* and worship at the temple, he considered this a courtesy extended to outsiders by the lineage, not a right bestowed by virtue of residence in the settlement.

Besides those affairs in which the *li chang* is so interested—the rotating *pai-pais*, the Tho-te-kong opera, the road repairs—there are other organized activities, involving the lineage more than the residential community, in which he takes part. In these, however, the *li chang* is on the margins of activity, seemingly drawn in because of his prominent position in the community. Unlike all the other lineages in Ch'inan, the Ongs have few regular lineage affairs that need organization. There is no corporate property in the form of paddy fields that must be tilled by someone or rented out to someone.* Since there is no rice land, there is no income that has to be managed. And since there is no income, there are no funds to finance corporate worship of ancestors, so that activity does not need organizing. Because there is no source of regular surplus earnings, there is no capital to invest in expensive projects, such as a water tower to bring running water to all households or a cement courtyard in front of the hall. Regular duties

---

* Corporate rice land, *kong-chan*, is land that is considered to belong to the lineage as a group. Usually it is rented to the highest bidder within the lineage, who may till it himself or rent it to someone else. Rent from the land, either in cash or in grain, becomes the property of the lineage. Part or all of it is rotated to lineage members to pay for lineage feasts.

involving lineage property, such as sweeping and dusting the hall, operate automatically, following the circulation of a plaque from household to household. Whoever holds the plaque on any given day is responsible for cleaning up the hall and lighting incense for the ancestors. That evening the plaque is transferred to another household. Payment for the electricity used in lighting the hall is handled in much the same way; each month one household is responsible for paying the bill. Because there is no standing fund for lineage leaders to draw on to finance some lineage project, any group endeavor requiring money is dependent either on a rotation system, as in the case of the electric bill for the ancestral hall, or on an assessment of each lineage member. This in itself may well act as a deterrent to group action. Since each household has to give up cash for the project, each presumably looks to its other expenses and wonders whether the lineage project is more important than buying clothes or otherwise providing for the family. If there were a common fund expressly for group projects, with no question of the money being used for family expenses, people would be less likely to object to a proposed project.

Despite the lack of a common fund, the Ongs do manage to keep the ancestral hall in repair by means of periodic assessments on each household. They fare less well, however, with another item, the written genealogy, which is often the common property of a whole lineage. In this case, the state of the Ong lineage genealogy is symptomatic of the divided state of the Ong lineage. As one might expect, there are two major genealogies, one tracing the ancestry of the *thau* and one tracing the ancestry of the *be*. Neither document is in the safekeeping of Ch'inan residents, but has rather been put in the hands of more educated, mobile lineage members who have moved out of the village to the market town or city. Consequently, it was only with some difficulty that I located and copied them. Before I succeeded in doing so, I attempted to construct a genealogy with the help of Ong lineage members. The task was not easy. Although many people could name their lineal ascendants all the way back to the founding ancestor, most of them did not know how their line was related to collateral lines.

Again, the relevant distinction is between *thau* and *be*; subdivisions within these two segments are usually unknown and are considered unimportant.

Similarly, the genealogical documents themselves are of little interest to the lineage as a whole. In the case of the *be* genealogy, no new names have been added for three generations; in the case of the *thau* genealogy, the man who is keeping it has filled in ancestors in his line of direct ascent but no collateral lines for the last three generations. Genealogical relationships are not relevant politically or economically below the level of the *thau* and *be* ancestors, so the document that could be used to elucidate or manipulate these relationships is not of much concern.

Although the Ongs were not particularly successful in carrying out joint enterprises, they did attempt some lineage projects during the time I was in the settlement. If these varied in the degree to which they succeeded in gaining group support, they were all alike in exposing the raw edge of antagonism between the *thau* and the *be*. The first project I became aware of began at the abortive meeting called by Hai-a at New Year in 1969. One of the issues he was most anxious to have discussed was the management of a large area of mountain land owned corporately by the Ong lineage. I was unable to ascertain exactly how much land this involves, but it is apparently an enormous tract. Hai-a claimed the Ongs own all the mountains near them, starting about half a mile up the valley from the main settlement and ending about two miles farther on. For many years sections of that land have been used profitably by a businessman from Sanhsia to mine coal. (Most lineage members still use parts of it also, for fruit trees, camphor trees, or tea plants. Any lineage member can lay claim to use part of the land by clearing and planting it.) Hai-a's primary goal for this land was to make it as financially profitable for the lineage as possible. He hoped to accomplish this by forcing the Sanhsia businessman to pay rent for all the years he had used the land for mining coal. In fact, Hai-a and other *be* representatives confronted this man with their demands and managed to get from him what Hai-a called a token amount of NT $20,000* for the three years 1966–68. Hai-a assured me that the Ongs were legally due a like amount for the rest of the 20 or more years the man had operated the coal mine, but he refused to give them any more.

According to government officials in Sanhsia, the only way the Ongs can force the coal-mine operator to make additional payments is to present the government with a document stamped by all lineage members affirming that the man had used their land for a stated period of time. It was at this point that Hai-a's plan ran afoul of the conflict within the lineage. He argued, "If we could get the money we would be able to carry on all kinds of lineage projects. Some people want to build a bigger hall, and others thought of building a playground for the children." But he was unable to get all the lineage members to stamp the necessary document. Some of the *thau* members simply refused. They told me, "Nobody trusts Hai-a. He has lost so much money failing in his business that he has to come back here and get money from the lineage lands to start up again. We don't want that money to go into his pocket." In face of this opposition, Hai-a abandoned his plan. If nearly half of the lineage did not trust him enough to let him act on behalf of the group, there was no way he could force them. There was no sanction to support his role of leader; he was dependent on consensual support.

On most occasions the *li chang*, backed by the *thau*, and Hai-a, backed by the *be*, were at loggerheads on matters at issue within the community. But in the course of one long series of incidents involving the repair of a road, their conflict was finally suppressed when the lineage came under attack from outside. The problem began when part of the road from the highway to the Ong settlement was badly damaged. Some parts of the section involved, the portion paralleling the Hengch'i River, had been protected from the river current by a stone wall built some years ago. But the wall had weakened over the years, and during the winter rains of 1969–

---

* In 1969–70 the exchange rate was 40 New Taiwan dollars (NT $) to one U.S. dollar.

70 it was completely washed away. The unprotected bank was then
eroded by the swollen river, undercutting the road. About a third
of its surface fell away, leaving a path wide and safe enough for
a pedestrian or cyclist but dangerous for even the smallest car.

The *li chang* made a trip to talk to members of the *hsien* government about getting a government subsidy for the repair of the
road and the construction of a retaining wall for the bank of the
river. When he returned he told me, "We have to raise NT $8,000
before the government will pay anything. It's awfully difficult to
come by that much money these days. I guess the people who are
using the road will have to be assessed." At the time I thought
he meant that as usual all the residents of the settlement would
have to pay a fixed amount in order to make up the needed sum.
But a week later I learned that he had another plan in mind.

In spite of the condition of the road, Hai-a had started up production of the brick kiln again as soon as the worst of the winter
rains were over. This meant that heavy trucks loaded with bricks
had to cross the damaged road to and from the kiln. The *li chang*'s
plan was to demand payment from Hai-a for the use his trucks
were making of the road. Predictably enough, Hai-a and others in
the *be* felt the demand was unreasonable. One of our neighbors,
an elderly man who often acted in Hai-a's place when he was not
in the village, said, "The *li chang* and the *thau* people just want
to ruin Hai-a. They know that the kiln hasn't earned much money
so Hai-a can't afford to pay anything. If he isn't allowed to use the
road free he will certainly have to close down. The *li chang* just
wants him to fail." The struggle continued for some time, groups
of *thau* Ongs meeting in the *li chang*'s house and groups of *be*
Ongs meeting in Hai-a's house, each to discuss and reaffirm their
position. I have no way of knowing how the conflict would have
been settled between the two segments, because at this point in
the dispute the interests of both segments were threatened from
outside, and they were diverted from their quarrel.

Late one evening the *li chang* came to our house and sat down
to have a talk with Hai-a. Hai-a, on guard at the almost unprece-
dented visit, relaxed as soon as he heard what the *li chang* had to

say. Mr. Tiu:, a rich businessman who lived across the river in Ch'ipei, had decided to construct a flood wall to prevent the river from rising so high that it would flood his house and others in Ch'ipei. The *li chang* and Hai-a were equally incensed at this news. In the first place, an existing wall, built on the Ch'ipei side of the river many years before, had changed the course of the river so that it had eroded the bank on the Ch'inan side. A new wall, perhaps farther out in the river bed, would turn the current even more toward Ch'inan; with the road almost washed out already, any further encroachment would be intolerable. More to the point, as Hai-a put it, "The river used to run much farther north than it does now. In fact, it used to run just where Tiu:'s house is built now. At that time, all the land to the south of the river belonged to us Ongs. But now all that land has been eaten away by the river and thrown up on the other side in front of Tiu:'s house. The land now on the other side of the river, between the water and the houses, is ours! How does Tiu: think he can use it to build a wall and push the river over even farther?"

In fact, the Ongs had a legitimate case. According to a cadastral map, they had once owned much land between the present Ch'inan road and the river. Since both *be* and *thau* had lost land in that area, both felt cheated and disadvantaged by Mr. Tiu:'s activities. Perhaps because of this the two leaders, Hai-a and the *li chang*, forgot their differences and their competition for influence among the Ongs. On the contrary, they used their dual power blocs to confound the common enemy. In the following days, Tiu: or his son made several trips to the Ong settlement to attempt to prevent the Ongs from making trouble for them. If the Tiu:s approached the *li chang*, Pau-a told them that he could not make any commitment and sent them to see Hai-a. Hai-a in turn sent them back to the *li chang*. As a result, the Tiu:s' pleas and threats were of no avail. The division in leadership within the Ongs, once their greatest weakness, was now their greatest strength.

In addition, the members of the *thau* and the *be*, who normally gathered separately for gossip or entertainment, now formed large mixed groups by the side of the river to watch as the work proceeded on Tiu:'s construction project. When the steam-shovel operator who was preparing the foundation for the wall moved over to the Ong side of the river to take fill dirt for the area behind the wall, a roar of rage went up from the group of Ongs watching from the bank. Almost continuous discussion, both in houses throughout the settlement and in the ever-present group on the riverbank, led to a fever pitch of excitement.

Emotions reached an especially intense level during a night meeting of the entire lineage, which was jointly called and organized by the *li chang* and Hai-a. Gathered on benches in the open space in front of the *li chang*'s house were representatives of every Ong household, *thau* and *be*. The meeting was called to order and run by the *li chang*, but Hai-a and his brother were seated at a table by his side, where they added comments from time to time. The group's leaders were clearly united and of accord. Various people, including the *li chang* and Hai-a, hotly expressed their conviction that Tiu: must not be allowed to continue building his wall. There was virtually no disagreement within the group. Each speech simply reinforced the one before and increased everyone's state of excitement. The *li chang* suggested that a group be sent to consult the *hsien* government; Hai-a agreed but added that if this produced no results, the Ongs should arm themselves and bodily attack the workmen at the construction site. The outcome of the meeting, besides increasing everyone's anger and indignation, was that all the adults stamped their seals on a document stating their case, which was to be presented to the *hsien* government by the *li chang*, Hai-a, and other members of the group the next day.

The trip was duly made, and the government responded by sending a representative to Ch'inan to look over the situation. Eventually, after continuing pressure from the Ongs, the government began construction on a retaining wall for the Ongs' side of the river. Even though Tiu:'s wall was completed and the land behind it reclaimed for his use, the Ongs apparently felt satisfied as long as they lost no more land in the process.

Relations between the *thau* and the *be* may have been somewhat improved as a result of their successful cooperation in opposing Tiu:. There were no further conflicts or cooperative enterprises in the settlement before I left in September so I was unable to judge whether they were getting along any better than before. The fact that the *li chang* dropped his demand to make Hai-a pay for his trucks' use of the road may attest to an easing of relations between them.

Whatever the importance of all this so far as the future conduct of the group is concerned, the incident is enlightening for what it reveals about the lineage. Even in a lineage with a low level of corporate organization, no rotation of the income from common land, and lack of support for those who claim to be the lineage leaders, an attack on lineage land was sufficient to make the members of the lineage function as a well-organized, solidary unit. It is doubtful whether a community of heterogeneous elements, without even a dormant lineage organization to pull them together, would have unified in the same way. Certainly the other settlements in Ch'i-nan, though closely allied to the Ong settlement in other ways, felt no interest at all in the wall incident. Nor did residents of the Ong settlement who are not members of the lineage take an active part in the affair. Yet many individuals within the Ong lineage stood to lose nothing personally by the threat to the land along the riverbank, since they had no land of their own in that section of the settlement. Nevertheless, they were just as concerned over the possible loss of the land as those who owned it. All the land in that area of the settlement was originally cleared and claimed by the ancestors of the present members of the Ong lineage. Regardless of whether or not a particular person had inherited part of the land in question, each member of the lineage could feel that some of the original land of one of the two focal ancestors was being threatened. This seemed sufficient to give them an impetus for common action. All the sentiments that Hai-a tried to awaken in his attempt to "save the land the ancestors handed down to us" were finally aroused when lineage land was threatened in a real, not a hypothetical, context, by real enemies hoping to gain from the Ongs' loss.

   The material I have presented about the Ongs to this point characterizes them as a group afflicted with a deep, internal division,
its members in many circumstances unable to unite behind a single
leader. Some might object, perhaps, that the incidents I have
chosen to discuss emphasize the conflicts among the Ongs out of
proportion to the way the Ongs themselves see them. Yet, I think
not, for toward the end of my stay in Ch'inan, some of my informants told me about a way they have of perceiving their social
relationships that leads me to think my presentation of the Ongs
conforms to their own view.

   The new information I received about how the Ongs regard
their own social group involves *te-li*. This phrase, which can be
translated as geomancy, is used in Ch'inan only in reference to
the orientation of buildings inhabited by living men. It is distinguished sharply from *hong-cui*, which refers to the geomancy of
graves. When I first questioned people on this subject, I often
confused the two terms, asking about the *hong-cui* of buildings or
the *te-li* of graves. My error always brought stern reprimands and
the instruction that graves have *hong-cui* but never *te-li*, whereas
houses and temples have *te-li* but never *hong-cui*. *Hong-cui* belongs to the dead, the *yin* (*im* in Taiwanese); *te-li* belongs to the
living, the *yang* (*iong* in Taiwanese).

   Beyond this distinction, most residents of Ch'inan could tell me
little more about the theory of *te-li*. If I asked "What is *te-li*?" or
some similar question, I got only puzzled claims of ignorance. If
I asked "What is the *te-li* of X?" filling in the variable with some
social unit such as Ong *chu* or Li *chu*, I usually got a prompt reply
in the form of the name of some animal, a lion, perhaps, or a dragon, or the name of some object, for example, a fishnet or a rice
winnower. If I asked "How do you know the *te-li* of X is the object
or animal named?" I was told that some configuration of land or
hills resembled the thing in question. If I then asked "Is the *te-li*
of X good?" I might receive one of three types of responses. One

sort of answer was a comment about whether the *te-li* of a certain animal or object was generally good or bad, together with some remarks about its specific character. For example, the *te-li* of a sleeping tiger is very good for producing government officials, whereas the *te-li* of a rice winnower is better for producing many male offspring. Another sort of response dealt with the question of whether or not the social group under discussion, say the Ong lineage, had successfully captured the *te-li* of the surrounding environment. In the case of the four Ch'inan lineages the means to such success is available in the advice of a professional "professor of *te-li*" on the correct orientation of the ancestral hall. If the hall is oriented in the proper direction, the benefits of the *te-li* will flow through the hall to the members of the lineage and sometimes to other residents of the same territory as well. If the hall is oriented incorrectly, the benefits of the *te-li* are lost. But this sort of fault is easily corrected. Whenever the hall is rebuilt it can be re-oriented in a direction better designed to capture the *te-li*. These first two responses both assume that a *te-li* is present, and that its benefits can be obtained under proper conditions. A third kind of response involved the state of health of the *te-li*, that is, whether or not it had been injured. Since the Ongs most commonly gave this response, we must see what it means to have a damaged *te-li*.

But before we come to that, a brief note about the other sorts of questions I asked on this subject. Inquiries about whether the "soul" (*lieng-hun*) of the animal or object in question resides in some sense in the land seemed silly to my informants. They had no opinions about this matter at all. More relevant to them were questions about whether a social area had its own *te-li* or shared in the *te-li* of a neighboring unit. As we will see, opinions on this question, as on all the others, vary from settlement to settlement within the *li*.

The Ongs, for example, declared unanimously that their settlement has its own *te-li*—that of a lily flower. One can only see the shape corresponding to the lily flower from a high place; the level land between the river and the mountains forms a rough circle with the main Ong settlement in its center. Everyone agreed, too, that the lily flower had been injured sometime in the past. Ciouq-kim, an elderly, well-informed member of the *thau*, told me, "Some time ago our *te-li* was ruined by the construction of the brick kiln. Our *te-li* is ruined; we can't get along or organize to do anything together." *Thau* and *be* alike agree that the *te-li* is ruined. Chiu-a, a middle-aged farmer in the *be*, said, "Our *te-li* is injured, prob-ably because of one of the irrigation ditches. Digging in the wrong spot just ruined the *te-li*. Now, you see, we Ongs cannot seem to cooperate at all. Our heart is divided; we are unable to get along."

The state of the *te-li* seems to be an expression of the current state of affairs within the group. If something is fundamentally wrong in the affairs of a group in social space, then something must be wrong with the *te-li* of that space. This sort of trouble is not as easily set right as that involved in a wrongly oriented hall and the consequent loss of the *te-li*. There the trouble is merely a result of bad technique, a mechanical problem easily correctable by mechanical means. Fix the orientation, and the *te-li* can auto-matically be obtained. But when the Ongs discussed the injury of their *te-li* in terms of the discord within their group, they did not seem to be thinking of two states of affairs that were causally or mechanically related. When I asked whether the injury to the *te-li* brought about the discord in the Ong lineage, or whether the reverse happened, people only looked puzzled. I think it is neither that the injured *te-li* causes the discord, nor that the discord re-sults in injury to the *te-li*. It may be rather that the relationship between the two is just one of correspondence; something wrong in the state of society means that something is wrong with the natural setting, the *te-li*, of the group. It is not that one causes the other, but that one implies the other, that one is an expres-sion of the other. Perhaps this is the reason why no one ever attempted to "fix" the injured *te-li*. I asked the Ongs why they did not just fill in the ditch or remove the offending brick kiln. They were quite sure that such measures would do no good. "Once a *te-li* is broken, it cannot be fixed so easily. It is very delicate."

So long as the discord remains in the social group the *te-li* will be said to be injured. Neither the delicate balance of power and interests within the group that makes cooperation easier, nor, therefore, the injured *te-li*, can be repaired with something so simple as the filling in of a ditch.

CHAPTER 3

The Other Settlements

THE OTHER three settlements have more in common with each other than they do with the Ong settlement. For one thing, they occupy contiguous territory at the base of a low line of hills that jut out from the higher mountains behind the Ong settlement. Also, in contrast to the Ongs, all three lineages in the other settlements possess corporate rice lands and a fairly well-developed lineage organization. Moreover, they are all without the kind of deep, internal discord that plagues the Ongs. Certainly, part of the reason I saw less conflict in the other settlements was because I lived in the Ong settlement. Yet I spent part of every day in each of the other *chu* and had some of my best informants there. In addition, my assistant was a member of the Lou lineage; she often related to me incidents involving conflict that she had witnessed or heard about. More significant is the fact that I did see conflicts arise in each of the other settlements. Yet in none of them did the trouble seem insoluble, nor did it always open the same line of cleavage in the group, as was the case in the Ong settlement. Still, despite the general similarity of the three *chu*, there is not a little variation among them, principally in the exclusion of nonlineage residents and the way their leaders operate. In this chapter I will discuss each settlement briefly, pointing out similarities and differences as we go along.

If one takes the right branch of the fork in the Ch'inan road a few yards from the highway, one winds through paddy fields, passes one or two isolated houses along the way, and arrives eventually at the Li settlement. Unlike the Ong settlement, which is located in the center of a circle of fields, the Li settlement is flanked by tea-covered hills at the rear and by the steep banks of two streams in the front and on the sides. The main settlement, like the Ongs', clusters around the Lis' ancestral hall. There are five rows of rooms jutting out from the hall, still easily identifiable as connected wings. To the right and in back of the hall there are several separate houses of more recent construction. This central part of the settlement contains 23 households with a population of 163. Residents in 20 of the 23 are lineage Lis; of the other three households, one consists of outsiders, another of the offspring of a uxorilocal marriage, and the third of Lis who are not descended from the lineage ancestors, and so are not members of the lineage. To the northwest of the group is a small cluster of houses, the residences of five households of Peqs; and over a hill to the northeast are four households, two of lineage Lis, two of other surnames. Residents of all these households are considered part of the Li settlement. The settlement is smaller in area and population than the Ongs' and more compact.

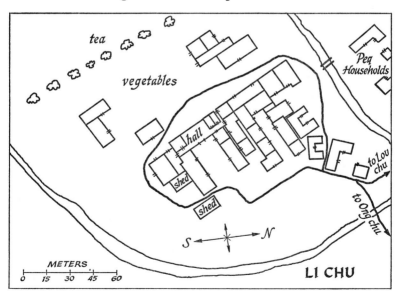

The corporate paddy land set aside by the ancestors of the Lis is still in existence though reduced in size. Formerly, the Lis possessed a large tract of land that produced enough income to finance many corporate feasts for the ancestors. Part of it was sold, and what is left today does not yield enough income to cover the cost of even one feast; whoever is in charge has to make up the difference out of his own funds. The corporate paddy land is rented permanently to one family of Lis. At each harvest they keep a portion of the grain and deliver the rest to the branch in charge of the corporate feast that year. These branches, or sub-lineages, are formed by the descendants of the sons of the founding ancestor. Since the Lis' founding ancestor had three sons, the lineage is said to have three "great branches," or great *fang* (*tua-pang* in Taiwanese).

Each year one of the three *fang* is in charge of the corporate feast for the lineage. Organization varies within the *fang* in charge, but usually the responsibility for the corporate feast devolves upon the descendants of one of the sub-*fang* formed by the sons of the great *fang* ancestor. Operation of the system is automatic, following the genealogy as shown in Fig. 1. The numbers show the temporal order of precedence of responsibility for organizing the corporate feast. In each case, all the descendants of the sub-*fang* ancestor share responsibility and must pay part of the costs for the feast. Usually the grain from the corporate land is consumed rather than sold because no Lis own or cultivate other rice land. When they receive the rice from the corporate land, they use it to replace part of the rice they would normally purchase. Whether resident in Ch'inan or living elsewhere, all lineage members are held responsible for the feast when responsibility falls on their sub-*fang*. The least those who have moved away do is pay their share of the expenses; most return to help if they live in Taipei or closer.

Usually the corporate feasts are very loosely organized with no one holding a formal position of leadership. In fact, there are no standing positions of authority within the lineage at all. I was told that earlier, when the Lis had surplus income, each *fang* had a permanent "representative" to take charge of the funds left from

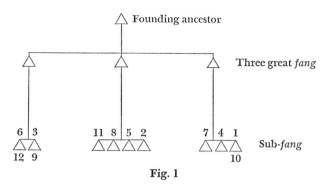

Fig. 1

the previous year. Now that there is no surplus, there is no need for the office. Apart from this one corporate feast, there is no other organized activity involving the lineage and exclusive to it. The annual meeting of the lineage, which I was told was once a matter of great concern because questions about the disposal of surplus income could be discussed, is now merely an adjunct of the corporate feast; in 1970, at least, no lineage business was discussed. The Li lineage emerges as a group whose lineage organization and activities have been considerably reduced with the decline in prosperity of the lineage members. Forced to sell much of their corporate lands to cover lineage expenses, having lost, in addition, all of the other paddy land originally owned by their ancestors, the Lis speak of themselves as "once rich, now poor."

Their poverty is only relative, however, for none of the Lis is exceptionally poor. Often their complaints about their decline in prosperity seem to mean that they have no paddy land and must depend on wages entirely. Still, in most cases, the Lis have found some alternative to farming to make ends meet. Many households rent or buy knitting machines with which the young men make piece goods for the textile factories near Taipei. In addition, there is a tea-processing operation in one home. Because many Lis still own mountain land planted in tea, they can sell green leaves to the processor as a source of cash income. Only three or four households display wealth above the rest of the lineage; in every instance the source of their prosperity is their own business success. For example, one household is said to be wealthy because a son owns a profitable candy factory in southern Taiwan. Another is thriving because of the household head's successful restaurant in Taipei. Although there is more economic differentiation among the Lis than in the Ong lineage, just as in the Ong case it does not reinforce political or genealogical divisions within the community. Each of the three Li great *fang* can boast some exceptionally wealthy members.

The great *fang* are more differentiated than their equivalents in the Ong lineage but, as we shall see, less so than in the other lineages. All Lis know which great *fang* they belong to and usually their genealogical relation to other members of the same *fang*. If there is any question, they can easily consult the written genealogy, which is kept in the ancestral hall. But the great *fang* do not have leaders to represent their interests, nor, outside the corporate feast, do they function as organized units. There are no strong ideas about the "character" of each *fang*, such as that one is rich or another prolific. The *fang* are important because they determine the rotation of the grain from the corporate land; otherwise, they have little significance.

Operating as a whole unit without reference to separate *fang*, the Lis carry on several organized activities with a lack of conflict unheard of among the Ongs. Over the years the Lis have purchased three large images of gods, which are housed in the ancestral hall. Each was obtained at the instigation of some lineage member or other who had had a dream that some god, say Co-su-kong, wanted an image made in a certain way. Acting on this report, the Lis had thereupon ordered an image like the one in the dream from a carpenter. These images are frequently used in ceremonies to cure the sick. My informants told me, "If someone in the lineage dreams of a god it means that the god wants to come to us here often and help us. So if that happens, we all contribute money to pay for the image." The implication is that if any one member of the lineage can benefit from the god's attentions, so can any other member; perhaps as members of the same lineage their social position is similar enough that they can be substituted for one another.

Nearly all matters that involve the gods' images or require healing consultations with one of the gods are handled and organized by a vigorous old man, a member of the second great *fang* of Lis, always referred to as the *tang-ki* (the shaman). If Co-su-kong is to be consulted about some illness, for example, the *tang-ki* will recite incantations in front of the image in the hall. Modest and unassuming, despite his eighty years, many healthy grandsons, and great knowledge, the *tang-ki* seems pleased to handle such affairs simply out of pride in his own capability. He is regarded as an expert who organizes the purchase of a god's image out of interest in the proceedings; there is no suspicion that he might gain politically or financially from his activities.

The *tang-ki* is also the organizing force behind a small group of five or six Lis who play horns and other instruments in an ensemble used for major *pai-pais*. In this enterprise, too, he is active simply because he enjoys it. The group includes men from all three Li *fang*. It is possibly significant, though perhaps only a matter of circumstance, that no similar group exists among the Ongs. At any rate, the Lis clearly have no trouble organizing groups of lineage members cutting across *fang* boundaries.

The young people, also, reflect the Lis' relative ability to cooperate. Virtually all the young male adults in the lineage, young men finished with school but not yet middle-aged, club together into a loose gang. They spend most of their time together hunting rabbits in the mountains with a pack of dogs or entering carrier pigeon contests, and keep a dog pack and pigeons specifically for those purposes. Sometimes the young Lis get into fights with similar groups from other areas, but internally there is never a sign of dissension. I often heard people from the other settlements criticize the gang members for these fights, but at the same time praise them for getting along so well together.

Activities requiring leadership other than those involving gods or ritual, which are automatically referred to the superior abilities of the *tang-ki*, are handled by people from different *fang*, principally two men, one from the first *fang* and one from the second. They differ from the two main Ong leaders in that they neither stand to gain personally from wielding power in the community, as Pau-a, the *li chang*, does, nor hope to change radically the emphasis of the entrenched leadership, as Hai-a does. Both of the Li leaders are upwardly mobile, one hoping to move up in the Agricultural Association, the other in the *hsien* government. They are occasionally in a position to help the lineage members politically, but the rest of the lineage is not particularly in a position to help them. Unlike the *li chang*, who is old and has no political ambitions beyond the *li* and who is dependent on support within the *li* for his reelection, these two leaders have goals that cannot be furthered very greatly by support within the lineage. Certainly they would not be furthered at all by building up a faction of strong support based on part of the lineage. Thus, when some lineage project needs direction, as, for example, when the courtyard in front of the hall had to be laid with cement, one or the other of the two men collects the money and hires the help. They do it as a favor, to fulfill an obligation they feel to the lineage, not as a means of gaining politically. In no case I observed or heard about did they act as heads of some faction within the lineage or even as heads of their own *fang*.

The community *pai-pais* for the Ang-kong and the other gods are organized in much the same manner as described in the last chapter. *Lo-cus* are chosen by throwing divination blocks in front of the god's image. But the Lis' organization of the *pai-pais* differs in one important respect from the Ongs': although participation in the selection of a *lo-cu* for the Tho-te-kong and Ang-kong *pai-pais* is open to all household heads in the settlement, Lis as well as those bearing other surnames, the Co-su-kong *pai-pai lo-cu* is closed to all but Lis. This is managed rather neatly: whichever sub-*fang* is responsible for managing the lineage's corporate feast chooses a Co-su-kong *lo-cu* from among its members if responsibility for that *pai-pai* falls to the Li settlement that year. In this way the responsibility and benefits of managing the Co-su-kong *pai-pai* are kept within the lineage and not extended to the rest of the community.

In order to assert that this exclusion is an expression of the power of the lineage, I must show that nonlineage members would like to participate in the *pai-pai*, and that excluding them is in the interests of the lineage. If the affair were one in which other people would just as soon not participate, even though the lineage preferred them to do so, their lack of participation would hardly be an expression of lineage power; indeed, a better interpretation would be that since the lineage is unable to force them to take part, it is a weak power in the settlement. But in the existing situation, there is no doubt that those outside the lineage would eagerly participate in the Co-su-kong *lo-cu* selection if given the opportunity. Being chosen *lo-cu* increases a man's prestige because he was chosen by the god; further, it gives him a chance to please the god by providing him with a splendid *pai-pai*. If he does a good job, he can only stand to gain the god's favor. The task of *lo-cu* does not require expenditure on the individual's part, either; all expenses are collected by assessment from the rest of the group. The *lo-cu* for Tho-te-kong in 1971 was in fact to be head of one of the poorest households in the settlement, a Peq family of five members. Yet he could not have been more pleased and excited; he had everything to gain and could lose nothing at all.

Thus, keeping the Co-su-kong *lo-cu* tied to the rotation of the responsibility for the corporate lineage feast ensures that only Li lineage members have this chance to please the god. Since a god is thought to relate to the lineage as a group, each time a Li presents a *pai-pai*, the whole lineage is bound to gain the favor of the god. Hence, keeping the *pai-pai* in the lineage is certainly in the members' interest. In contrast to the Ong case, where under the aegis of the *li chang* all three rotating *pai-pais* are extended to every member of the community, in the Li case the lineage comes into evidence as a political power, securing resources for itself and denying them to outsiders.

As in the instance of the Ongs, the Lis' own perception of themselves as a group is revealed in what they said about *te-li*. The *tang-ki* told me that the Lis' *te-li* was that of a fishnet because of the settlement's enclosure by mountains. "That *te-li* isn't bad at all. It can lead to great wealth and many offspring, but only if the people work hard and make a great effort to improve things themselves. So you see, we Lis are going downhill all the time because no one works very hard. All the young men play around with dogs and pigeons, and never go out to look for work. Our ancestors were the same way—playing around and gambling all our land away." Other Lis declared that the settlement does not have a *te-li* of its own but shares in the *te-li* of the Lou settlement, adjacent to them. A-chan, an elderly man whose life was made unhappy when his daughter-in-law ran away before bearing him any grandsons, said, "We are on the same line as the Lous. But people say that the reason our *te-li* is bad and we are so poor is because the hills behind our settlement are too high."

The *te-li* reflects the primary problem the Lis feel they have: their wealth has declined and left them landless and poor. The fact that some Lis declare they have no *te-li* uniquely their own is symptomatic of this problem. Here, as in other cases, if a weak group is adjacent to a more powerful one, the weaker group will say it shares in the *te-li* of the more powerful one. It is as if the weak group wanted to plug into the power line of the stronger one. Hence the Peqs, peripheral to the Lis and even poorer than they, claimed to share in whatever *te-li* the Lis had. Likewise, some of the Lis, perhaps having given up hope in the future improvement of the lineage on its own, claim a share in the *te-li* of their much richer neighbors, the Lous. Yet in spite of the Lis' decline in wealth, the retention of even a small piece of corporate land provides enough incentive for them to keep at least a vestige of their lineage organization and to make use of that organization to withhold advantages from nonlineage members.

The Lou settlement, lying between the Li settlement and the highway, overlooks an expanse of paddy fields in the front and is flanked by a hill covered with tea bushes in the back. Dominating

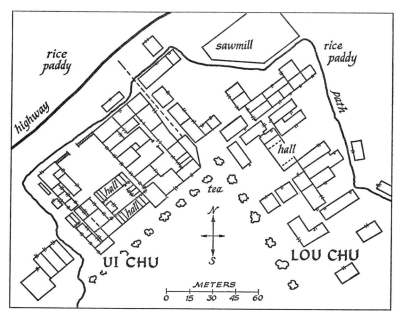

its houses and rising above all of them is the Lou ancestral hall with its soaring, curved eaves. The central settlement population of 242 includes 25 households of Lou lineage members living closely packed around the hall, either in apartments in its wings or in houses adjacent to the wings. Interspersed among these Lous are seven households of other surnames. Members of four of these households are long-time residents with permanent employment in the area. The other three are made up of recent arrivals who have moved in temporarily. Between the Lou and Li settlements is a household of Lous who are not related to the lineage Lous. They are actually closer to the Li settlement, but their front door faces the Lou settlement, and they consider themselves part of it. Across the highway are four widely separated compounds that are all considered part of the Lou settlement; two belong to lineage Lous and two to people of other surnames. Thus, the physical arrangement of the Lou settlement is very similar to the Lis': a central core of houses occupied primarily by lineage members surrounding the lineage hall, plus several outlying houses that are considered part of the settlement.

The organization of the Lou lineage is also very like the Li lineage's, though more elaborate, perhaps because of its more extensive possessions. Unlike the Lis, who are wont to complain sourly about losing most of their corporate land, the Lous proudly claim that all their original corporate paddy land (approximately one *chia* or 2.39 acres) is still intact. Tendered out to the highest bidder within the lineage, this piece of land yields the lineage NT $3,000–4,000 per year. Part of this income is used to finance two corporate feasts, one on the fifteenth day of the eighth month, and the other on the day of the grave festival in the spring. Responsibility for organizing these feasts, following the pattern in the Li lineage, rotates among each of the seven *fang* formed by the seven sons of the founding ancestor. Each *fang* is, however, more clearly distinguished from the others than in the Li lineage. All have an official "representative," and pictures of these seven leaders hang in the ancestral hall. In addition, each *fang* is said to have its own unique character. For example, it is said that members of the sixth *fang* produce many sons but few rich and famous ones, and that members of the fifth *fang* produce the most famous and wealthy Lous. The Lous identify strongly not only with their lineage, but also with their particular *fang*. They see themselves as affected by the nature of their *fang*, that is, as likely to have many sons if they are sixth *fang* or as closely related to many famous people if they are fifth *fang*. Also, they are apt to consult the representative of their *fang* in order to see that their opinions are expressed at the lineage meeting or to voice some complaint. In contrast, among the Lis, though everyone knows what *fang* he belongs to, the *fang* as such are not politically important, nor are they distinguished from one another through the attribution of different characteristics.

The lineage organization of the Lous has still another complexity beyond the *fang* representatives. One of the representatives, the head of the fifth *fang*, is considered to be the chief representative, the head of the entire lineage. This man, a medical doctor educated during the Japanese occupation, resides in Sanhsia. His family is wealthy, once having owned extensive tracts of land. Although most of this land was confiscated as a result of land reform, the family still has large capital assets, among them a thriving medical clinic in Sanhsia run by Dr. Lou's son.

Dr. Lou's primary formal task as head of the lineage is to manage the income from the common lands. He collects the rent from the person who tills the land, distributes what is necessary to pay for the corporate feasts, and retains the rest. He also heads the lineage meeting on the fifteenth of the eight month, when the representatives together with household heads from all the *fang* discuss how surplus funds are to be allocated. He does, in effect, what Hai-a's constitution for the Ong lineage would have the business manager do. Besides managing the corporate income, he is responsible for keeping the written Lou genealogy up to date. I do not know how Dr. Lou came to be the head of all the representatives. He told me he had held that position ever since he took primary responsibility for organizing the rebuilding of the hall in 1926. Other members of the lineage do not seem to resent his leadership but, on the contrary, to appreciate his willingness to manage things and act with authority.

The kind of leader Dr. Lou is can be illustrated by an incident in which his behavior and that of the Ong *li chang* were in direct contrast. On one occasion the *li chang*, finding the funds collected from the Ongs falling short by NT $200, canceled plans to send a band to accompany the presentation of a plaque to an Ong relative who had achieved political office. Reacting quite differently in a similar situation, Dr. Lou advanced NT $2,000 out of his own pocket to make up the amount needed to complete repair of the Lou ancestral grave, reimbursing himself the next year out of surplus income from the lineage lands.

Not only does Dr. Lou take more personal responsibility for the lineage than the Ong *li chang*, he also exercises more authority over lineage affairs. In one incident, several households of seventh *fang* Lous were quarreling over the disposition of the ancestral tablet for their uxorilocally married ancestor two generations back. Because the tablet could not be placed in the main hall with the tablets of the Lou ancestors, it had been kept first with one, then with another family of the ancestor's descendants. The last family to have it had kept it for many years. Finally, the members of this family laid down an ultimatum: if someone else would not take the tablet, they were going to nail it up outside their door. Many discussions took place, but no one else was willing to take the tablet, mostly because they had no room for the large altar necessary to display it. Eventually the representative of the seventh *fang* came up with a solution: they could clean up one of the rooms adjacent to the main hall and set up the tablet there. But before this plan could be carried out, Dr. Lou heard about it and immediately ordered the seventh *fang* representative to abandon the idea. "The hall is corporate property," he argued. "It cannot be used to serve the private interests of any subsegment of the lineage." The representative and the rest of the seventh *fang* capitulated at once and sought another solution. In this case, conflict was avoided because the lineage members respected the authority and leadership of the doctor. He is a strong leader because the lineage members and especially the other representatives are willing to accept his leadership. And they are willing to do so because, among other things, it is usually to their benefit. Although following the doctor's dictates sometimes causes inconvenience, as in the case of the ancestral tablet, at other times, as when he paid for the completion of the grave, his actions benefit the group.

Another important aspect of the doctor's leadership is his willingness to act as mediator in quarrels within the lineage. In one incident, he mediated a dispute between neighbors over whether the path between their houses had been made too narrow as a result of the remodeling of one of the houses. In this case, the *fang* representative of the disputants refused to have anything to do with their quarrel, saying, "I don't have time to pay attention to all your problems. Besides, whatever I do someone will be dissatisfied and hold it against me. It only makes trouble for me." The doctor, however, perhaps because he resides outside the community, and is not enmeshed in its everyday affairs, was willing to help the neighbors resolve the difficulty. On another occasion, the representative of the second *fang* went into the Lou hall and noticed to his irritation that it had not been swept or dusted in some time. Instead of going directly to the person he knew was responsible, he made a trip all the way to Sanhsia and complained to the doctor. He preferred to let the unpleasant task of criticizing a relative fall on the doctor, who was less apt to have regular social contacts with the offender. Having someone to mediate disputes and to see that responsibilities are fulfilled seem to be the most important benefits the lineage members obtain from submitting to Dr. Lou's authority.

Yet by no means are all lineage affairs managed by the doctor. Most local projects involving cooperation between community members are run without help from him. One important undertaking was the assessment of residents to pay for the paving of the footpath that runs through the settlement. Cui-tho, the representative of the seventh *fang*, though sometimes reluctant to act as mediator in quarrels, was the sole organizer for this project. He collected a contribution from every resident of the settlement, Lou lineage members and others alike. After the road was built, he made a plaque with all the names of the contributors on it and hung it in the Lou ancestral hall. The positioning of the plaque in the hall is highly significant when compared with the disposition of such lists in the Ong settlement. There, lineage leadership and activities are separate from community leadership and activities, so the contribution lists for the two sets of affairs are hung in different places. In the Lou settlement, the community and the lineage leadership are one and the same, so all lists, even for community projects, are hung in the same place, the lineage hall. This is true for the Lis and Uis as well.

Many other projects of a community-wide nature were also originally organized by Cui-tho. A large cement trash receptacle is open to use by any resident, regardless of surname, who wants to pay a few dollars each month toward hiring a truck to haul the garbage away. The use of an irrigation pump is open to anyone with fields located below the pump provided he paid a share of the original cost and continues to pay for the electricity needed to pump his fields full. A water tower and pump provide running water for every house in the main settlement, regardless of who resides there, as long as the residents pay the monthly charge.

Still, many as the Lous' community projects are, there are signs that some of them may be falling into disuse, not, as might have been the case if this were the Li settlement, because of poverty, but because of increased prosperity. In the spring of 1970, five households of Lous moved into a new, relatively luxurious row of houses on the northern edge of the settlement. Since each of these houses was equipped with its own water pump, five households simultaneously stopped using the community water tower. At the same time, the old pump broke down. Since Cui-tho was one of those who had moved into a new house, he was not interested in organizing the group to repair the old machine. And several other Lous said, "Times are good and we can afford our own pumps now. The common pump was a bother because it was always breaking down and you had to wait for someone else to fix it." As a result, before long nearly every household in the settlement had purchased its own pump and installed a pipe to the nearest well. There was no quarrel or difference of opinion; when people could afford it they preferred to abandon the inconvenience of a cheap, common water supply for a convenient, expensive system.

The Lou lineage has prospered by taking advantage of newer, more modern ways of making money while maintaining the traditional ones. Nearly every household still owns some rice land handed down from the ancestors, and most manage to farm it. In addition, Cui-tho and another Lou man have developed a successful sawmill located at the north edge of the settlement. It provides work and materials for many Lous, and three Lou household heads, besides the owners, are paid living wages for their work there. The mill also provides low-cost lumber for another enterprise operated by a Lou household, a carpenter shop that specializes in heavy cabinets and chests. Still another family owns a machine that twists straw into heavy rope, which the sawmill purchases to bind sawn lumber. Beyond this, three brothers have become successful building contractors. Almost all the houses that are built or remodeled in the *li* are contracted by them; they were responsible for building the new row of houses in the Lou settlement. When they need lumber they purchase it from the Lou sawmill, obtaining it conveniently and at a reduced price. By using one another's services, each of these Lou enterprises helps increase the others' profits.

There is one other major business in the settlement, a candy factory run by four brothers. They, too, have been successful and have even managed to save enough to purchase a pickup truck, with which one brother delivers candy all over Taipei *hsien*. When the truck is free for other uses, they often drive to one of the textile factories near Taipei and pick up a load of yarn, which many Lou and Li youths use in knitting machines. The brothers turn a small profit from this service as well. All this activity involves a large proportion of Lous in the settlement in a general prosperity. No family can be said to be poor, and most are able to afford luxuries like motorcycles and television sets.

Although the Lous' increased prosperity may lead to the abandonment of some of their community enterprises, it is doubtful whether it will influence their management of the community rituals for Co-su-kong, Tho-te-kong, and the Ang-kong. Where a community project like the water tower is concerned, it is to everyone's advantage for large numbers of people to cooperate, as long as thrift is an important consideration. But where the rotating rituals are concerned, as we saw in the Li lineage, the lineage gains supernatural protection and patronage if it can limit participation in the leadership of the rituals to lineage members. The Lis have succeeded in doing this for the Co-su-kong *pai-pai*. As we might expect, given the well-organized, strong leadership of the Lou lineage, so have the Lous. But the Lous' monopoly on feasting the gods is even more strict: *lo-cus* for both the Co-su-kong *pai-pai* and the Ang-kong *pai-pai* are limited to members of the Lou lineage. When responsibility for either of these *pai-pais* falls on the Lou settlement, whichever *fang* is responsible for managing the corporate feasts that year is also responsible for selecting a *lo-cu* from within its ranks, either by mutual agreement or by competition in throwing the divination blocks. Only the *pai-pai* for Tho-te-kong, god of the earth and protector of the residents of an area, is not limited to the Lou lineage. All residents of the settlement participate in the competition to be *lo-cu* for Tho-te-kong. Partly because of the Lous' strong leadership, resident both locally and in the market town, and partly because of their relative wealth, they dominate the households of the outsiders in their midst. The others are not persecuted or ostracized from social interaction in any way; they are simply prevented from encroaching on the benefit to be gained from organizing the *pai-pais* for the Ang-kong and Co-su-kong.

Judging from the Lous' comments on the *te-li* of their settlement, they consider themselves beneficiaries of better circumstances than the other settlements. I was often told that the Lous have a *te-li* of the dragon, the rarest and most excellent *te-li* to be had. Some Lous pointed out that the main ceiling beam in the ancestral hall "sweats" or exudes beads of water—an infallible sign of a dragon *te-li*. But the most important evidence of the existence of the dragon *te-li* is the state of prosperity and good fortune in the Lou lineage. During the year I lived in Ch'inan five Lou households moved into modern houses by the road, two others built new houses near the hall, and six more completely remodeled their old houses. In contrast to the other settlements, no Lous live in houses with mud floors or mud-brick walls; and television sets and motorcycles abound. The lineage is not beset by a crippling division into antagonistic segments, and its population is expanding rapidly. All these things—wealth, many offspring, and harmonious relations—are thought to be signs of a dragon *te-li*.

If the homogeneity of the settlements were to be represented on a scale, the Ong settlement would be at one end, the Lis' and Lous' in the middle, and the Uis' at the other end. Unlike the Ong settlement, with its relatively high proportion of non-Ong households, the Ui settlement has only two households whose residents bear another surname. One is a product of a uxorilocal marriage with a Ui woman; the second is not related to the Uis. The other 29 are all Uis and belong to the Ui lineage. Hence, 241 out of a total settlement population of 253 are lineage Uis. The residential compactness of the settlements could be put on a scale in this same order. The Ong settlement encompasses a wide area and includes two centers of population as well as some scattered compounds; and the Li and Lou settlements are less spread out, with one main center and a few houses outside it. The Uis, again at the other extreme from the Ongs, have a compact central settlement with several outlying houses, but only one of these is as far removed as the outlying houses in the Li and Lou settlements.

More important, the character of the living units around the Ui hall is different. In the other three settlements, the apartments close to the hall are recognizable as wings of the hall, but many of the connections between the wings have fallen away so that living units of different families have become physically discrete. In the Ui settlement, not only have all the original connections between the wings been preserved, but over the years many more connections have been added. Indeed, in some cases the wings have merged into one another and are virtually indistinguishable. In consequence, walking through the main settlement is like walking through a huge, single compound. From an outer entrance at the left side of the settlement, one passes through a kitchen, a bathroom, another kitchen, and a bedroom before emerging into the central courtyard. Because the rooms are directly adjacent, one never passes through an unroofed area along this route. In fact, the Uis say proudly that you can walk all the way from one end of the settlement to the other in the rain without need of an umbrella. To a large extent this is true, for in many cases the once empty spaces between the wings have been filled in with additional rooms. The result is a solid maze of rooms all opening into each other. (The map on p. 49 shows this compact residence pattern.) If one were to draw a hasty conclusion from the residence pattern of the Uis, one would guess that they are a close-knit group with little internal differentiation. Unwarranted as that conclusion is, based on residence pattern alone, it is borne out by other aspects of the local organization of the lineage.

The Uis' official lineage managers do not represent each *fang* as a separate political element, as the Lou representatives do. The two managers were chosen by popular demand because of their interest in lineage affairs and ability to organize people. They are managers of the entire lineage, not of their own particular *fang*. Hence, the oldest Ui genealogy is in their keeping and kept up to date by them. In addition, it is their responsibility to handle the funds received from rent of the common rice lands, an extensive tract that yields about NT $10,000 annually. Each year part of this money is doled out to whichever one of the nine great *fang* is in charge of managing the corporate feast and the four corporate worship *pai-pais* for the ancestors. As in the Lou lineage, the corporate feast is also the occasion for a lineage meeting at which members discuss the disposition of surplus funds. In 1970, the group decided that if the feast were held only every five years, instead of yearly, the money not spent on the other four years could be used to enrich the lineage in more important ways—for example, to provide for the continued education of the brightest lineage youngsters. "We Uis don't have very many members with high education as the Lous do. In this way we can ensure that the smartest children will go on as far as possible and not be held back by lack of money. The whole lineage will benefit by the gain in prestige."

Although there is evidently a strong sense of identity with the lineage as a whole, the genealogically founded subsegments, the great *fang*, are not as clearly distinguished as among the Lous. Certainly, everyone knows what *fang* he belongs to, but no one mentions any distinguishing characteristics of the nine *fang*, nor are they represented by leaders appointed to protect their interests. As among the Lis, the great *fang* are important chiefly because the responsibility for the corporate feasts rotates among them.

In addition to the two managers who officially represent the lineage, there are other men who take an interest in lineage affairs and who handle some of its problems. One is a man in his sixties whose three sons jointly manage a family noodle factory, which has its headquarters in the Ui settlement. For years this man has been in charge of the pump that takes water from a well to a water tower on the hill behind the settlement, from whence drinking water is piped into every house in the settlement. In the spring of 1970, the water pump, at the end of its mechanical life, broke down. Some of the Uis suggested that since the pump had originally been bought with surplus money from the corporate lands, it should be replaced from that source. Others thought the old pump should be fixed. No one suggested the Lous' solution to the same problem—that the old system be abandoned in favor of separate private wells. In part this was because the Uis are not on the whole so wealthy as the Lous; several families lead a marginal existence, and for them purchasing their own pump would be out of the question. But in addition it was a matter of leadership. As we have seen, once the Lou leader in charge of the settlement water supply got his own pump he was not interested in organizing the repair or replacement of the community system. The Uis, however, still had a responsible person, namely the Ui noodlemaker, to see that the problem was solved. After hearing the opinions of all the lineage members who cared to express them, he took it on himself to see that the pump was fixed, assessing the households who used it. He was able to gain the cooperation of everyone in the settlement even though some people held opposing opinions. Unlike the leaders in the Ong settlement, he was not hampered by the existence of inveterately opposed segments suspicious of his motives.

If the factory of the Ui noodlemaker were large enough, he would probably hire fellow lineage members as helpers, forging still other links among the Uis. As it is, he can handle all of the work with the help of his three sons and their wives. Another village business, however, is thickly populated by Uis. This is an antivenom and vaccine factory, which raises horses in the *li* (between the Li and Ong settlements) and produces serums from their blood. The factory is owned by businessmen who are not natives of Ch'inan, but two Uis are highly placed in the management. In addition, four Ui household heads earn an adequate wage from more menial tasks, such as grooming and feeding the horses. Further, just as some Lous have based their occupations on the needs

of the sawmill, so some Uis provide services the antivenom labora-
tory is willing to buy. Two Ui men support their families by cutting grass that grows wild along the riverbanks and carting it in
for fodder.

Except for one man who makes a living constructing ritual
offerings to the dead out of bamboo splints and paper, these are
the only enterprises in the Ui settlement. Many Uis are busy
enough with their rice land not to need full-time employment for
wages. On the whole the Uis are richer than the other lineages in
corporate land but poorer than the Lous in individual income.
Many of them still live in mud-brick houses, and many cannot
afford expensive luxuries.

The Uis emerge as a close-knit residential group able to cooperate under official and unofficial leaders. Since only two households
in the settlement do not belong to the lineage, the issue of including and excluding outsiders is not as important as in the other
settlements. Nevertheless, those two households are excluded from
the Co-su-kong *pai-pai*. Here, just as in the Li and Lou settlements,
whichever great *fang* is responsible for the corporate ancestral *pai-
pais* is responsible for the Co-su-kong *pai-pai* in the years when
the Ui settlement is in charge of it. The lineage manages to exclude outsiders from one *pai-pai* but does not exclude them twice,
as the Lous do. It may be that the smaller number of nonlineage
residents makes excluding them less important.

Again, as in the case of the other three lineages, the Uis' views
about the *te-li* of the settlement provide important clues about the
nature of the group. What is interesting here, however, is not so
much people's statements about their *te-li* as the steps they have
taken to improve it. The Uis say that theirs is the *te-li* of the lion,
and that their hall is positioned precisely right to benefit from this
te-li. Yet pleased as most of them seem to be with their lot, during
the winter of 1970 there were several conferences between the lineage managers and an expert on *te-li* from Taipei. He assured
them that if they built a wall to enclose the courtyard in front
of the hall, their *te-li* would be even better. The primary result
would be that all the wealth and prestige attained by the Uis

would be held in the group and would not flow out to other people: "As the teeth in the mouth hold in the saliva, so the wall and gate in front of the settlement will hold in our riches and good fortune and not let them escape." Acting on this advice, the Uis used surplus funds from the corporate lands to build a high brick wall and gate across the front of the settlement. In this instance, as in others, the Uis found it very important that they were in a position to pay for this lineage project with money earned by the corporate lands. They felt that if an assessment had to be made from every household, the project would be an agglomeration of separate elements, rather than an unambiguously corporate enterprise. They always spoke of the wall (and of other settlement projects, such as the water pump and tower) as having come from the ancestors; that is, they were financed out of the proceeds from land that had been set aside as corporate property by the ancestors.

The completion of the wall set the Ui settlement off from the other settlements even more distinctly. Before the wall was built, the Uis were already huddled together, closely packed into a compact unit with few stragglers. The wall merely sealed off the only break in their defenses. In the next chapter we will uncover some historical reasons for the Uis' tendency to close themselves off from the others. For the present it is enough to note that the wall is a physical representation of a posture taken by the group, a turning inward and presenting of a united front to the outside. One symptom of this tendency is revealed in a practice that became possible only after the wall was built. It is customary, on the day of a wedding, for the boy's parents to hang a piece of red cloth over the door of their house. This represents their happiness and good fortune in gaining a daughter-in-law. But after the wall was finished, the Uis began hanging the cloth, not over the door of the family concerned, but over the gate in the wall. For them, the marriage, though it actually affects only a segment of the group, draws them all into interaction with an outside group. When one family takes a daughter-in-law, the whole lineage is involved in the happy event; hence, the red cloth is hung above the gate to the entire settlement, not over the door of any single family.

CHAPTER 4

Within the Circle of Bamboo

A T T H I S P O I N T, having had a look at the four lineages in their settlements, we might usefully discuss the relationship of the four settlements to one another. I have said that they occupy a common territory, conceived as such by the residents, and that during their early history they were closely allied. But have these early ties fallen away over the years, leaving the four settlements isolated units, like villages? Or have they remained associated, so that the *li* is neither one village nor four villages, but rather four groups more closely connected than four villages yet less bound together than four parts of the same village? In fact, the four parts of Ch'i-nan cohere as a social unit in an unusual way, as discussion of the rotating *pai-pais* and earth-god temples will disclose.

In discussing the rotation of *pai-pais* among the four settle-ments, what concerns us is not the Ang-kong *pai-pai*, in which Ch'i-nan cooperates with Ch'ipei and Ch'itung, but the two *pai-pais* in which the four settlements alone are involved, those for Co-su-kong and Tho-te-kong. Let us take them in that order. The festival for Co-su-kong is held on the fourth day of the first month. On that day the settlement or lineage in charge must fetch an image of the god from the Sanhsia temple. Once in the settlement, the image is placed in a sedan chair, which is either rented from the temple or borrowed from one of the Ch'inan lineages. A procession forms behind the image, composed of a small band of horn and drum players, usually from the Li settlement, and three men to carry and beat a huge brass gong. In the rear walks the *lo-cu* and any-one else who is interested. Starting from the lineage hall of the settlement in charge, the procession "beats the bounds," which is to say, marches along a path that marks the geographical boundaries of the *li*. Usually, as the procession marches slowly past isolated houses, the residents dash out to *pai-pai* the god with incense. If they are slow to come, the procession waits; the *lo-cu* may even go inside to fetch them. When the procession reaches a densely populated cluster of houses, such as the area surrounding a lineage hall, it stops and waits until everyone has had a chance to worship.

In 1970, the Ui *lo-cu* and the procession he organized toured the *li* in the following order. Beginning at the Ui ancestral hall, they proceeded to the Lou settlement, then to the Lis', and on to the lower Ong settlement. They next marched up to the farthest house in the upper Ong valley that is considered a part of Ch'inan, then turned around and marched out to the road. From there, they proceeded slowly, waiting for each isolated household on the other side of the highway to send out a representative to *pai-pai*. Eventually, the procession made full circle and ended at the Ui settlement, where the god's image was placed inside the hall.

The god is said to be touring his realm, overseeing a small part of his domain, during this procession. The territorial unit that he surveys on this occasion corresponds to social boundaries established by the residents of the *li*. Whereas the earthly authorities sometimes establish governmental divisions on the land that are at odds with socially defined territories, the supernatural authorities are thought to recognize only units that are socially relevant to the residents. Hence, the god was not escorted all the way up the valley behind the Ongs even though the last houses are not far beyond where the procession stopped. According to the government classification, in fact, the farthermost houses belong to Ch'inan *li*, but they do not belong to it according to where their social interaction occurs. It is Ch'inan seen as a social unit by the residents that is surveyed by the god on his tour.

It is also Ch'inan that the god is beseeched to protect for another year. Each year, only one of the settlements or lineages provides an opera for the god. Yet all the residents regard the person holding the position of *lo-cu* as their representative before the god.

In addition, every resident trusts the *lo-cu* to dispose of funds honestly and wisely, for the cost of the opera is shared by each household in the *li*. There is thus a relationship of interdependence among the four settlements for supernatural favor. For three out of four years, each settlement is content to rely on the efforts of another settlement to please the god and obtain his protection for another year. To be sure, residents of settlements that do not have the opera may make their own offerings to the god, but he is thought to be especially pleased by opera performances. Only the first day of opera is financed by the entire *li*. After that, the settlement in charge is supposed to continue the show by taking up a collection among its residents. Consequently, the other three settlements are at least partly dependent on the willingness of that settlement to please the god with opera. But this fact reacts in turn on the settlement in charge. In 1970, there was much talk among the Uis to the effect that they would be criticized by the rest of the *li* residents if they failed to provide a good enough show. In this way the four settlements remain tied together by their interdependence in ritual affairs.

Virtually the same account could be given for the rotating Tho-te-kong *pai-pai*. Like Co-su-kong, Tho-te-kong is feted by each of the four settlements in turn. Yet his relationship to the *li* is both more intimate and more complex than Co-su-kong's, for the only locus of Tho-te-kong relevant for the residents of the *li* is within the *li* itself. In order to discuss the present location of Tho-te-kong images I must outline the history of former Tho-te-kong temples in the *li* as best I could piece it together from my informants' accounts.

Originally, perhaps in the early 1900's, there was a small Tho-te-kong temple housing an image that belonged to the entire *li* on the banks of the Hengch'i River. As the course of the river moved southward, eroding land, the original site of the temple was washed away. Another temple was then built by the *li* residents approximately equidistant from all four settlements, and there it stands today.

The next major change for Tho-te-kong occurred about ten

years before my visit. At that time, the fortunes of the Ongs were
in decline. In particular, their rice harvests had been scanty, and
their chickens and pigs were dying. According to the Ongs, "We
were having a lot of trouble with our crops and livestock because
the door of the Tho-te-kong temple didn't face us. Tho-te-kong
couldn't see us very easily and didn't know what trouble we were
having. So we built ourselves another temple right in our settlement facing us directly so that Tho-te-kong would be more likely
to protect us. Since then everything has been fine." Virtually
everyone in the *li* I questioned about the existence of two temples
to the earth god gave me this same story for the first several
months of my stay, in spite of my suspicion that there was more
to be told.

Finally I obtained evidence of a conflict that could not be denied, and as a result, I was told a more complete tale. My evidence
came from the list of contributors to the temple building fund
that hangs in the Ong Tho-te-kong temple. Listed are the names
of all the household heads for both Ongs and other surname hold-
ers in the area of the Ong settlement with one exception: none of
the three Ui households in the upper Ong settlement is represented. When I confronted several members of the Ong *thau* with
this fact, they told me:

We felt that the position of the temple was unfairly beneficial to the
other three settlements because it faced them more than us. So, because
we were having economic troubles, the *li chang* called a meeting of the
li and asked the others to agree to finance another temple that faced
more in our direction. But some of the Uis wanted the temple left where
it was because they were not suffering from bad times. Since they wouldn't
agree to move the temple, we Ongs had to build our own. We felt that
since the temple is supposed to be for the whole *li*, it should be oriented
so as to benefit us all equally.

The Ui noodlemaker corroborated this story and added:

Those Ongs wanted to grab away all of the god's protection for themselves. Of course we wouldn't agree to let them change the temple's
direction. It was an Ong geomancer who originally recommended that
the temple be oriented the way it is now. We went along with them
once, but they can't always expect to run things their way. The temple
belongs to the whole *li*, not just one settlement.

The Uis felt very strongly about this and were apparently able to exert so much pressure on their relatives in the Ong settlement that they refused to contribute to the Ongs' protest action, the construction of their own temple. Neither do those Uis participate in the rotation of a plaque for the new temple, which circulates only within the Ong settlement. By refraining, they have demonstrated that they are members of the Ui lineage first, and bound to follow policies set by it, and that their residence in the Ong settlement clearly comes second. What may have been partly an attempt by the Ong *li chang* to exercise power within the whole *li* did not succeed. Far from succeeding, it managed only to cement more strongly the lineage ties of the Uis in the Ong settlement and weaken their territorial ties to their place of residence.

It is difficult to know how to interpret the Ongs' building of their own temple. Since they already had an image of Tho-te-kong in their ancestral hall prior to the dispute with the other settlements, the move does seem largely an act of protest and defiance. It is as if the Ongs were saying, "You won't go along with our plan, but that won't stop us; we'll build a temple that faces us anyway." When the temple was built, they simply moved the old image from the lineage hall into it. In the Ongs' case, this separation of the hall and the Tho-te-kong is particularly appropriate. As we have seen, the *li chang* regards the settlement as a territorial unit, whereas others are trying to reestablish lineage dominance. The physical separation of the Tho-te-kong image, the god of earth and protector of all who live on it, from the lineage hall is in accord with this basic separation of interests.

As we saw earlier, the Ong settlement differs from the other settlements in hanging lists that concern exclusively lineage matters in a separate place from those involving all the residents of the settlement. Paralleling this difference, the Tho-te-kong image is separate from the lineage hall in the Ong case but inside the hall in each of the other three settlements.

It is not easy to say what the true significance of these images is. Certainly the four of them, each in the appropriate settlement, mark off the four territorial divisions within the *li*. Beyond these and the one in the main *li* temple, there are no other images of Tho-te-kong in the *li*. Yet these are not the only locations at which Tho-te-kong can be worshiped. I was assured that anyone at all could obtain an image and set it up in his house if he so desired. In fact, various households in all the settlements have pictures of the god that seem to function as convenient places at which offerings can be made to him without going all the way to his main temple.* One informant told me it was like telephoning someone. Each picture or image is a telephone extension from which the god can be reached. Going to the main temple may in some cases be considered better insurance of making contact, but ordinarily the site does not matter much.

Given the multitude of locations at which offerings can be made to Tho-te-kong, as well as the fact that people tend to go only as far as the closest image or picture to make their offerings, one is prompted to wonder whether the main *li* Tho-te-kong temple plays any important role at all in the *li*. It occurred to me that the already decrepit temple might simply be allowed to crumble away altogether, perhaps symbolizing the decay of the ties between the four settlements and the loss of their identity as a single social unit. But in the winter of 1970, the *li chang* began talking about plans to finance the rebuilding of the old *li* temple. Throughout, as the project took shape, though the instigation and planning were largely the *li chang*'s, he received much support and cooperation from people in the other settlements.

When the *li chang* began talking of rebuilding the temple, he had funds from two sources in hand. A couple from Taipei who often hiked in the mountains behind Ch'inan claimed that an old man with a long, white beard had emerged out of a torrential rainstorm and had led them to safety in the Tho-te-kong temple, thereafter immediately disappearing. Out of gratitude for what was an obvious act of Tho-te-kong's, they had given the *li chang* NT $2,000 toward the reconstruction of the temple. In addition, there was a corporate *li* fund of NT $6,000. This money was said to

---

* Pictures of Tho-te-kong and other gods are commonly found on domestic ancestral altars, which are discussed in Chapter 7.

have come from the sale of a piece of land owned in common by the *li* residents before the Japanese occupation. It had once been the site of a public building, I was told, where a kindergarten for the *li* children was held. Although this story was repeated independently by informants in all four settlements, I was not able to find any documents or other hard evidence to back it up. But if such a piece of land did exist, there was plainly cooperation among the settlements to the extent of holding property and a building in common, much as lineages hold property in common. In fact, as we shall see, there are elements of the Tho-te-kong temples that make them like the territorial equivalent of a lineage hall.

Besides the single contribution from the Taipei couple and the corporate *li* fund, the *li chang* also took advantage of a government campaign to increase voter participation. Any *li* producing a turn-out of better than 80 per cent for the local and national elections was entitled to a prize of NT $10,000. The *li chang* and many others encouraged everyone of age to vote "so that we will win that prize and increase our fund for the new Tho-te-kong temple." So many people cared about this goal that the *li* succeeded in passing the necessary 80 per cent, thus adding NT $10,000 to the Tho-te-kong fund. Finally the *li chang* proposed an assessment of NT $10 on each person registered in the *li*. As far as I know, everyone in the *li* paid at least this amount, and certainly some exceeded it by a considerable sum.

With all this money in the till, it became apparent that there would indeed be enough to begin construction. Accordingly, the *li chang* called a meeting of *li* residents to discuss the style of the new temple. This led in turn to the appointment of a committee of residents from all four settlements to make a tour of the most beautiful Tho-te-kong temples in the immediate area and select from among them the most appealing style. Significantly, from beginning to end there was never any mention of changing the direction of the temple; it was taken for granted that the temple was to remain oriented in its original direction. The goal of the *li chang* was now clearly not to garner any special advantages for the Ong settlement but rather to "make a bigger and more beautiful temple. People can see it from the road so it will be much more impressive when it is remodeled."

As I accompanied the men who toured the nearby temples, it became even clearer that a primary motive for rebuilding the temple was to represent the community to the outside world in as impressive, expensive, and ornate a manner as possible. The wealth put into the Tho-te-kong temples we surveyed was taken as an indication of the wealth of the residents of the community; the residents share in the admiration excited by an elaborate and expensive Tho-te-kong temple. It is highly significant and strong proof of the extent to which the four settlements still feel they form a single social unit that they are willing to raise and contribute money for a single temple representing all of them. The temple is inconveniently far away from all four settlements. Probably on most occasions people will not trouble to walk all the way to the main temple to make offerings. Yet in the future, as in the past (and even when the temple was quite decrepit), a representative of one household in the *li* must walk to the temple each day to light candles and burn incense. Responsibility is delegated by the circulation of a wooden plaque from household to household day by day. It passes from the Lou settlement to the Lis to the Ongs to the Uis, tying each resident to a temple that represents them all as members of Ch'inan.

The new temple was not complete before I left the village. Although it was clear there would be two functioning Tho-te-kong temples in the *li* before long, I had little hope of finding out what the eventual relationship between the Ong Tho-te-kong temple and the new *li* temple would be. Just before my departure, however, there was a ceremony for the raising of the ridge pole and there I overheard a conversation that may give us some hints. An elderly man from the Ong lineage angrily confronted a man from the Ui lineage saying he had heard that the Ui noodlemaker was telling people the Ongs had no right to take part in the building of the temple at all. "Oh, that can't be right," said the Ui man. "This temple belongs to the entire *li*, not just to some of us. Of course the Ongs have a right to take part. No matter how many different Tho-te-kong temples you build you always have a share in the earlier or bigger ones. So, of course the Ongs can belong to their own temple and this one as well." Finding at least this Ui in agreement with him, the Ong man relaxed and repeated that the new temple belonged to the whole of Ch'inan. Apparently the relationship of the two temples within the *li* is open to interpretation, depending on one's point of view. As far as the Ui noodlemaker is concerned, when the Ongs went off on their own they opted out of the joint temple. Their own separate temple should replace their part in the other one.

In fact, if the trend of development within the *li* were otherwise, that is, if the *li* were tending to fragment into four separate parts, each with no desire to cooperate or be associated with the other three, this attitude might well have been adopted by the Ongs too; they perhaps would not have wanted to be included in the plans for the new temple. But in that case, each of the other settlements might also have built a temple to house its Tho-te-kong image and represent it separately as a territorial unit before the outside world.

This is all pure speculation, of course, for there was no such fragmentation. The Ongs were among the most eager to see the new temple built and certainly were willing to contribute their share to the temple fund. They view themselves as members of two territorial groups, one inclusive of the other. The two temples mark off the two groups. On this theory, the two temples are in some ways like the territorial equivalent of two lineage halls for two segments of a lineage, one of which is inclusive of the other. In a lineage, all members share in a hall at the level of the founding ancestor. So, by rough analogy, it is with a *li*: all its residents share in the *li* temple. If, in the lineage, there is another hall for an ancestor who is a descendant of the founder, those who have a share in the second hall keep their share in the first. So, continuing the analogy, if a subgroup within a larger territorial group builds its own temple, then it may be said to have a share in both temples, one for the largest group of which it is a part and one exclusive to itself.

Events involving Tho-te-kong and Co-su-kong are the major occasions on which the settlements expect to cooperate, though, as we have seen, cooperation may sometimes give way to conflict. The primary conflicts that have occurred in the *li* were between two lineages, pitting whole groups rather than particular individuals against one another. About the first of these conflicts, I have very little data. People seemed to feel that it happened a long time ago, and because it does not still affect relations among the settlements, they did not seem very interested in discussing it. I was told that some time before the Japanese occupation, the Lis challenged the Ong ownership of the mountain directly behind the Li settlement. The Ongs rose up in a body to defend their land, perhaps much as they did in their dispute with the Tiu:s over the river wall, and, consequently, the Lis withdrew their challenge. There was much bad feeling, but the two groups never came to blows. For a time they did not intermarry, but after about two generations, the ill feeling subsided, and today there is intermarriage between them.

In this dispute no substantial loss was incurred by either side. There was no loss of life or injury, and not much change in the status quo. In another case, this one involving the Uis and the Lous, the outcome was far different. Since I have no written records of this conflict, the following narrative has been pieced together from my conversations with members of the respective groups, as well as with men who served as officials during the Japanese period. Everyone is in agreement that the trouble started with a dispute over the ownership of some land. Originally, though the Uis and the Lous came over from the mainland together, the Uis settled in a nearby *chen* while the Lous cleared land in Ch'inan. At that time some people named Kou lived next to the Lous. The Uis say that when this family decided to move away from Ch'inan, the Lous contacted their friends the Uis, asking them to buy the Kou land and move in, thus helping the Lous defend their land against the still unpacified aborigines; and that as a favor to the Lous, the Uis did so. The Lous, for their part, claim that they owned the land the Kou people lived on, and that after it was

vacated, they offered to give it outright to the Uis in return for
their help in defending the area against the aborigines.

After the Uis moved in, a dispute arose over a piece of land.
The Uis claimed it belonged to the Kous and hence, through purchase, to them; the Lous claimed it was still theirs. Unlike the dispute between the Lis and the Ongs, which never came to blows,
this conflict ended in a pitched battle in which lives were lost
on both sides. Afterward, all social intercourse between the two
groups stopped. It was said that members of the two lineages spat
and looked away whenever they happened to pass each other. The
Uis diverted the stream that had been watering the Lou land after
passing through their own, forcing the Lous to find another source
of irrigation. In addition, the combatants swore that in the future
none of their descendants could ever intermarry with the other
group. This edict is still taken very seriously by both Uis and Lous.
Although cases of intermarriage have occurred in spite of the inter-
diction, they have supposedly ended in infertility or crippled children.*

The enmity between the groups did not end with the battle. It
was continued for many years during the Japanese occupation.
Both Uis and Lous now agree that when the Japanese began to
occupy Sanhsia *chen*, the Uis were leaders of a local "self-protec-
tion organization" that attempted to fight off the Japanese. The
Lous, on the other hand, offered no resistance. Their hall was
probably burned as part of a general attempt to quell insurgence
in the area, not in an attempt to single them out for special punishment. Indeed, after the area was occupied, the Lous managed

---

* Except in the Ui-Lou case, intermarriage or its lack does not affect relationships among the settlements in a substantial way. But though there are no
other prohibitions on marriage between lineages in Ch'inan, the vast majority
of Ch'inan girls and boys who marry in the major fashion (in which the girl
is transferred to the groom's house as an adult) take partners from outside.
This is probably because, as people say, if the girl comes from within the
community she will always be running home to her natal family. To illustrate,
of 137 major marriages contracted by Ongs from 1900 to 1949, only seven
partners had their natal homes in Ch'inan. When lineage families do occasionally contract marriages within the *li*, they do not forge exclusive links with
one or two other lineages. For example, among these seven Ong marriages,
there was at least one person from each of the other settlements.

to obtain several positions of importance under the Japanese administration. Dr. Lou, current head of the lineage, was one of the Taiwanese physicians who served the Japanese. Several Lous told me that their fathers and grandfathers were policemen under the Japanese. Further, during one period the *ch'ü chang* for the area was a relative of the Lous.* Beyond this, the Japanese used the ancestral hall of a Ch'itung branch of the Lou lineage for their regional headquarters.

The Uis, meanwhile, were subjected to harsh treatment at the hands of the Japanese. The lineage members attribute their troubles to the Lous, claiming that they acted as informers and falsely accused the Uis of every crime and misdemeanor in the area. In consequence, they contend, Uis were unjustly imprisoned and subjected to harsh punishment. In addition, according to the Uis, the Lous used their privileged position to assert false claims to some of the Uis' land. As a result, they were able to redraw the land records so as to include Ui land under Lou ownership. The Lous, without denying that the Uis were unfairly treated, claim that this harsh handling was a logical consequence of the Uis' armed resistance when the Japanese began to occupy the area.

Whatever the actual facts, the events of this period served only to increase the antagonism between the Lous and the Uis. In addition, there is some indication that the other two settlements were more closely associated with the Lous than with the Uis. The Lis claim they have always been on good terms with the Lous and, as evidence, they substantiate the Lous' account of events during the Japanese occupation. Although the Ongs presently take a position of impartiality toward the dispute between the two sides, we know that an Ong held the governmental post of *ch'ü chang* during the occupation, so the Ongs must have been in the favor of the regime. All this points to a period in which three of the settlements were at odds with the fourth, the Uis. The antagonism of the Uis was largely directed against the Lous. But if the Lis and

---

* During the Japanese period the *ch'ü* was an administrative area larger than the *li*. In this case the *ch'ü* included some villages farther up the valley as well as Ch'ipei, Ch'itung, and Ch'inan.

Ongs were also in the favor of the Japanese, the Uis might have felt persecuted by them as well. Even if this were not the case, the Uis would have been neatly cut off from normal contact with the rest of the *li* by their conflict with their only neighbors, the Lous, who occupy the land between them and the other settlements. There is enough evidence, certainly, to warrant the hypothesis that the Uis were somewhat isolated from the rest of the *li* during this period. This experience may have formed their tendency to view themselves as an enclave within the *li*, connected still through rotating rituals and the Tho-te-kong temple, but also separated, living packed close around their hall and sealed behind a high wall.

In spite of the Lou-Ui battle and the lasting antagonism it produced, the four *chu* still maintain enough sense of their unity as residents of Ch'inan to contribute to a common temple for Tho-te-kong. Perhaps because of their long history of cooperation in fighting off a common enemy and their simultaneous development of irrigated rice paddy, they have forged links that bind them inextricably as residents of Ch'inan, "Within the Circle of Bamboo."

CHAPTER 5

Some Parameters of the Lineage System

Now that we have completed a separate discussion of each of the lineages we can begin to determine why they are similar in some ways but different in others. I will attempt to do this by showing the relationships between some of the variables that are relevant to these Chinese lineage communities. Maurice Freedman provides a list of such variables, which he uses to formulate models of two types of lineages, A and Z (1958: 131–32).

Type A is a lineage with a small population whose members live at a low economic level. Its members possess no corporate property except perhaps the gravesite of the founding ancestor. Because of its weak position the lineage may be under the control of a stronger lineage and pay it tribute in return for protection. Ritual care of the ancestors is relatively simple, since there is no worship except before domestic shrines and the tomb of the founder. Both written genealogies and segmentation below the level of the sublineages formed by the sons of the founder are absent. Leadership is in the hands of the eldest men in the senior generation; they serve as heads of their respective sublineages and handle disputes within the lineage.

Type Z, at the other end of the scale, has a population of 2,000–3,000 people, among whom are officials and successful merchants. Most lineage members are poor, but the lineage itself owns much corporate property. The segmentation within the lineage is asymmetrical, meaning that some sublineages and branches of sublineages possess more ancestral halls and more men of wealth and distinction than others. There are both written genealogies and

elaborate ancestral rites. The latter reflect the existence of segments within the lineage. Leadership may belong nominally to
genealogical elders, but gentry—men of wealth and social standing—exercise much of the actual decision-making and conflict-
resolving power.

As Freedman presents them, these are descriptive types showing
the range of variation that is known to occur among Chinese lineages. This variation is a result both of the presence or absence of
certain traits, such as corporate property, and of differences in
form of other traits, such as leadership (i.e., the leaders are gentry
in some cases and elders in others). Freedman (p. 132) claims that
these "are explanatory models in the sense that, by implication,
they show the interconnexions between elements; in A smallness
of scale and a rudimentary genealogical segmentation go with a
low level of corporate property and a lack of social differentiation,
while in Z the complementary correlations are shown." But he
could not show, given the data available, more precise relationships among the variables.

One way to do this is to formulate a list of those traits identified as characterizing the Chinese case that can vary from instance
to instance. Here, following Freedman's example, we might list
size of local population, economic level, economic differentiation,
corporate property, ancestral cult, genealogy, leadership, and segmentation. These are traits whose presence, absence, or varying
forms describe the variation among Chinese lineages. This list of
variables is incomplete as it stands, however; as we will see later,
there are other traits that vary importantly from case to case and
that should be included. For now the most important task is to
determine the interrelationship of the listed variables, ascertain-
ing where possible which are dependent and which are independent. Often the data available are not sufficient to reach a definitive conclusion; hence, this is only a preliminary analysis. Freedman began this endeavor with his discussion on lineage types A
and Z, showing that certain traits seem to go naturally together
in Chinese communities. Where possible, I will try to show more
specifically the nature of the connection between related traits and

to explain why they are associated. In the present discussion, only some of what I will eventually attempt to analyze will appear. Leaving to the next chapters the complex problems of the relationship of ancestor worship and segmentation to other variables, I shall present here a tentative analysis of five traits that can appropriately be discussed at this stage in the essay: corporate property, genealogy, the size of the local population, leadership, and corporate activity. My conclusions are based on evidence gathered from the four lineage settlements within Ch'inan.

For convenience, let us begin with corporate property, a variable that is itself independently related to other variables. The Ch'inan evidence shows that corporate property set aside in the name of the founding ancestor depends for its maintenance on the continuation of an adequate economic level among lineage members. As the Lis' case demonstrates, when the wealth of a lineage as a whole has declined, its members who are in need of funds may force the sale of all or part of the corporate lands for a share of the profits. The Uis and Lous, who have never gone through a similar period of economic deprivation, have never sold any of their common lands. Probably, if the decline in wealth were limited to a small segment of the lineage, the rest of the members could not be persuaded to sell part of the lands to provide relief for a few. Generally speaking, corporate land is highly valued as a heritage from the ancestors and will not be easily relinquished. When some people to whom certain Lous had rented the common lands attempted to claim it as their own after the Land Reform Act in 1949, the Lous responsible promptly bought it back at the price set by the government rather than risk loss of the land.

Besides economic necessity, other factors have led to the loss of corporate land in Ch'inan. Although the Ongs often say their focal ancestors were two brothers, at other times they claim that the first Ongs to settle in Ch'inan were four brothers in the second ascending generation from the focal ancestors. I will discuss possible reasons for this discrepancy in the Ongs' account of their ancestry in a later chapter. Here I am concerned only with the fact that the four brothers are said to have formed four *ku*, or parts, and to have set aside corporate land in the name of their father. This land and responsibility for several corporate events rotated as it does in the other settlements today. Most of the Ongs were unclear about how long the rotation continued. At some point, at least several generations ago, the land was sold. As far as the Ongs could remember from what they had been told, one *ku*, composed largely of Ch'inan residents, had increased in population well beyond the other three *ku*. As a result, there were many more Ongs from the Ch'inan *ku* attending the yearly feast financed by the income from the corporate land than from the other *ku*. Eventually, the income from the land was insufficient to pay for the feast, and the person responsible had to add funds of his own. Finally, the members of the *ku* with the fewest members refused to participate any longer. Far from benefiting from the responsibility for corporate events, they felt that they were being asked to bear an intolerable financial loss. In the first place, those who had responsibility for the feast had to provide funds that were needed for other expenses. This is much like the existing situation, in which the Ongs have had trouble carrying out projects that depended on assessments. In the second place, the least populous *ku* bore a disproportionate share of the responsibility, since the fewer the sub-*fang* formed by sons in the third generation from the founder, the more often each sub-*fang* becomes responsible.

Once the members of the disgruntled *ku* declined to take part in the rotation the other three *ku* lost interest in the rotation too. The Ongs say that in the end the representatives of the four *ku* sold the corporate land and divided the profits among themselves. A similar process might occur in the Li settlement unless the Lis increase their holdings of common land. Some of the lineage members are already complaining that the amount of rice they receive as compensation for providing the corporate feast is insufficient. If the economic loss becomes severe, it is conceivable that a disruption of the rotation similar to that experienced by the Ong lineage might happen in the Li case.

Thus far we have related the preservation of corporate land to economic benefit and loss alone. But in some cases there are quite different factors involved. The Ongs, for example, are potentially as rich in income-producing corporate property as any of the other three lineages. If they wanted to, they could force the man who operates the coal mine on their mountain land to pay his back rent. With that money, they could purchase land or equipment or make some other profitable investment, and use the proceeds or interest to carry on corporate activities, as the other lineages do. Yet, as we have seen, the prospects of their doing this are very dim. The deep division within the Ongs prevents them from corporate action, even when, as in this instance, it might bring material benefit to all. Unless that barrier is removed, the potential of their corporate property will probably remain unrealized. This points to the conclusion that any assumption of a simple, direct relationship between economic benefit and the use of corporate property is oversimplified. Plainly, the Ongs need do very little to acquire substantial corporate funds; that they do not do so is related to their lack of unity and the split in their leadership, not to the possibility of economic loss. In the presence of division within the group, the promise of economic benefit is insufficient to spur them to take corporate action.

In summary, we may say that in some cases either economic necessity growing out of a general decline in the standard of living of the group or economic loss experienced in providing feasts may result in the loss or decrease of the corporate land. Probably in most cases, the converse—that attaining profit from the land will result in its maintenance—is also true. But as the Ong case illustrates, other factors may intervene, so that the profit the corporate property might yield is not realized. Those other factors, conflict in the group and in its leadership, may even lead to the loss of the corporate property.

Corporate property, depending for its own maintenance on other factors, may itself influence still other aspects of the lineage, such as the importance placed on the genealogy. Before discussing the relationship between corporate property and genealogies, however, we should note that in most cases literacy is probably a precondition for the acquisition of a written genealogy. To be sure, if all the members of a lineage were illiterate, they could still hire an outsider to write a genealogy for them (provided they could afford it). But the resulting document would be virtually useless; they would be unable to add to it or to change and manipulate it without seeking the help of an outsider. The inconvenience involved in having to rely on an outsider even to read the document makes it seem unlikely that an illiterate group would have much use for a written genealogy.

In traditional China and the early period on Taiwan, when literacy depended on the wealth to provide leisure, it would be fair to suppose that the existence of a genealogy could be tied to a degree of economic wealth sufficient for some lineage members to free themselves from labor long enough to be educated. All four Ch'inan genealogies were begun on the mainland or were copied from the originals prepared there during the time before universal literacy. Although I can produce no independent proof that some lineage members were literate, my informants were sure that the documents had been drawn up by literate lineage members and safeguarded over the years by their literate descendants. If so, attainment of literacy must have depended on some lineage members amassing enough wealth to attain education. The presence of one variable, a written genealogy, can be related to another, an economic level sufficient to allow education. But the literacy made possible by economic wealth is merely a precondition for the existence of a genealogy. We cannot draw the conclusion that if there is literacy in a group of agnates, there must perforce be a genealogy. Written genealogies can be more or less useful, play an important or unimportant role, depending on other circumstances.

There is some reason to think that the genealogy itself varies in importance among the four lineages. At present the Uis' genealogy is the most complete and the most often consulted. The Lous' is complete except for the most recent generation. It is less accessible than the Uis', but the situation will be improved if some of the *fang* carry out a tentative plan to copy it. The Lis' genealogy is very accessible but is incomplete for the last three gener-

ations. The Ongs again lie at the far end of the scale. Their genealogies are neither accessible nor complete from three generations
back.*

This variation corresponds well with another factor: the amount
of corporate land owned by each lineage. The Uis possess the most
common land and have the most surplus capital from it. The Lous
and Lis lie in between, and the Ongs fall at the other end with
no regular corporate income at all. This suggests that a recorded
genealogy is more important or less important depending on what
can be gained from a particular genealogical connection to the
lineage. In the case in point, what there is to be gained is a turn
in the rotation of the corporate land. For the Ongs, no land rotates, so particular genealogical ties that would determine the order of rotation are relatively unimportant; the genealogy has declined as a relevant document. Further, in the absence of access to
the genealogy, the Ongs tend to forget many genealogical connections. For the other three lineages, a turn at receiving the profit
from the corporate land is still important and still dependent on
one's genealogical position in the lineage. The Uis stand to gain
most from a turn at handling the corporate responsibilities. At the
least, whichever Uis are responsible obtain a large supply of feast
foods three times a year. Because only one of the four corporate
pai-pais involves a feast for the entire lineage, the food used to
pai-pai the ancestors on the other three feast days is retained by
the segment responsible. Besides, an enterprising Ui can always
find ways to spend less cash than he is given, keeping the rest for
himself. The very definite benefits obtained from managing the
corporate income may account for the Uis' extensive use of their
genealogy: the document would plainly be essential to settle disputes and questions over the correct order of rotation. Thus,
though the existence of a written genealogy may depend on literacy in turn made possible by wealth, the importance of a genealogy may depend in part on the existence of some advantage to

* I am estimating the relative accessibility of the genealogies on the basis
of whether they are kept in Ch'inan or elsewhere. The Uis' and Lis' are stored
in Ch'inan; the Lous' and Ongs' are not.

be gained by a particular genealogical connection to the rest of
the lineage.

We have seen in the first discussion how the use of corporate
property may depend on a modicum of unity in the group, and
in the second how the importance of genealogies may be increased
by the possession of corporate property. Corporate property may
have some relation to the size of the locally effective population
as well. By this term I mean neither the absolute population size
of the lineage nor the size of the population resident at the original settlement, but rather the percentage of lineage members not
resident in the original settlement who still maintain ties with it.
These ties may vary greatly from case to case, involving anything
from an obligation to return periodically or to contribute to lineage projects, to a mere acknowledgment of kinship with the
people living at the original settlement. The latter is a tenuous
connection indeed unless it is accompanied by an obligation to act
in some context or other.

It is perhaps obvious by now that members of a lineage with
corporate property who take up residence elsewhere would more
readily remain part of the lineage's locally effective population
than would those of a lineage without corporate property. Whenever a member of the Li, Lou, or Ui lineage moves away from
Ch'inan, he maintains at the very least a responsibility for managing the corporate activities when his turn comes around. Most
people return for this occasion when it is their responsibility; if
they find it impossible to do so, they must discharge the obligation in some other way, possibly by finding a substitute or sending money. The Uis and the Lous both estimate that they have
effective local populations of approximately 900 people, and the
Lis put theirs at some 500.*

There is no apparent reason why the same kind of obligation
might not be maintained in the absence of common property, but

---

* If these figures, which are only the rough estimates offered by informants,
are anywhere close to the true figures, they suggest that there are more lineage
members outside Ch'inan who maintain ties with their lineages than there are
lineage members resident in Ch'inan. This in itself is a measure of the strength
of people's attachment to lineage concerns.

the experience of the Ongs suggests that this is not likely to occur. After the representatives of the four *ku* sold the corporate land, the Ongs continued to worship the ancestors on the dates when the corporate activities used to be held. But since there was no corporate income to defray the cost, had the responsibility for the worship been assigned to a specific segment of the lineage each year, the cost would have been prohibitive. Hence the rotation stopped, and it became the joint responsibility of each household to make a small offering to the ancestors on the appropriate days. The responsibility was thus splintered among the households. But after this change, households that moved away from the original settlement felt no need to return on the dates for corporate worship. They could carry out their share of the worship equally well in their own residences.

It is difficult to reconstruct the process in detail, but it is clear that eventually nonresident lineage offshoots felt entirely self-sufficient and under no obligation to the rest of the lineage. Even nearby groups of lineage members lost touch with one another completely. There are several groups of Ongs descended from the four *ku* living in Ch'ipei and Ch'itung. All of them I spoke with knew of the four *ku* and, vaguely, of their connection to them. But none of these local populations have preserved their ties with the Ongs in Ch'inan. The lineage focused on the father of the four *ku* has ceased to exist as a social group. The loss of the corporate property contributed in some measure to this development. No longer bound by the rotation of responsibility for it, people tended to lose touch with the original settlement once they broke away. And it may be that a similar trend is in process among the Ch'inan Ongs today. Without corporate property to finance joint feasts, the responsibility for the various ancestral *pai-pais* is shared by each household. The 600–700 Ongs who have moved away do not return to Ch'inan to worship, but simply mark the occasion wherever they live.

Another variable that can be taken up at this point is leadership. But first a brief look at the criteria for leadership, those factors that determine who becomes a leader. As Hugh Baker suggests (1968: 132), leadership in a small, poor agnatic group tends to be gerontocratic because no members are marked off by special wealth or experience; but in a differentiated lineage, in which some members are more wealthy or educated than others, it is those members who commonly hold the political leadership of the lineage. This fairly simple correlation is well-substantiated by the evidence from Ch'inan. Each of the four lineages has produced at least a few members who have more wealth, experience, or knowledge than the rest. In each case some of these men are the political leaders. Seniority by itself is considered an insufficient criterion for leadership. Preferred leaders are those who "know a lot about things."

From here on, the issue becomes more complex. Granting that leaders will probably be drawn from among the most capable men, there is still no clear way of determining why a given individual becomes a leader in a certain context. In the case of the representatives of the seven Lou *fang*, wealth and success in business appear to be the outstanding characteristics. To some extent, the Lou doctor may have personally influenced the choice of leaders, for as the elderly representatives die, he appoints replacements. But these do not seem to be the qualifications the Uis look for. Although one of their managers is a rich businessman, the other is a humble wage earner. He is said to be a manager because he knows a great deal about lineage history and how the traditional lineage affairs should be run. Although he is literate, he is not as well educated as others in the lineage. In the Ong case, neither the *li chang* nor Hai-a can be counted among the wealthiest lineage members. Hai-a is probably a leader because of his experience outside the *li*, and the *li chang* because of his long experience as a government official.

All of these leaders are outstanding in some way, but in each case for different reasons. One characteristic most of them share, which perhaps gives us a way of understanding why they are leaders, is a willingness to take on the task of leadership and an enjoyment of the responsibilities that accompany it. Of the men in the *li* who are qualified to be leaders but are not, I have heard several profess lack of interest in the sort of affairs that must concern leaders. They seem to prefer to remain turned inward to their own problems and interests. Other people's business and quarrels, lineage responsibilities and difficulties, they are glad to leave to others.

It is much easier to pinpoint the criteria for leadership in Ch'inan than to judge its strength and particularly its extent in each of the four lineages. Since there are no written codes that delimit the powers of a leader (save the document drawn up by Hai-a, which was an unsuccessful move in this direction), one must rely on observing the exercise of power. Yet this can be misleading, for the cases observed may represent neither the most authority a leader is capable of wielding nor the least. For example, the Lou doctor was able to exert considerable control over the affairs of the Lou lineage on several occasions. But I have no way of knowing whether he has always succeeded in exercising authority or whether these instances were atypical; perhaps people gave in to his wishes on these occasions because they cared very little about the affairs at hand. What does seem clear is that the ability of leaders to exercise authority depends on a combination of things: on the degree of division within the lineage, on the leader's persuasiveness and ability to elicit support and trust, and on the extent to which the leader is willing to attempt to control other people. Because of the difficulty of measuring such intangibles, I hesitate to attempt to account for variation in the strength of leadership among the four lineages.

However, I can comment briefly on another aspect of authority that is indicative of well-developed leadership: institutionalized positions of leadership, or political statuses. In two cases, the Lous and the Uis, there are institutionalized positions of leadership. The Lous have seven standing positions of "representatives," one for each of the *fang*. When an incumbent dies or retires, either the head representative, Dr. Lou, appoints a replacement, or the members of a *fang* choose one from among their ranks. The Uis have only two standing positions of "representatives"; these positions are filled when necessary by an election among the adult lineage members. The key to understanding the importance of standing positions for leaders is revealed in the rationale behind the *be* Ongs' attempt to institutionalize such positions. Hai-a's reason for trying to establish formal and permanent positions of authority was to ensure that the common lands would be managed properly. Conversely, the Lis say they no longer have any *fang* representatives because there is no surplus income from the lineage lands to be managed. Income from corporate property is perpetual and needs constant care lest it be misused; perpetual positions of authority ensure that lineage funds will always be protected.

The last variable I will discuss in this section is also related to corporate property. This variable, which Freedman does not mention, might be called corporate or joint activity; I mean by this any project, organization, or activity undertaken by a lineage as a group. The applicable questions here are whether there is variation in the degree of corporate activity among the four lineages, and if so, whether it can be related to other factors.

We have seen that in the past, under abnormal conditions of duress, in particular under threat from outside the lineage, each of the four Ch'inan lineages has united as a group to meet the threat. The Lis once joined as a unit to challenge the Ongs. Both the Lous and the Uis formed solid groups in their confrontation. The Ongs united as a single lineage to face a challenge to their land. Apparently under these conditions any of the lineages is capable of one form of joint activity, that in which the lineage members unite under a common bond of kinship to protect their interests. Under threat from nonkinsmen these lineages always have one basis on which they can unite as a group: their relationship as agnates based on their descent from a common ancestor. Whether or not they will in fact unite probably depends on the nature of the threat and on internal relations in the group. If the threat appears likely to harm only a segment of the lineage, if it is not seen as an attack on the whole lineage or its common property, the unthreatened segments may or may not rally to the support of the one in danger depending on the group's internal relations. Years ago, when the upper Ongs claimed that a house built by outsiders moving into the area had damaged their *te-li*, their fellow *be* members in the lower settlement did not support them. The members in the lower settlement did not see the building as a threat to all the *be*, so prior strained relations between the two groups took precedence and prevented them from meeting the threat jointly. Although all four lineages have the potential for acting together under duress, whether or not they do so depends on the political situation. If they do so it is in part because of their common agnatic descent from a single ancestor, which links them as members of the same lineage.

Under normal conditions, the four lineages display some difference in the degree of corporate activity they undertake. The Ongs, as we have seen, do not carry on any of those corporate activities that are associated in the other lineages with the possession of corporate property. They have no corporate feast, no yearly meeting, and no projects using corporate income. Hence, it appears that the possession of corporate property is one factor that increases the incidence of corporate activity. The Ong case is useful for illustrating two other points as well. First, what joint activity the Ongs did attempt, for example, Hai-a's attempt to make full use of their mountain land, sometimes failed because of the hostility between the two segments of the group. This demonstrates the obvious point that deep cleavage into antagonistic segments reduces the possibility of successful corporate activity. Second, the Ongs do not attempt to restrict either the Co-su-kong *pai-pai* or the Ang-kong *pai-pai* rotation to the lineage members, as all of the other lineages do. This may be a function of the division in the Ongs' leadership, that is, the *li chang* may be led to extend these *pai-pais* to the territorial group, Ong *chu*, in an attempt to increase his electoral base. Hence, a leadership internally divided can also reduce the extent of corporate activity.

The Lis perhaps engage in somewhat fewer joint activities than either the Uis or the Lous simply because they have a smaller amount of corporate land than the one and a lower level of prosperity than the other. They have no common water tower or trash receptacle, nor do they need to make plans to dispose of excess funds from the common lands. The Lous and Uis, with their vigorous leadership, relatively large amounts of funds to draw on, and lack of persistent internal conflict, engage in more joint activity than the other two lineages: each holds two corporate feasts with profits from lineage lands; each has a commonly organized water supply; and each has carried out extensive building projects financed by lineage funds.

This is as far as I can go in my discussion of the interrelations among the variables that characterize the Chinese lineage until I take up the subject of ancestor worship in Ch'inan. In the course of analyzing that topic, I want to resume this discussion.

PART TWO

The Cult of the Dead

Even if no tab -
CAN be worshipp
to point
air.

CHAPTER 6

Ancestral Halls

[handwritten margin notes:
ne: - Dragon in east
- Tiger in west
- Nice View

① Funeral
② Burial - w/ goods / time
③ Rebury
④ Death days
⑤ Calendrical Holidays
⑥ Show relation engagement / marriage

Incense
Food
Paper money
cars
etc.]

THIS INVESTIGATION has dealt so far with the political and
territorial community of Ch'inan. I can now begin to analyze the
relationship between this community and the cluster of institutions involved in ancestor worship. A more apt term might be
"the cult of the dead," for as we shall see, something more than
"the ancestors" and more than "worship" is involved. The foregoing depiction of the community will serve as parentheses around
the institutions in the cult of the dead, providing the setting in
which the cult occurs and allowing me to relate the cult to certain
facets of community and lineage organization.

The cult of the dead in Ch'inan can be seen as a code that,
once deciphered, reveals how groups are articulated and how they
are subdivided along economic and political lines. We must consider many phases of the cult: large corporate lineage halls, tablets
for individual dead persons, and the reciprocal obligations between the living and the dead. In studying the reciprocity that is
at the heart of ancestor worship, we shall find that the living are
expected to care for the dead in payment of the debts they owe
them. Beyond this, in the act of meeting this obligation, the living
hope to inspire a further reciprocal response from the ancestors,
to obtain through them the good life as they perceive it: wealth,
rich harvests, and offspring who will ensure undying memory and
sustenance in the afterlife. Following tenaciously the many threads
of ancestor worship leads one over the warp and woof of the social
fabric in Ch'inan, showing the alliances and tensions between
groups, the desires and fears of individuals. Far from being merely

[handwritten right margin:
Ancestors
① Actual/potential contributors of wealth (property) or offspring
① Unmarried women
② Pre-mature boys/girls]

[handwritten bottom margin:
Women - domestic
men - ancestral; priveledge have surname (most)
④ Uxorilocal
⑤ Posthumous
③ Not nec. same surname (But not in hall)]

an abstract expression of agnatic relationships, the cult of the dead decoded reveals the basic design of society in this Taiwanese village. All the most important social relations can be related to each other through this medium.

One aspect of the cult of the dead, the corporate lineage hall, is more deeply entwined than any other in the nature of the territorial community. To emphasize the unique character of the halls, I will describe them comparatively, using Maurice Freedman's analysis of ancestral halls as a standard. Although Freedman's conclusions may be generally true for other areas of China, they cannot be applied without modification to the halls in Ch'inan. In this chapter I have centered the discussion around one main theme in Freedman's analysis, his distinction between the domestic and hall cults of the ancestors. According to Freedman (1970: 175–76), the domestic cult revolves around tablets for the recently dead, which are worshiped in order to preserve the memory of the dead, to serve their needs, and to satisfy the demands of their slight authority. Partly because of the location of these tablets within residential units, the women of the house are often responsible for carrying out worship services for them. In addition, Freedman suggests that men may avoid dealing with their recently dead ancestors because the ancestors are capable of punishing their descendants under certain restricted circumstances: "They cannot be in too intimate a relationship with domestic ancestors because of the latter's potential power to inflict harm" (p. 174).

Worship of each tablet continues in this way for three or four generations. Then the tablet is destroyed and its place in the domestic cult comes to an end. In some cases, when there is no worship of the ancestors outside the domestic cult, the ancestor whose tablet has been destroyed is never worshiped again. In other cases, when there are ancestral halls, another tablet may be made and placed in the hall. This cult, the "cult of descent group ancestors," differs markedly from the domestically centered "cult of immediate jural superiors" (Freedman 1967: 91). In the hall where the most remote ancestors are enshrined, men conduct all worship activities. The tablets have come to represent agnatic ascendants in an abstract sense, not well-remembered fathers and grand-fathers.

In order to relate this model to the Ch'inan case, I will begin by discussing those aspects of the halls that are domestic according to Freedman's view. The physical structure of the Ch'inan halls is fairly simple. The Lis' consists of a single large room, about 12 by 20 feet. The adjoining side rooms are now used as living quar-ters. The Ong and Lou halls, somewhat larger than the Lis', are flanked on either side by a room used for storage of lineage prop-erty and records. The Uis' hall is composed of two large rooms, one in front of the other, separated by an open courtyard. In the central room of the Lou and Ong halls, and in the rear room, in the case of the Uis, there are several large pieces of furniture and a number of ritual objects on display. In each case a large, high altar made of carved wood is located in the center of the rear wall. Directly in front of the altar is a table (or tables) for the dishes of food that are offered to the ancestors. On the left side as one faces the altar are boxes for ancestral tablets and an incense pot for the ancestors. The right side of the altar is reserved for the worship of the gods. The Lis have images of gods there, four in all. Rather than images, the Ongs have an incense pot used for worshiping the gods. Both the Uis and the Lous have an image of Tho-te-kong.

Although there is some variation among the four lineages in the form of the boxes for their ancestral tablets, the general pattern is the same. All have wooden boxes about two feet high and a foot and a half wide that contain small slips of wood or large boards on which the names of ancestors are written. As we shall see, the number of boxes and the form of the tablets vary. But for now, I am concerned only with what the four lineages have in common, especially in regard to the placement of tablets for agnatic an-cestors under ordinary circumstances. In most cases, such tablets are placed in the appropriate hall box about one year after the person's death. Ordinarily (we will come back to the exceptions in due course), there are no tablets in the living units of the lineage members, that is, in the rooms in which they cook, sleep, or enter-tain guests. Shortly before or immediately after a lineage member dies, his body is placed in the ancestral hall. Here the rites for the recently dead are carried out; here the coffining takes place. The funeral rites are held both within and directly in front of the hall, and the funeral procession leaves from the hall. After the burial, a temporary paper tablet is set up on the hall altar along with a separate incense pot. In about a year, this tablet is burned, and the name of the deceased is written on a wooden tablet and placed in the correct box. At all times, both immediately after death and after the permanent tablet has been made, the descendants make offerings in the hall in front of the tablet. Just as there are ordinarily no tablets in the home, so there is no worship of the ancestors in the home. Once ensconced in the hall, the ancestral tablets are not removed to be burned after three or four generations according to some regular procedure, nor are they transferred to any other place. The hall box becomes their permanent resting place.*

Certain other ritual activities are also carried out in the ancestral hall in Ch'inan that elsewhere in China are the business of families and households, and take place in domestic dwellings. On the occasion of an engagement, when the groom's family brings goods and money for the bride price, all the items are set up for display in the ancestral hall. Often the ring ceremony, in which the bride receives a ring from her mother-in-law, is held in the hall, with the bride seated facing out the door. Afterward, her father worships the ancestors in the hall, informing them of the event and offering the goods to them. Sometimes the feast for the groom's family is held in the hall as well. At weddings, when a daughter-in-law comes into the family, her ritual introduction to the lineage

* A somewhat similar pattern has been described by Myron Cohen. According to him (1969: 170), among the Hakkas of the Meinung region in southern Taiwan "domestic worship is merged with that at the level of the compound. A founder of a compound...may build a hall and place tablets within it. Until such time as his family divides, of course, worship of this sort may be considered 'domestic.' Thereafter, however, there is no proliferation of tablets corresponding to increasing numbers of families. In any given compound there can be only one set of tablets, located in the cheng-t'ing [the central room of the compound]." As in Ch'inan, separate domestic units worship at a single altar, but in the Hakka case the unit with only one altar is the compound rather than the settlement.

and family ancestors also takes place in the hall. Usually on the day of the wedding, the bride and groom stand before the tablets in the hall and offer incense to the ancestors, bowing three times.

At this point, it looks as though the domestic cult of the ancestors described by Freedman has simply been moved into a central location. The tablets are all in one place, so care and worship of the ancestors must also occur in one place. Engagement and marriage both involve worshiping the ancestors, so they are naturally carried out in the same place as well. Yet there is strong evidence that more is involved, for the domestic cult *par excellence*, the worship of the kitchen or stove god, also takes place in the hall. In most other areas of China, the kitchen or stove god is inextricably associated with an individual household and its separate stove. A picture of the god or a sheet of paper bearing his name is posted near the stove; this is the only location at which he is worshiped (Fei 1939: 99–100). In Ch'inan, however, this is not the case. Although there is some variation in the extent to which different households carry out their worship of the stove god in the hall, the majority of people in lineage households say they do not worship the kitchen god at all before their domestic stove but worship him only in the ancestral hall along with all the other gods at New Year. Some indicate they burn incense at their domestic stove twice a month but in addition worship the kitchen god in the hall at New Year. Further, none of the other practices that involve the household and its stove god are important in Ch'inan: almost no one had heard of the custom of smearing the mouth of an image of the stove god with sweet rice so that he would report only the good conduct of the household when he returned to heaven each year. Nor is the stove god replaced by some other supernatural being associated with each separate household. In many cases, then, the unit of the household is without regular ritual demarcation. The domestic symbol of the kitchen god has only one primary location for all the households in each lineage. It is as though the ritual idiom for delineating the distinctness of households is used to demonstrate their common place within a single lineage. When, at New Year, all the household heads present offerings to the kitchen god in the same place on the same day, they are expressing their common identity in the lineage, not their separate identity as distinct residential and economic units.

One might be tempted to conclude that the hall is nothing but the locus for domestic and household rituals for a large number of households. In other words, is it possible that the building should not be called a "hall" at all, but should rather be given a name that ties it more closely to the domestic sphere? One might wonder further whether the Ch'inan case is similar to an alternative form described by Freedman (1970: 167) in which one domestic altar is used by a broader group than that living in the house in which the altar is located. Answers to these questions will emerge from a discussion of those aspects of the Ch'inan halls that make them more than a place to which many separate domestic cults have been transferred.

But first let us look at the alternative form described by Freedman:

> By an extension of the principle that families resulting from a recent division may come together at the altar maintained by one of them, one such altar may continue over many generations—well beyond the "standard" four—to house tablets serving as the focus for a large group of agnates scattered over numerous houses. Such an altar is physically domestic, and it is ritually domestic for the people in whose house it stands; but acting as a ritual center for a long line of agnates, it has become akin to the altar constructed in an ancestral hall (*ibid.*).

The essential difference between this form and the Ch'inan halls is that in Ch'inan the hall is not physically domestic. It is not owned by any domestic unit, nor is it used as a living area by any group. Aside from the ritual objects and furniture, which are the common property of the group, there is nothing stored in the hall that would indicate its use as a domestic area. There are no sacks of surplus grain, soy sauce bottles, television sets, desks, or anything else that belongs to private individuals or single families. The building itself is the property of the lineage as a whole and doubtless has been repaired or even rebuilt by the group. It cannot be used to serve any solely private interests. The activities that single families carry on in the hall, such as weddings and death-day offerings to the ancestors, are related to the interests of the whole group. The acquisition of a daughter-in-law, for example, points toward the future addition of sons to the lineage and, in that sense, satisfies and glorifies the entire line of ancestors of the family whose son is marrying. Since even the earliest ancestors stand to gain from this event, all their descendants, including the entire lineage, are involved. Death-day offerings, though intended for one or more specific ancestors, please all the ancestors. Incense is placed in the single incense pot used for all ancestor worship; all the ancestors are thought to be aware that the filial rites of caring for deceased forebears are being carried out. Hence, it is clear that the Ch'inan hall is not physically domestic, nor is it ritually domestic for one family more than any other. It is physically distinct from domestic areas, but it is the locus for what Freedman calls the domestic cult for all the domestic units in the lineage.

Having seen that the hall is not physically domestic for any household, we may suspect that certain aspects of the hall involve more than an agglomerated domestic cult. Besides serving as a locus for the internal business of domestic rites, the hall serves also as a representation, a symbol, of the lineage as a whole when facing the world outside and, in particular, the other lineages in Ch'inan. Evidence of this function of the hall comes in many different forms. Perhaps most obvious to an outside observer is the pride with which members of some of the lineages speak of their hall. Shortly before my arrival in Ch'inan the Lis' hall had been painted inside, and the walls decorated in many different colors. In the first weeks of my stay, nearly every time a Li found me in the hall he or she would point out all the fine points of the decoration, telling me how much it had cost, who had painted it, and so on. The conclusion was usually that the Li hall was now decorated more beautifully inside than any of the other Ch'inan halls. The Uis, too, were particularly proud of their hall. Since the front room of the hall, open in front and rear and shaded by a high roof, was a cool place to sit during hot weather, Uis often gathered there in their idle hours—an ideal situation from my point of view, for they were most willing informants in these circumstances. People in these gatherings often volunteered information about the hall, perhaps inspired by its proximity. The unique qualities of the hall with its two connected rooms and high roof, of the box for the tablets, and of the Tho-te-kong image were all pointed out with considerable pride. I was to understand how much each had cost, where each had been obtained, how beautiful and unique each was, and how much more impressive than anything in any of the other Ch'inan settlements.

Feasts given for the gods and ancestors are especially fruitful occasions for gathering information about the way Ch'inan residents view their lineage halls. This was especially true of the *pai-pai* for the Ang-kong, on the twenty-sixth of the eighth month, when only Hengch'i residents have feasts for the gods. Since all other areas have their *pai-pais* on different days, the people of Ch'inan are able to invite outside acquaintances to be their guests. On this occasion I often saw lineage members giving their guests a tour of their hall and explaining carefully each of its unique and beautiful aspects. Likewise, many guests are invited to the *pai-pai* for Co-su-kong, on the fourth day of the first month, which is also marked with a feast. During the year I lived in Ch'inan, the Ongs had responsibility for this *pai-pai*, which rotates not among communities but among selected surname groups. For about six days after the first of the year the Ong settlement was full of the sounds of pigs and fowl being slaughtered for the feasts that were held by each Ong household. In addition, the settlement was crowded with out-of-town guests come to stay for a few days. Because these guests had arrived at least a day before the *pai-pai*, they were present for the entire series of worship offerings to the gods and ancestors made before the feast, and so witnessed the many grand offerings made to the ancestors in the lineage hall. Lavish offerings in enormous quantity were presented by the men of each household to demonstrate to the ancestors and visitors alike that they were prospering and able to afford such expenses. On this occasion and others, such as weddings, the hall is a public display place where men can both glorify the ancestors and impress onlookers from outside the lineage. The men, more often in evidence when matters of extra-domestic authority and prestige are concerned, almost always make these offerings.

The men also ordinarily take charge when offerings are made on the death-day anniversaries of the most distant ancestors. The remote character of the earlier ancestors would lead us, according to Freedman's scheme, to expect men to take precedence here. Yet on death-day anniversaries for the recently dead as well, men rather than women commonly make the offerings to the ancestors. In addition, remote and recent ancestors receive the same type of food—cooked, seasoned dishes prepared as for an ordinary meal. Likewise, there is no difference in the manner of offering the food. Men make the offerings, burn the incense, communicate with the ancestor, and throw the divination blocks to see whether or not the ancestor is satisfied.

Not unexpectedly, it is the men who remember the death days of the ancestors, both recent and distant. One of the things I requested in a questionnaire I administered to each lineage family was a list of its death-day anniversary dates; men could almost always reel off a long string of dates, whereas women almost never could. Elderly widowed matriarchs were the only exceptions. The worship of all the ancestors in the lineage hall, both recent and distant, is the business of the men. I suspect this is partly because of the public nature of the hall, separate from any domestic unit and visible to any passerby. When the hall is involved, as it is for worship of the dead, the lineage is facing both inward to its ancestors and outward to outsiders, members of other lineages. The character of the hall as a publicly visible symbol of the lineage makes it appropriate for men, concerned with extra-domestic affairs, to play a dominant role.

Just as the beauty of a large, well-decorated hall is a matter of pride for lineage members, so the ugliness of a decrepit hall, or one that is lacking in some way, is a matter of shame for the lineage. A case in point is the Ong group residing just upstream from the main Ong settlement. The upper Ongs once had their own ancestral hall in which they kept all the ancestral tablets of their line. But over the years it grew more and more rickety, and by 1967 it was in need of major rebuilding. About that time the group held a meeting to decide whether or not to fix the hall before it was too late to do anything with it at all. Some members felt they could not afford the assessment of several hundred dollars when they were having trouble enough just keeping their families fed and clothed. Others argued that even if some members had to borrow money, the group should find a way to repair the hall. "Otherwise all those Lis, Lous, and Uis will come up here and laugh at us." Although everyone agreed this would happen, many members simply could not produce the needed funds, and the hall was not repaired. It was no surprise when it collapsed entirely during a typhoon in the fall of 1969. The upper Ongs were extremely loathe to discuss the hall; they seemed to find its condition very embarrassing. Their inability to repair the hall is visible proof to any observer of their poverty and lack of resources. The state of the hall corresponds to the state of the lineage; a fallen hall is an embarrassing proof of the declining fortunes of the lineage.

A similar case involves the lower Ong hall, a building with a more complicated history. Until the early 1920's the lower Ongs had a small hall like the Lis'. Since the lineage was then prospering greatly, the Ongs wanted to build a bigger, more impressive hall to fit their improved status. So, in front of the old hall they built a much larger and taller hall, with curved eaves on the roof. But then, not long after the new hall was finished, the lineage's economic situation worsened. After many conferences, the majority of Ongs agreed that their decline was due to the new hall—it was in the wrong place to capture the *te-li* of the Ong settlement—and that, accordingly, the front hall should be razed and the back hall rebuilt instead. But one man, A-iong, who had been living in one of the rooms adjacent to the new hall, refused to acquiesce. What is more, he moved his personal belongings into the side room of the hall and insisted he would not move out. The rest of the group began the rebuilding of the back hall, razing all of the front hall except the section where obstinate A-iong was living. And here the situation remains to this day: looming in front of the smaller rear hall, and partly blocking it from view, is a third of the abandoned front hall, one segment of its soaring eave still sticking up into the sky.

Most of the Ongs intensely resent A-iong's failure to conform. One man, A-cui, wants to report him to the government authorities for maintaining a private residence in a corporately owned build-ing. But he needs the signatures of all the Ongs in order to do this. As we might expect, not all of the Ongs will cooperate, so A-cui cannot carry out his threat. Still, almost all the Ongs agree with A-cui on why they so deeply resent A-iong's actions: "What will all the others, the Lis, Lous, and Uis, think, seeing that ridiculous segment of the old hall still standing. They will laugh at us and make fun, saying we don't know how to do things right. We have lost a lot of face because they don't know it is just one man who insists on keeping the old hall there. They will think it is all of us Ongs who don't care about face."

It is apparent from these cases involving the hall as a symbol of pride or shame to the lineage that the members of each lineage in Ch'inan see themselves in opposition or in contrast to the other three lineages. When they brag about the fine points of their hall, their standard of comparison is the other halls in the *li*; when they are ashamed of their hall, they are worried only about what the other lineages will think. I gathered much more evidence of this, mostly from casual remarks made spontaneously by the villagers. For example, many offhand remarks showed me that the members of each lineage were aware of what the other lineages had in their halls. They often used me to check on their information, for they knew that I circulated among all four settlements. Several Lis showed me the paintings of their apical ancestors, which hang on the wall of the ancestral hall. They usually stated that none of the other halls had such a thing, and then hesitantly asked me if that was not so. They were worried lest one of the other lineages had recently acquired similar pictures. Many of the Lous took much the same tack with respect to the photographs of the seven *fang* representatives on the wall of their hall. They seemed pleased and gratified when I assured them that none of the other lineages as yet had anything of the kind. Each lineage tries to outfit its hall with some different ornamentation or ritual object in order to claim superiority to the other three lineages. Yet none of the variations depart widely from social forms familiar to all the lineages. That is, all the lineages have *fang*, though only the Lous have photographs of each *fang* representative in the hall. Likewise, all the lineages have founding ancestors, though only the Lis have their portraits in the hall. Each of these cases is a unique but not radically innovative variation on themes common to all the lineages.

Another instance of the variation among lineages became clear to me at a feast for the god Co-su-kong. Although feasts are often occasions for introducing outsiders to the Ch'inan system of ancestor worship, they are also occasions for discussion of the system among members of different Ch'inan lineages. Both purposes were served one evening during the Ong *pai-pai* for Co-su-kong, when Hai-a, my landlord; Lou Cui-tho, representative of the seventh Lou *fang*; several other Ongs; and a guest from Taipei and I sat together at one table. The conversation centered on the variation among the ancestral tablets in the four Ch'inan halls. Hai-a explained his lineage's arrangements in detail. He reported that the Ong hall has a single large wooden box, on the outside of which are written the names of the founding *thau* and *be* ancestors and their wives as well as those of the three sons of the *be* and the four sons of the *thau* and their wives. Inside, the box is divided into seven horizontal layers, with one shelf for each of the sons of the *be* and the *thau*. The ancestral tablets themselves are small slips of wood about two by three inches; the name of the deceased lineage member and in some cases the date of death are written on one side. The finished tablet is placed on one of the seven shelves depending on which of the three *be fang* or four *thau fang* the deceased belongs to.

Hai-a then turned to the Lis' system. In contrast to the Ongs, the Lis keep the ancestral tablets of their three *fang* in separate wooden boxes. On the outside of each are written the names of the founding ancestor and his wife as well as the names of one of the *fang* ancestors and his wife. Inside each box are wide wooden boards labeled according to generation. By this system, then, a man who belonged to the first *fang* would have his name written on one of the boards in the box for his *fang* along with the names of all others in the first *fang* who were born in his generation.

Lou Cui-tho observed that the Lous have eight large boxes, one bearing the names of the founding ancestor and his wife, and the others bearing the names of each of the *fang* ancestors and his wife. But instead of single boards for each generation in the seven *fang* boxes, they have a drawer at the bottom containing little slips of wood for each ancestor, much like those the Ongs keep in their box. The Uis have still another variation. Like the Ongs, they have a single box, but theirs is labeled not just with the names of the founding ancestor and his sons, plus those of their wives, but also with the names of the grandsons and their wives. Inside are generation boards like the Lis'.

My table companions reviewed and discussed all four lineage halls both to educate me and the guest from Taipei and, seemingly, to confirm their own knowledge of one another's system. It is remarkable, and perhaps not random, that two variables, the boxes and the tablets, take two forms in the four cases. In the first instance the two forms are a single box for all the lineage and a separate box for each *fang*. In the second, the two forms are a single slip of wood for each individual and a board for each generation. There are thus altogether four possible combinations of tablets and boxes. As Table 3 shows, each of these combinations occurs in one of the Ch'inan halls.

TABLE 3
Variations in Tablets and Boxes in
the Ch'inan Ancestral Halls

Lineage	Ancestral box		Ancestral tablet	
	By lineage	By fang	By generation	By individual
Ong	x			x
Li		x	x	
Lou		x		x
Ui	x		x	

I would like to suggest that there is a certain correspondence between the variation a lineage shows in this case and its other aspects. For example, it seems very appropriate that the Uis, the most closed and solidary group, would choose the variant with least divisions: their single box has no divisions into *fang*; their generation boards group individuals together. Likewise, the Lous, with the best developed differentiation into *fang* and the most economic differentiation between individual families, seem to have chosen the system with the most divisions: the *fang* are grouped separately into seven boxes; individuals are represented separately on small tablets. Yet such an analysis seems risky. I have no way of determining when the boxes were constructed except on the word of the lineage members themselves—the Lous and Ongs say the boxes were constructed around 50 years ago; the other lineages claim theirs were built more recently—and in any event no way of knowing whether, at the time the boxes were made, the character of the lineages was the same as it is today. Hence, I will merely suggest this analysis as a possibility.

Another possible interpretation, which is also difficult to substantiate but which seems to be corroborated by the lineages' tendency to celebrate differences among their ancestral halls, is simply that the first lineage to build a box became a model for the other lineages; and that each of the other three lineages attempted to create a different solution while staying within the same system. "The system" itself is defined by the primary ways in which a lineage member can be viewed: as an individual member of a *fang*, an individual member of a lineage, a member of a generation within a *fang*, or a member of a generation within a lineage. As each Ch'inan lineage in turn built its box or boxes, each rang the changes on these possible combinations, choosing something different but still consistent with the overall system. This method makes sense only if the four lineages see each other as like units competing with one another for a beautiful, unique hall. Only if they are acutely aware of each other and intent on distinguishing themselves from one another would they be so concerned to develop halls that are basically alike yet distinctively their own. It is as though they are playing a game in which the rules are the same for all and accepted by all, and in which the winner is the one who makes the most ingenious use of the rules.

The material I have presented points to two conclusions. First, ritual marks of differentiation internal to the lineage at the domestic level are largely nonexistent in Ch'inan. Those rituals that are characteristically associated with separate households elsewhere in China are lifted up to the level of the hall in order that they may serve as an expression of the unity of the domestic units in the lineage as a whole. Second, the halls are symbols of the wealth and prestige of the lineage. They are relevant in Ch'inan especially in relation to the competition among the four lineages in the community. The four lineages set themselves off against one another, vie with one another, represent themselves to one another through their respective ancestral halls. But before attempting to account for this situation, we must explore another aspect of the halls, again taking Freedman's view as a starting point.

According to Maurice Freedman, ancestral halls often serve to demarcate segments within a lineage. "Ancestor-worshipping segments might emerge in relation to a series of halls" (1958: 47). Segmentation that is marked in this way is unevenly distributed throughout the lineage. A rich sublineage might have several halls at different genealogical points, so that a man would belong to several branch halls, each subsumed within the next higher one; whereas in a poor sublineage a man might belong to no unit other than the family in the household and the sublineage (p. 49). By virtue of their uneven occurrence halls are not distributed symmetrically; a hall for one son of the lineage founder need not be matched with halls for all the other sons of the founder. The existence of halls depends on the availability of adequate economic resources. A sublineage with money to spare might build many halls and endow them with corporate property to express its relative prosperity as compared with other segments of the lineage. Poor sublineages would build none at all.

We already know that each Ch'inan lineage has at least one hall, and that three of them have income-producing corporate property. Are there other halls or pieces of land that serve the purpose Freedman suggests? Except for the estate established in the name of the founding ancestors, I was not able to discover any pieces of corporate land set aside to provide worship for the ancestors. Significantly, when I asked about the possible addition of estates in recent generations, I was told that such a thing would be impossible. Li A-pieng, who runs a tea-processing operation in his settlement, explained, "The Li settlement in Ch'inan has its piece of corporate land. Why would there ever be another, separate piece? No one would ever want to set up another piece. Maybe if some Lis moved away to settle in another place, they would set aside a piece of their own. But as long as you are talking about the settlement in Ch'inan, there could only be one piece of corporate land."

The implications of this statement are twofold. A-pieng is saying first that the lineage which traces its ancestry from the founding ancestors who settled in Ch'inan would not segment itself by means of corporate land set aside to worship ancestors below the level of the first generation. Just as the lineages do not use domestic rituals to differentiate units within the lineage, so also they would not use corporate land to form segments. The ideology is of a whole lineage presenting an undivided face to the outside. Second, he is saying that another piece of corporate land to mark a sublineage or segment could be established only if there were another, separate *settlement*. I believe this suggests that the establishment of corporate land and ancestral halls is related to the attainment of a separate identity as a territorially based community facing other like communities.

To substantiate this claim, I will begin with the development of ancestral halls as it has occurred in Ch'inan. The following tentative sequence is based on informants' accounts of the histories of the four lineages and of other more recently settled groups. For the Lis, Ongs, Lous, and Uis, one of the first steps in their settlement of a new area, Ch'inan, was the construction of a building—a single rectangular room or, more ambitiously, a room with a wing or two forming an L-shaped or U-shaped compound. As the population increased and more housing was required, wings were extended from the original building. This pattern was perhaps set in the early period because of the desirability of a compact group to fend off attacks from the aborigines. As the population grew still larger, the original room, used from the beginning to display the ancestral tablets of the whole group, became in need of repair. Since the room was of use to the whole group as a place to store ancestral tablets and since it had probably been abandoned as a private dwelling, the entire group saw fit to contribute to its repair either by assessment or by using income from the common lands. At this point, when none of the lineage members used the room for private purposes and when it had been renovated by the whole group, its name changed. What had once been the *su-thia:*, or private hall, now became the *kong-thia:*, or common hall. This name change is generally the pattern in other cases also, though as we will see, certain factors may intervene to prevent it.

The halls of the four main Ch'inan lineages underwent another change as well. At some point, the diverse collection of separate shrine boxes for tablets that had been accumulating in the hall from the start was replaced by a single box or boxes. In most cases the old tablets were copied and then burned. Uniform slips of wood or generation boards took their place. The motive was the same in each case: "to make the hall more orderly and beautiful. When we had guests they would laugh at the dusty, disorderly collection of boxes, all shapes and sizes. So we made the tablets uniform and neat to improve the appearance of the hall." As we have seen, another motive was probably to keep up with improvements the other lineages were making. Although in Ch'inan there is no transformation such as Freedman outlines—from a tablet in a domestic cult to a tablet in a hall cult—in a sense the entire lineage has undergone a transformation from having separate domestic cults in one place to having both a domestic cult and something beyond, a hall cult, in the same place. The name of the place changes when it is no longer physically domestic and when it becomes common property either by being linked with the corporate lands or by being the object of joint investment for its repair; *all* the tablets are burned and transformed at once from separate boxes for each household to a single box for the entire lineage.

The pattern followed by the four main lineages has not to my knowledge been exactly duplicated by any other lineages in the area. Two factors seem of paramount importance in understanding why the outcome has been different in other cases. First, the economic state of the group is important. There are at least four cases of agnatic groups in Hengch'i that had once had a *kong-thia:* but had allowed it to crumble, partly because they could not afford to repair it. The case of the upper Ongs discussed above is one instance. Another is the Peq group, whose houses are adjacent to the Li settlement. Much earlier than the upper Ongs', the Peqs' *kong-thia:* needed repair, but, like the upper Ongs, they could not raise the necessary money to fix it. Their hall was leveled by the next typhoon, and the spot where it stood is still vacant. There are two parallel cases involving Lous from the fifth *fang* who moved to Ch'itung.

The second important factor is the lineage's perception of itself as a territorially based community that is set off politically from other, like groups. For example, there are several cases of lineage members who have built their own U-shaped compounds outside the main settlement. There is one such compound behind the Ong brick kiln and another near the river. The Lis have one on the other side of the stream that bounds their settlement. The Lous have two, located across the highway, and the Uis three, located to the west of the main settlement. The residents of these compounds moved away from the central hall for many reasons; population pressure on the land near the hall and a desire to live near outlying rice fields seem to be the most common ones. Yet even though these families may have lived away from the main settlement for many generations, and even though their central room may no longer be domestic, they continue to call it a *su-thia:*, private hall. The hall at the main settlement with which they continue to maintain many ritual and social connections is still their *kong-thia:*. It seems clear that they do not see fit to call their own hall a *kong-*

thia: because they still regard themselves as subsidiary members of their original community, as parts of the indivisible lineage community that already has a *kong-thia:*. They are not separate political communities.

In other cases, in which offshoots of the lineages have become the focus of a separate community in one way or another, they do call their hall a *kong-thia:*. The upper Ongs, for example, are the leaders of a community separate from the lower Ongs. The area is referred to by a separate name, *tieng-chu* (upper settlement), as opposed to *kong-chu* (lower settlement). The 17 Ong households living there and those of other ancestry together form a fairly large group of 31 households. Often they are subsumed within the larger unit, Ong *chu*, which includes both the upper and the lower settlement. They share one turn with the lower Ong *chu* in the rotation of the *pai-pais* for Tho-te-kong, Co-su-kong, and the Ang-kong. In such contexts, the two areas, upper and lower Ong *chu*, form one unit facing the other three settlements. But at other times, the upper settlement unites as a separate community to protect its own interests. When trucks from the brick kiln were using the paved road to the upper settlement to transport clay, the residents objected as a group, led by the lineage Ongs, and demanded recompense from the kiln owners. The upper Ongs, who have a political identity separate from the lower Ongs, do refer to their hall as a *kong-thia:*. Although it has collapsed from lack of care, they regard this as only a temporary embarrassment to be rectified as soon as possible. Their hall has become akin to the hall of the lower Ongs, representing them as a political unit within the larger community.

The Peqs' case is similar, though they have given up hope of ever replacing their hall. At one time, they were so strong a political community as to be referred to as Peq *chu*. In addition, they had one turn in the rotation of the Tho-te-kong *pai-pai*. Over the years, however, they failed to prosper or to produce many offspring. As a result, their hall, once called a *kong-thia:*, collapsed. Further, they are now fully amalgamated with the Li settlement and only share a turn in the rotating *pai-pais* with that lineage. In this case,

what was once a lineage and a political community became merged
into another community, losing its symbol of distinction, the *kong-
thia:*, along the way. The upper Ongs could conceivably follow
the same path if their population and wealth decline and they
cease to exert themselves as a separate political entity.

When segments move outside Ch'inan the same pattern occurs.
In the late nineteenth century the first and fourth *fang* Lous moved
to Ch'itung together. Their descendants still reside there in a
large settlement centered around their ancestral hall. The ancestral boxes in this hall express the separation of the new settlers
from the original Lou hall: instead of boxes for the founding ancestor and his seven sons representing the seven *fang*, there are
only two large boxes visible on the altar, one for the first *fang*
ancestor and one for the fourth. The tablets for deceased members
of the two lines are kept in drawers at the base of the boxes, just
as in the original Lou hall. The close ties between the two *fang*
are expressed in the use of a common incense pot by worshipers
of ancestors in both lines. The single hall and single incense pot
correspond to the single settlement established at one time. In this
case, the move into new territory was the factor that set the
Ch'itung Lous off as a segment with a separate hall. They call this
Ch'itung hall a *kong-thia:*, just as the upper Ongs do theirs. Like
the upper Ongs, too, they are members of a political community
distinct from their Ch'inan settlement of origin. Ch'itung has its
own affairs, apart from Ch'inan, and the Lous there play a prominent part in them. They refer to their hall as a *kong-thia:* because
it represents them as a separate group in a wider political arena.

A new hall can be built, then, when a group of agnates forms a
distinct political force, operating to further its own ends and to
gain power either independently of or in opposition to the original
settlement. Could a group of agnates that has become a distinct
political group but is still resident within the original settlement
build its own hall? Or is a separate territorial settlement also a
necessary condition for the building of a hall? I cannot give a
definite answer here, because my informants could not. They
seemed to feel strongly, however, that there should be only one

hall for each of the four original settlements. Certainly the Li tea-processor's statement would indicate that corporate property for the worship of the ancestors, of which a hall is one form, could not occur twice in one settlement. Further evidence is that when separate political groups do form within the same *chu*, as in the lower Ong settlement, the lineage still has only one hall. Even though the *thau* and *be* show few signs of reconciling their differences, there has been no discussion either of letting the hall go unrepaired or of building two halls. The hall was completely redecorated in 1964, and minor repairs were made in 1970. In the Ong case a split would mean the lineage would divide into two equivalent halves. If each was to build a hall, the two halls would be a visible proof of their final inability to cooperate. One thing that may operate to prevent this is the Ongs' concern with what the other lineages would think. Aware that the neighboring settlements would consider their inability to cooperate a failure, the Ongs may try to keep up the appearance of harmony as long as possible.

Suppose that a political division between two segments occurred below the level of the founder, and one segment wanted to build a branch hall in the settlement that would be subsumed under the original hall. In this case another factor would come into play. It must be kept in mind that the descendants of the original settlers in the area hold their residential area as undivided common land. The land the Ong, Li, Ui, and Lou founding ancestors staked out as house-building land continues to be owned jointly by all their descendants. For example, the area around the Ong hall that is encircled by the path around the settlement is *kong-e*, or commonly owned. It is not divided into plots by ownership or according to *thau* and *be*. By rules that all the lineage members accept, the land can be used either for commonly financed buildings, such as the hall, or for private dwellings. No provision is made for a nondomestic building that some lineage members, but not others, hold in common, in a word, for a branch ancestral hall. If a subgroup wished to construct such a common building, they would have to move away, that is, make a new, separate settlement.

At this point it may be helpful to gather together the evidence I have presented to show that in Ch'inan the ancestral hall is a concomitant of a lineage based in a separate political community, not of agnatic segments within a lineage. First I have tried to show that the hall is used by the lineages to represent themselves to other lineage communities. It is a symbol of the lineage as an indivisible social entity when facing other, like units. To be sure, on the basis of this alone, there is no reason other halls might not be focused on ancestors within the lineage at levels below the founder to mark differences between agnatic segments. Yet, as I have demonstrated, halls occur only when a segment of the lineage forms another settlement, another community, and not as long as segments are still closely connected to the lineage community of origin. One might object, then, that it is basically only a matter of economic differentiation, that the groups in a position to move away from the original lineage are probably just wealthier than the others. Their halls would simply be marks of their economic status. Yet, as we have noted, the upper Ongs, too poor to keep their hall in repair, and never in the past rich enough to construct a very fine hall, persist in seeing themselves as having a separate hall, a *kong-thia:*, even though it is currently in disuse. On the other hand, the Ongs who live behind the brick kiln, some distance from the central settlement, are said to be exceptionally rich. Their brick compound is well-decorated, and they could probably afford to erect an impressive hall. Yet, they insist that they only have a *su-thia:*. Hence, I conclude that in Ch'inan the *kong-thia:* is a concomitant of a lineage community with a separate political identity. Communities use the hall to express their separate identity and to compete with one another. The hall is not a means for agnatic segments of a lineage to express their superior economic status regardless of whether or not they have formed a separate political community.

Some might object that the Ch'inan lineages, five to seven generations in depth from the founding ancestors, are still too shallow to support segmentation; that this, rather than the reasons I have outlined, might account for the lack of segmentation. What needs to be explained, however, is not a complete lack of segmentation but rather the existence of segments (such as the upper Ongs and the Ch'itung Lous) located in political communities separate from the original settlement, and the lack of segmentation within the original settlement. Segmentation has already occurred, even though the lineages are relatively shallow; it has not occurred except where lineage members have become part of political communities separate from the original settlement.

I would like to suggest that the distinctive character of segmentation and ancestral halls in Ch'inan may be partly a result of the way the area developed. The founding ancestors of the four lineages settled there at about the same time. They were bound together physically by the rivers and mountains that make Ch'inan into a natural amphitheater; they were bound together socially by the experience of constructing irrigation works and defending themselves against the aborigines. In these circumstances, the settlements came to view each other as four like units. They competed for prestige through their ancestral halls, yet at the same time cooperated through the Tho-te-kong temple. A system developed in which the groups of ancestor-worshiping agnates that were set off from one another became separate lineages in separate communities. According to Freedman (1970: 176), ancestral halls set off groups of agnates within the same lineage "in distinction from other groups of like order." But in Ch'inan the groups of like order are separate lineage communities, not segments within a single lineage. Freedman says further (1966: 39) that "political and economic power, generated either within or outside the lineage itself, urges certain groups to differentiate themselves as segments." In Ch'inan the political situation outside the lineage, the nature of the territorial community itself, produced the opposite effect: the lineages, seeing themselves as units set against other lineages, do not differentiate themselves internally by means of the ancestral cult unless they subdivide into two settlements. The lower Ongs, for example, are deeply divided into two segments based on genealogical differences. Yet they have but one hall, because in the face of the wider community they are all Ongs living in one settlement. To be an Ong in this context means to be non-Li, non-Lou, non-Ui. In some contexts it also means to be non–upper Ong. Because they see themselves as set off from other lineages, the Ongs feel it is appropriate to have only one hall. The form of the ancestral cult has been affected by the nature of the wider territorial community.

Like reasons may also explain why the rituals ordinarily associated with the household are not used to express internal differentiation. The cults of the stove god and of worshiping the recently dead are lifted out of the private domestic area to the public sphere of the hall. The symbolism of the household units merged in one place is used to represent the unity of the whole lineage. Perhaps because of the importance of presenting a unified ritual face to the other three lineages, the internal differences implied by separate stove gods and domestic cults are not emphasized. Lineage members pour all their concern and energy into the lineage hall, the one object that is a visible symbol of the lineage. The halls grow larger and more ornate in response to competition among the groups while the domestic rituals continue to be merged within the hall. The households, residential groups composed mostly of agnates, express their unity in the lineage community, also a residential group composed largely of agnates.

Another reason for the lack of internal segmentation and differentiation in lineages located in multilineage communities has been suggested by Burton Pasternak. He holds that a "need for cooperation across agnatic lines for economic or defense purposes (or both) works to inhibit the structural elaboration of localized lineages, especially where families exert more or less equal control over subsistence resources" (1972a: 149). This statement can be aptly applied to Ch'inan in its earlier days. There was then a need for cooperation among its surname groups to defend their homes and build an irrigation system. Yet once the irrigation network was built, extensive cooperation in maintaining it was not required; and cooperation for defense was not necessary after the pacification of the aborigines in the 1920's. In spite of this, feeling about the inappropriateness of lineages segmenting within the four original settlements is still strong. The people's conception of the larger community, Ch'inan *li,* as a quadripartite unit lives on.

In conclusion, the ancestral hall as part of the cult of ancestor worship can be related to our on-going discussion of variables relevant to the form of Chinese communities. According to Freedman's analysis, halls depend on economic differentiation within the lineage, rich segments building halls to express their relative wealth. Although this is undoubtedly the case in some Chinese communities, the evidence from Ch'inan indicates that another form is possible. As we have seen, the members of a group such as the upper Ongs may insist they have a hall, a *kong-thia:,* even though they cannot afford to maintain it. Other groups that have moved to the outskirts of a settlement have the resources to purchase land and build expensive dwellings, yet they do not consider any part of their compounds, even the commonly used rooms, to be *kong-thia:.* Only segments grounded in political communities separate from the community of origin will build a *kong-thia:.* The existence of halls for segments is dependent on the political relationship between the community centered around the original hall and the members of the segment. This means that another significant variable should be added to the original list. The political relationship between territorially based communities is important in understanding one facet of the ancestral cult in Ch'inan, the ancestral hall.

CHAPTER 7

Ancestral Tablets

THE ANCESTRAL tablets, which are one locus of worship for the
dead, operate in two ways within the cult of ancestor worship. In
one way they are like the ancestral hall, showing outsiders the
public face of the lineage. In another way they represent the lineage as a body of individual members. In this respect they are
useful for delineating the criteria necessary for complete lineage
membership and showing how membership in the lineage can be
earned or lost, since there are rules governing the placement of
tablets for individuals in the hall: those whose tablets cannot be
placed there are not full lineage members. I will show that the
question of membership turns on whether the people involved
have contributed in certain ways to the wealth and size of the lineage; that the right to full participation in the lineage is not simply
ascribed automatically to males by birth or to females by marriage
into the lineage.

Before analyzing which tablets of the recently dead are allowed
in the hall, I will discuss the publicly visible names written on
the outside of the hall boxes. These names, representing the earliest ancestors, are closely related to the internal structure of the
lineage. In the halls of the Lis and the Lous, for example, the
names of the founding ancestor and his wife and of all his sons
and their wives are visible on the outside of one or more of the
boxes. In this way the apical ancestor of the lineage, who in these
instances is also the first settler, and the *fang* that focus on each
of his sons are publicly represented. Each member of the lineage
fits into this framework as a descendant of one of the *fang* ances-

tors, and, therefore, as a descendant of a single founding ancestor. The distinction between these names, externally visible, and the tablets concealed within the boxes seems to accord with Freedman's distinction between hall tablets and domestic tablets for the recently dead. First of all, the founding ancestors named on the outside of the boxes are the focus of the feasts and worship services financed by the corporate lands of the lineage. In addition, the sons of the founding ancestor delineate the *fang* focused on them, the only important genealogical subgroups in the lineage. In these respects, the ancestors whose names are visible on the boxes are akin to ancestors forming a "cult of descent groups." The earliest ancestors, too remote from the living to be remembered as individuals, are worshiped by the group as a whole as symbols of its agnatic unity.

But the distinction between the kinds of tablets is not carried through with a distinction in means of worship. Although the founding ancestor and his wife are worshiped with proceeds from the corporate land of the lineage, the *fang* ancestors whose names also appear on the outside of the box are worshiped by each *fang* separately in the same manner as the recently dead. In the case of the Uis especially, the distinction between the names on the outside of the box and those inside does not correlate with a difference in the way the ancestors they represent are worshiped. The Uis have three generations of names on the outside of their box: the founding ancestor, his sons, and his grandsons. Only the founding ancestor is worshiped with the corporate funds of the lineage. Between the next two generations represented on the outside of the box and the ancestors whose tablets are inside the box, there is a continuum. They are all worshiped in the same manner. In addition, the ancestors in the third generation on the Ui hall box are close enough to the oldest members of the lineage to be remembered, albeit vaguely, as distinct individuals. At death-day *pai-pais* for these ancestors, I have seen Uis make special offerings that were said to be the favorite foods of the deceased.

The founding ancestors, then, are the only ancestors who are worshiped differently from the recently dead. Does the worship of these ancestors function in all cases as a cult of descent groups, "a set of rites linking together all the agnatic descendants of a given forebear"? (Freedman 1966: 153.) In the Lou, Li, and Ui cases, it does seem to serve this function. The entire lineage is descended from the focal ancestor; the local lineage was founded and settled by him. The one man who began settlement in the territory, built the first houses in the area, and fathered sons who founded all the lines of descent in the lineage is worshiped corporately by the entire group.

The tablets for the earliest ancestors in the Ong hall, however, present a subtle difference. Drawing on the historical development of the Ongs as revealed in their genealogy and in the *Taipei Hsien Gazetteer*, we can establish with some certainty that the first Ong settler in the area lived two generations before the two brothers who are the focal ancestors of the Ong lineage. But neither the first settler nor his son is represented by a tablet in the Ong hall. Since the original settler is said to have returned to the mainland, it is understandable that he has no tablet in Ch'inan. His son, however, the father of the two focal ancestors, is said to have remained and died in Ch'inan. When the Ongs designed their hall tablet box, they could have used his name as their focal ancestor to demonstrate their unity as the descendants of a single forebear. Instead they chose to represent themselves as the descendants of two brothers, the ancestors of the two groups, *thau* and *be*. The father of these brothers has no tablet because he is no longer a relevant symbol of the composition of the group. That is, if his tablet were ensconced on the altar it would signify the unity of the Ongs, both *thau* and *be*, as descendants of one man. But the Ongs are not a unified group; they are split into two distinct sectors. By saying they are descended from two brothers and consigning the father of the two brothers to oblivion, the Ongs emphasize their current political division. At the level of the most remote ancestors, where worship involves demarcation of descent groups, the political alignments of the group can affect which ancestors are represented by a tablet in the lineage hall.

At the level of apical ancestors, the composition of the entire

lineage may be a factor in determining which ancestors have tablets and which do not. We turn now to names that are not emblazoned on a publicly visible box as a symbol of a lineage. For the
purposes of this study, I copied the names and death dates from
the tablets inside the hall boxes and compared that information
to the lineage genealogies and the household registration records.*
The task of copying the tablets was a project involving both difficulty and risk. When I first broached the topic I was usually told
that the boxes of ancestral tablets could not be moved under any
circumstances, lest the ancestors become angry and cause harm to
their descendants. A few informants thought it might be all right
to copy them at New Year, the only time when new tablets can be
added to the boxes. They felt that since the souls of the ancestors
leave their seat in the hall box and journey to heaven (*thi:*) several
days before the New Year and do not return until New Year's day,
it ought to be all right to open the boxes during that time; the
ancestors would not be present and could not take offense.

My job was to convince the appropriate members of each lineage
that this line of reasoning was correct. I concentrated my efforts
on the leaders of each lineage and on the *fang* in charge of the
corporate activities for that year. That *fang* was responsible for
cleaning the entire hall from roof to floor on the day before New
Year; since the objects in the hall would be disarranged for cleaning, I hoped that opening the box and copying the tablets would
be more permissible at that time. In the end, I was allowed to open
both the Ongs' box and the Uis', and was thus able to copy all of
the tablets for those lineages. I managed also to copy the first and
second *fang* tablets of the Lis and the second and seventh *fang* tablets of the Lous. The members of the third Li *fang* and the representatives of the several Lou *fang* whose tablets I did not copy are
not resident in Ch'inan, and I was unable to reach them and obtain their permission before the New Year period. Since in the Li
and Lou cases, each *fang* has a separate box for its tablets, no *fang*
leader would take responsibility for letting me see the tablets of

---

* I am indebted to Professor Arthur P. Wolf for allowing me to use his
translations of these government records.

another *fang*. I was only allowed to copy the tablets of those *fang* whose leaders had given me permission.

The full tale of my efforts to secure permission and support would make an instructive essay in the workings of lineage politics. To summarize briefly, once I had gained the approval of the lineage leaders, I usually met no further opposition. Also, after I had obtained permission from the first group, the Lous, I used this fact to convince the other lineages. In discussions of the matter I often heard people say, "Well, the Lous are letting her do it, so why can't she do it here?" The four lineages' constant awareness of each other, as well as the competition among them, worked in my favor.

In the case of the Ongs, gaining unanimous consent was more complicated. Both the *li chang* and Hai-a had given me permission, and A-cui had agreed to take the direct responsibility for lifting down the box and opening it. But A-iong, the man who insists on living in the one remaining section of the abandoned hall, and A-lan, a woman who lives near him, objected strenuously. The rest of the lineage members seemed to feel that A-iong had no right to express an opinion because his continuing to live in front of the hall showed disrespect for the hall as it was. A-lan finally acquiesced as long as she and her husband were not involved, but A-iong never yielded. Since the rest of the lineage felt he was being unreasonable, I decided to copy the tablets anyway and risk his displeasure. In any event, the matter was out of my hands. A-cui made the copying an issue in his long-standing dispute with A-iong over the ancestral hall. He was fully determined to see that I copied the tablets if only to prevent A-iong from getting his way. In the end I copied them without incident under A-cui's surveillance.

After I had copied and identified the tablets, I was able to search for the basis on which some persons are allowed to have tablets in the hall and others not. This is a complex business best unraveled by discussion of specific cases. Hence I present material separately for different categories of people, for example, adult males or female children, showing under what conditions tablets for people in these categories can be admitted to the hall.

The lineage hall, as we have seen, is the center of the corporate life of the lineage. Built with lineage funds in most cases, it represents the material benefits left from the efforts of the ancestors. A tablet located in the hall is literally a seat for the soul of the person it represents. Only those persons who have a right to enjoy the legacy of the lineage ancestors can have a tablet, and hence a kind of reserved seat in the hall. That right comes to some sorts of people naturally. If they do nothing other than follow a typical course of life, their tablets will automatically be placed in the hall when they die. But under some circumstances even these people can lose their potential right to have a tablet in the hall. Other sorts of people do not ordinarily have this right, yet if they follow certain courses of action, they can gain it. In general, as I will demonstrate below, the right to enjoy a seat in the hall of the ancestors is dependent on two conditions: an actual or potential contribution to the property or membership of the lineage and possession of the lineage surname.

An adult man who is a direct descendant of the lineage ancestors and who has married, sired male children, and handed down property to his sons is a paradigm of the person with a right to have his tablet placed in the hall. His sons are obligated to make a tablet for him as a parent and as a bequeather of property. He has contributed in the fullest measure to the lineage, giving it new life in the form of sons and enriching those sons with property. Judging from the tablets I copied, tablets have been made for the great majority of such men after their death and placed in the hall. Everyone agreed that this is their right.

A man who differs only in that he begot no children is usually accorded the same treatment. To provide himself with a descendant he may adopt a son or daughter who will be obligated to make a tablet for him. (Of course a son is preferred, whether adopted or natural, for a daughter's remaining in the natal family for life involves the complexities of uxorilocal marriage.) Otherwise a childless man may arrange for some lineage member, say a brother's son, to worship his tablet in return for inheriting his property. The tablet is allowed in the hall whether or not such men actually add to the lineage by adopting a child from outside because they were at least potential fathers of lineage children. A man is not faulted for failing to produce children as long as any children he would have fathered would have belonged to the lineage. I know of no case in which a man without natural children did not have a tablet made for him provided he had adopted a child or offered his property as inducement for some lineage member to make him a tablet. Nor did anyone ever question the right of a man in this position to have his tablet in the hall.

A man descended from lineage ancestors who dies after reaching maturity but before marriage, or one who grows old without marrying, can also have a tablet in the hall. In the absence of any sort of initiation ceremony to mark social maturity, the line between childhood and adulthood is not all that clear-cut, but usually by the time a young man is over twenty years old, he is considered to be past childhood. If he dies any time after this point but before marriage, he can automatically have his tablet placed in the hall; if he grows old without marrying, he will probably adopt a son or daughter to continue his line and carry out the duty of making a tablet for him. The young man who dies before having a chance to marry is regarded in the same manner as the man who marries yet has no children. That is, some lineage relative, perhaps a brother or a brother's son, will make a tablet for him. In this case, as in the other, the potential contribution of the deceased to the lineage is emphasized. As one informant put it, "Whatever he might have done, he would have done as one of us. If he had fathered 12 sons or become president of the country, his accomplishments would have belonged to us." His actual failure to produce children is not sufficient grounds to deprive him of his right to a place in the hall after death.

Even though the childless man does not contribute new members to the lineage, at least he does not purposefully cause it loss. The man who deliberately deprives the lineage of members loses the right to have his tablet in the hall. For example, some men marry their wives uxorilocally, residing with the woman's family and allowing some of the children to take her surname. The greatest contribution a man can make to his wife's family, and consequently the greatest extent to which he can sacrifice the interests of his own lineage, is to reside with his wife's family permanently and allow all of his children to bear her surname. In return he will be given a share of his father-in-law's property when it is divided. The smallest contribution a man can make to obtain a uxorilocal marriage is to reside with his wife's family until her younger brothers are old enough to earn money. Until that time he contributes his own earnings or labor to the family, but retains the right to have his children bear his surname. Once his wife's brothers are old enough to support the family, he is free to return to his lineage with his children. By this arrangement, he gains a wife without the costly bride-price payments required in virilocal marriage.

If the terms of the uxorilocal marriage agreement require any of the sons to bear the wife's surname, a man may lose the right to have his tablet placed in the hall belonging to the lineage of his birth. People said, "Once you leave through the big gate, you can never come back." They did not mean that a uxorilocally married man would not be allowed to reside with his lineage again, but that he would not be allowed a seat in the lineage hall. His social position is like that of a woman: he leaves his home to live with the parents of his marriage partner; he devotes his energies to her family; his offspring belong to her line. Like a woman, too, he is thought to have transferred his interests to his marriage partner's family; at the least his loyalty toward his natal lineage is suspect. Because he not only has failed to contribute sons or labor to his lineage, but also has allowed the products of his labor and fertility to be diverted to another group, he no longer deserves a place in the ancestral hall. In this sense, he has lost membership in the lineage. Even if he returns to reside with his natal lineage later in life, breaking the terms of the marriage contract, he will be denied this right. When I asked about a small tablet located on a domestic altar in the dining room of an Ong household, I was told, "That man married out of the lineage when he was young and only returned to die here. We had to put the tablet here because it couldn't go in the hall."

On this issue the people of Ch'inan held very strict views. Most said that if a uxorilocally married man allowed any of his children to take his wife's surname, he would lose his right to a seat in the hall. The loss of children who might have belonged to the lineage would be enough to severely weaken his status. It is misleading, however, to suggest that the lineage members were able to provide absolute answers in this regard. I questioned one informant extensively, asking whether a man who married uxorilocally could have a tablet in the hall of his natal lineage if the majority of his children took his surname. My informant finally decided that in such event the man could have his tablet in the hall as long as he returned to live with his natal family after a few years, bringing the children named after him with him. Each case is judged according to its particular characteristics, not according to blanket rules. Moreover, individuals may interpret cases differently.

Although most people agreed that the tablet of a man who had produced children for another group would be barred from the hall, some felt that one who only contributed his labor to his wife's family could return to his natal lineage and have a place in the hall. Others would deny him that right. The difference of opinion seems to turn on the question of the man's loyalty or commitment to his lineage. Some feel that his willingness to devote the energy of his youth to another agnatic group lessens his commitment to his own lineage; others feel that if all his children bear the surname of his lineage he has made contribution enough. Change of residence alone is not the determining factor. Lineage members who move to the city to earn a living are nonetheless still lineage members with a full right to a seat in the ancestral hall. Uxorilocally married men lose status in the lineage because they siphon off resources that might have belonged to the lineage.

Ordinarily, even if a uxorilocally married man agrees to allow all of his children to be named after his wife's family and to reside permanently in his wife's community, his tablet will not be placed in the hall of his wife's lineage. This was the explanation for most of the tablets located in residential rooms of Ch'inan lineage members. No matter how valuable a contribution these men make to their wives' lineage, their tablets are barred from the hall on the grounds that they bear a different surname. The hall belongs to the lineage ancestors who all bear one surname; different given names can be written on hall tablets, but not different surnames. If a place in the hall is contingent on a contribution to the lineage and possession of the lineage surname, it should follow, then, that a uxorilocally married man can earn a place in the hall of his wife's family by giving sons and labor to that lineage and taking its surname. Although everyone agrees that in theory this is true, in practice men are seldom willing to take their wife's surname. I did, however, copy one hall tablet for a man who married uxorilocally into the Lou lineage, allowed his children to take the Lou surname, resided in the Lou settlement permanently, and finally took the surname Lou himself. So, a man can, if he chooses, give up membership in his natal lineage and attain full membership in the lineage of his wife.

We have dealt so far only with the conditions that allow mature males to have tablets on the hall altar. What of males who die before maturity? Freedman claims (1970: 165–66) that, "What the system rigidly excludes is the immediate entry [to domestic altars] of the tablets of dead children, for they are not considered potential ancestors and have committed an unfilial act by the mere fact of dying young." In Ch'inan, a boy who dies young is held to be the incarnated soul of someone to whom the parents owed a debt. "He is born and lives with us for a few years, eating our food until the debt we owe him is paid off. Then he dies, having no more to claim from us." Because the child is but a guise adopted for this specific purpose, when a boy dies lineage members need have nothing more to do with him. No one is further obligated to him; it is assumed that he lived only until the debt owed him was repaid in full.

As long as this interpretation of the death prevails, no one would make a tablet for the boy. If, however, some misfortune, such as the sickness of a lineage member, is attributed to the activity of the dead child, the interpretation of his death changes. If he is thought to be the cause of some ill, then it is assumed that he was not after all the incarnation of a creditor. A creditor come to claim money owed him would not die until he had been fully repaid; if the boy is still trying to get attention, he must be a genuine lineage member and so entitled to further care in the afterlife.

If this interpretation is accepted, regular offerings will be made to the boy and a tablet probably will be made for him and placed in the lineage hall. He is treated exactly like an adult male who dies before marriage. No matter how soon after his death misfortune is attributed to him, he will be regarded as a true lineage member. Food and money can be offered to him, and a tablet can be made for him by his parents or siblings, even though they are not in a lower generation than he. He is worshiped not because a son or daughter is obligated to him as a parent, but because, as a genuine lineage member, he is entitled to the privileges of a lineage member. Like the adult male who dies childless, he is seen as a potential contributor to the lineage; whatever he might have done would have given benefit to the lineage. His right to treatment as a member of the lineage is intact, so he will receive offerings and a seat in the hall.

Turning now from males to females, we find that the case of women who die after marrying into the lineage and bearing children is closely parallel to the case of a man who marries uxorilocally into the lineage. In both cases the individual changes residence and directs all labor and energy toward the new group. In both cases the person produces children for the new group; he or she may also take the surname of his or her spouse. The woman who marries into a lineage usually has no choice about taking her husband's surname, however. Since a married woman with children has produced much of value to the lineage and has also taken her husband's surname, we would expect to find her tablet placed on the altar in the lineage hall. In marriage a woman casts her lot entirely with her husband's family. It is fitting that she should be given full status as a member of his lineage. Even if she bears no children for her husband, and even if she is the second or third wife to fail in this regard, she is still given full lineage membership. In one case, an Ong man took four successive wives of which only the fourth bore him children. He and the first three wives are now deceased, and all have tablets in the hall box. The fourth wife, still alive, sees to it that the first three wives are worshiped. Even though the first three wives did not provide the lineage with new members, they are not denied lineage membership. Their commitment and hence potential contribution to their husband's lineage were never questioned. Like men who die without begetting children, they are given their due as lineage members.

A woman who dies before marriage but after she is socially mature receives very different treatment. Like an unmarried adult male, she has a tablet made for her as a matter of course. But unlike her male counterpart, she cannot under any conditions have her tablet placed in the hall. My informants all agreed about this proscription but explained it in various ways. Some said, "She does not belong to us. From birth on, girls are meant to belong to other people. They are supposed to die in other people's houses." Some even held that the tablet of an unmarried girl cannot be positioned anywhere on lineage property; they insisted that her tablet must be housed in a special temple for unmarried girls, or that the girl must be married posthumously so her tablet can be placed on her husband's family altar. One family evolved a variant of this view. They refused to allocate any space in their house for the tablet of an unmarried daughter but had not arranged for it to be permanently placed elsewhere. Their solution was to hang the tablet, suspended on a string, in a dark corner behind a door. Her tablet was literally in limbo without a resting place in her natal home. Other people give the tablet of an unmarried girl a place to sit, usually a small, high shelf in a dim corner. All agreed that her tablet can never be placed in the ancestral hall.

A woman's stay in her natal home is usually temporary, ending when she marries out of it. From her birth it is expected that she will give the children she bears and her adult labor to the family of her husband. In the usual course of things, she is not a potential contributor to the lineage into which she is born. More often she detracts from it by taking considerable wealth with her in the form of her dowry when she marries out. If she dies before being transferred to her husband's lineage, it is felt that she has been caught in the wrong place. She has no right at all to care or worship from the members of her natal lineage because she is not a permanently committed member of that lineage. She was born to leave it. Consequently, if her tablet is allowed a place anywhere in her natal home, it is an uneasy, nonpermanent arrangement. As soon as possible, her family will find a place for her among her own kind, either in a temple for unmarried girls or on the altar of a posthumous marriage partner. Until then she is left hanging, sometimes literally. No one is obligated to worship her as a parent, and no lineage members are obligated to provide for her as an actual or potential contributor to the lineage. Whatever they offer her is intended to propitiate her and prevent her from causing harm to lineage members.

If a woman circumvents the usual pattern of life for her sex by marrying uxorilocally, she attains something of the position of a male lineage member. Like a male, she continues to reside in her natal home after marriage. Depending on the marriage arrangements, she may keep her surname rather than taking her husband's. Almost certainly some of her children will bear the surname of her natal lineage. Under these circumstances, she acquires the right to have her tablet placed in the ancestral hall of her natal lineage.

There are no unequivocal rules governing the precise conditions a uxorilocally married woman must fulfill to gain this right. Most of my informants felt that if she had contributed any children to her lineage and had not changed her surname, she had earned the right to a seat in the hall. Some, holding a stricter view, insisted that all of her offspring must bear the lineage surname for her tablet to be placed in the hall. There are at least two tablets in the lineage halls for women who had made such marriages and who had given every child the surname of her lineage. There may be tablets there for women who allowed some offspring to bear their husbands' surnames, but I did not find any. At least it is clear that some women fulfill certain conditions expected of every male lineage member: residing with the lineage; retaining their original surname; and giving their children the lineage surname. If they do, they, like men, are allowed seats in the lineage hall. In this way, a woman, who is invariably considered a potential loss to the lineage unless demonstrated otherwise, proves that she can be a contributing, committed lineage member. In return, she is awarded lineage membership in the form of a place for her ancestral tablet alongside the lineage ancestors.

The theme that people who actually give to the lineage, as well as those who would have given had they not died prematurely, are allowed tablets in the hall appears again when we consider the tablets of female children. As in the case of boys, no tablet is made for girls unless they return after death to cause trouble. But not all dead girls can have a tablet placed on the hall altar, even when they have established that they are authentic lineage members. Just as women who die before marriage are not allowed a place in the hall, so young girls who die are barred from the hall if they are natural daughters of lineage members. These girls are destined to be other people's, so they are not allowed close association with the lineage ancestors. But a girl adopted as a *sim-pua* (little daughter-in-law) *is* permitted a tablet in the hall. My informants explained this seeming discrepancy as follows. A *sim-pua* will stay permanently with the lineage into which she is adopted because it is her fate to marry one of the sons of the couple who adopts her. If she does not marry her foster brother, a uxorilocal marriage will probably be arranged for her. Because *sim-pua* are potential lineage members in this sense, they are allowed tablets on the hall altar. My informants' feeling seemed to be that if a *sim-pua* had not died young, she would have remained with the lineage and contributed sons and labor to it. Her strong potential as a committed lineage member entitles her to a place on the lineage altar. The likelihood that a natural daughter will marry out of the lineage deprives her of that privilege.

We have seen that the admission of tablets to the hall is largely based on whether or not the persons they represent have or might have enriched the lineage. In one case I discovered, this principle was strong enough to partially override the second rule, that only the tablets of those who bear the lineage surname can enter the hall. In the Ui hall, directly in front of the large box that holds all the ancestral tablets for the lineage, stand two identical incense pots. I was told, "The pot on the more honored right side is for all the lineage ancestors. The other pot is for a man who is not a relation of any of our ancestors, but who had no descendants himself. Since he had no posterity, he told his friend, our earliest ancestor, that he wanted to leave his land to the Uis to be part of our corporate ancestral land. Because he did this, we are obligated to worship him. Even though his name wasn't Ui, because his gift is part of our common lands, we put an incense pot for him in the hall." This man's contribution to the corporate funds of the lineage was so substantial that though his foreign surname could not be written on a hall tablet, he was given the closest thing to a tablet, an incense pot in the hall. Other childless people who were not relatives of lineage members have also given property to lineage members, but later than the generation of the founding ancestors. Because their gifts did not become part of the corporate lands of the lineage, they were not given a place in the hall. Instead, whoever was responsible for making the person a tablet, usually the recipient of the property, placed it on a domestic altar in his private dwelling.

The tablets of other outsiders to whom a lineage member is obligated also find their way to domestic altars. All are barred from the hall because the people they represent have made no contribution to the lineage and usually bear the wrong surname. Most commonly these outsiders are parents of uxorilocally married men and parents of wives of lineage members who have no other descendant to care for the tablets. Sometimes a household acquires more than one tablet that cannot be placed in the hall. If the tablets represent people with different surnames, they cannot be placed directly next to each other on the same shelf or altar. Rather than trouble to set up different altars for each tablet, most people simply divide them from one another by standing a small wooden board a few inches square between them. One Lou family

Lower Ong settlement. The ancestral hall is in the center
of the cluster of houses.

Wall enclosing the Ui settlement. The curved-eave building
is the ancestral hall.

Lou ancestral hall. This is the hall of the most prosperous
of the four lineages.

Ong ancestral hall and remnant of the abandoned hall. A-iong's
house is in the right foreground.

Ancestral tablets in Ui hall, with the single incense pot in front

Ancestral tablets in Li hall, including two paper tablets for the recently dead

Ancestral tablets in Lou hall. The image to the right is of the earth god, Tho-te-kong.

Ancestral hall of the upper Ongs. Its dilapidated state, the combined work of years of neglect and a typhoon in 1969, is considered a temporary embarrassment; the upper Ongs hope and expect to rebuild it some day.

Carrying the image of the god Co-su-kong out of the temple in Sanhsia

Ch'inan temple to Tho-te-kong, rebuilt and enlarged in 1970–71

Image of the Ang-kong arriving by sedan chair at the Lou hall

Pig with raw fowl and entrails offered to the god Co-su-kong

Assorted dry foods offered to the ancestor in the grave at the spring grave-cleaning ceremony

Second burial: arranging the
cleaned bones in a ceramic urn

Rubbing the bones clean prior to
placing them in the urn

Young woman cleaning the bones of her father, a step that usually
takes place six to seven years after first burial

Young man carrying the *tau* and paper ancestral tablet of his father in the funeral procession to the grave

had a domestic altar with a particularly dense population. At the far right, as one faced the altar, was a tablet for a man who had married into the family uxorilocally. Next to it, separated by a wooden board, was a tablet representing the parents of a woman who had married into the lineage; she was their only descendant and hence responsible for worshiping their tablet. On the far left edge of the altar, against the wall and divided from the others by a high board, was the last tablet, representing a young Lou woman who had died before marriage. Each of the tablets had its own incense pot. The tablets for all the other deceased members of this family were, of course, in the Lou ancestral hall.

The rules governing the admission of tablets to the hall reveal both the limits of lineage membership and the lack of ritual marks of distinction within the lineage membership. The lineage is bounded by criteria of contribution to it; membership may be earned or lost on those grounds. Within the body of members it is not customary, as it is in other places in China, to mark internal distinctions by means of separate domestic altars for each household. As long as a tablet represents a lineage member, it can be placed in the same place as the tablets of all other lineage members. Distinctions must be marked by domestic altars only at the boundaries of lineage membership, not within it. Domestic altars for uxorilocally married men and other people who are not full lineage members are ranged like punctuation marks around the edges of the hall. Within the group of those who are allowed to have tablets in the hall, no punctuation marking distinct households at every point of division is necessary.

Although all lineage members who meet the criteria I have outlined have the right to have their tablets placed in the lineage hall, some tablets for lineage members are nevertheless located outside the hall. These domestic tablets mark, not every point at which a new household divides, but certain forms of distance from the main body of the lineage and the lineage hall. The kind of distance from the core of the lineage that leads some people to establish domestic altars for tablets entitled to a place in the lineage hall can be geographical, economic, or (for lack of a better term) genealogical. To illustrate I will present data from the Ong settlement, which has the most tablets located outside the hall. This circumstance may make the Ong case somewhat atypical, but it is a useful place to begin to study the several reasons tablets are not placed in the hall.

There are eight households in the lower Ong settlement with domestic altars for tablets that could be placed in the lineage hall according to the criteria for admission. The usual pattern for people wishing to set up domestic tablets is to remove from the hall only those tablets for direct ascendants to whom they alone are obligated. For example, a household head can remove the tablets of his deceased mother and father as long as he has no brothers. He cannot remove tablets for his grandfather and grandmother unless he is again the only descendant, but he can make a copy of their tablets as well as those of more remote ancestors. All these tablets are placed in a single small shrine box and arranged on a shelf or altar in the guest room of his private home. Under no circumstances is this room called a common hall, or *kong-thia:*; it is invariably known as a *su-thia:*, or private hall. If the household also has tablets for persons who have no right to a seat in the hall, they can be placed on the same altar or shelf as the Ong tablets and separated from them by a wooden board. The eight households with Ong tablets have transferred many aspects of the worship of the ancestors to the home: temporary paper tablets for the dead are placed on the domestic altar; weddings and funerals take place in the home; and worship of the recent and remote ancestors on their death days and on special holidays is conducted in the home in front of the domestic tablets. In contrast, the rest of the Ong households carry on all these aspects of the worship of the ancestors in the Ong ancestral hall; none have tablets bearing the surname Ong in their homes.

There are three factors that alone, or more often in combination, lead to the development of domestic altars for tablets eligible for a position in the ancestral hall. The first is geographic distance from the hall. There are seven houses lying outside the central square of Ong houses clustered around the hall but still within the lower Ong settlement. All of them have domestic Ong tablets. Ongs who live outside of Ch'inan, in Ch'ipei or Sanhsia, also often set up domestic tablets. Even if those who have moved out of Ch'inan do not remove their ascendants' tablets from the hall, they will carry away a pinch of ash from the hall incense pot, and thereafter will observe all aspects of the ancestral cult in their homes. Those who have domestic tablets are unanimous in explaining their presence in the home by complaining that "going all that way to the hall is too far. It's too inconvenient." When people live a certain distance away from the hall, carrying dishes of food, making frequent trips to burn incense, and so forth become too bothersome; it is simply more convenient to invite the ancestors to one's house. In these cases, the existence of domestic tablets is in part an expression of and a result of geographic distance.

The second factor that leads people to set up a domestic altar is economic superiority. One member of a family that was building a new house just outside the central Ong settlement and would soon invite the ancestors out of the hall expressed it this way: "When a family is able to build a really beautiful house with a special place in a front room set aside for the ancestral tablets, then one can invite the ancestors out of the hall. Only those whose houses are too small or too uncomfortable don't do this." In fact, seven of the eight Ong houses with domestic tablets are relatively new, with concrete floors and plastered walls, a guest room with upholstered chairs in it, windows, and in some cases a porch. They are definitely among the finer houses in the settlement. Hence, in some cases, economic superiority to one's neighbors, once it is expressed through the building of an especially well-appointed house, may be a reason for inviting in the ancestors. One feels set apart and above, able to afford a much better house and justified in inviting the ancestors to enjoy a more comfortable environment than the ancestral hall. There is also an element of social superiority present. One woman spoke with distaste of the crowds who wait in line to worship the ancestors at the hall on a big feast day, and maintained that anyone who has a special place to install the ancestors does so; it is more convenient, less bother and fuss. The existence of domestic tablets thus may be an expression of economic distance between the members of the lineage; those who can afford a beautiful house can avoid the common herd, so to speak, and worship in the privacy of their own guest rooms.

In many cases, economic distance and geographic distance coincide. In order to move away from the old houses around the hall, one must be able to afford to build a new house on the outskirts of the settlement. Likewise, many of those who have invited the ancestors to move with them out of Ch'inan not only have moved away geographically, but also have moved up economically to business ventures in the market center or town. In the Ong settlement, in fact, neither economic superiority nor distance alone is sufficient to lead to the development of a domestic altar.* Four houses in the inner cluster of Ong houses are as well furnished as those located farther away, yet none of them has domestic tablets for Ong ancestors. On the other hand, one family that lives on the edge of the settlement formerly lived next door to their present home in an old, dark house with a dirt floor. At that time they had no Ong tablets in their home. As soon as they moved a few steps away into their new, luxurious house, they set up domestic tablets and ceased to make trips to the hall. The distance from both houses to the hall is virtually the same; it was only when the family moved into an elegantly furnished house that they invited the ancestors to their home.

If neither economic distance nor geographic distance alone necessarily leads people to set up domestic tablets, the two factors operating together inevitably result in them. The first two columns in Table 4 illustrate this point. As the table also indicates, though one household is neither located far away from the hall nor especially well furnished, it too has domestic Ong tablets. This household does, however, share a certain characteristic with

* I did, however, find instances of these variables operating independently in the other settlements.

TABLE 4
Geographic, Economic, and Genealogical Distance as Variables in
the Possession of Ong Domestic Tablets

Household	Lives away from hall	Lives in well-appointed house	Includes a male Ong last of line
1	x	x	
2	x	x	
3	x	x	
4	x	x	
5	x	x	
6	x	x	x
7	x	x	x
8			x

two other Ong households possessing domestic tablets: there is a
man in each household who has no male Ong descendants to carry
on his line of descent. These three households are the only instances of the termination of a descent line in the settlement; and
all possess domestic tablets for Ong ancestors. In each case the
termination of the descent lines has come about because the man's
only child is a uxorilocally married daughter without children
surnamed Ong, the result either of no provision having been made
for this in the wedding arrangements or of the death of the children named Ong. Thus the daughter's children are the man's descendants and will worship him after death, but none of them are
named Ong.

I suggest that the possession of domestic tablets by three households including an Ong man without Ong heirs is another expression of distance from the rest of the community. Just as some
people are separated spatially and others economically, still others
are separated in that they have not provided for continuation of
their line of descent in the Ong lineage. Perhaps the parents'
knowledge of this failure and their appreciation that it is known
to their fellow lineage members, as well, have made them feel uncomfortable about participating in the public ancestral worship
ceremonies in the central hall. They supposedly stand there as
representatives of an Ong line of descent. Since theirs is not an

Ong line, they might easily find the fact embarrassing. Under these circumstances, a simple way of avoiding a difficult situation is to transfer worship of the ancestors to the relative privacy of the home. The domestic altar in such cases is thus an expression of distance from the genealogical core of the lineage; future generations of Ongs will not return to the hall to worship these Ongs along with the earlier ancestors. Worshiping the Ong ancestors in the home presages the time when the non-Ong descendants will have nothing further to do with the ancestors in the Ong hall.

Data from the other lineages support these conclusions. The eight Li households and three Lou households with domestic tablets either live at the farthest remove from the center of their settlements or possess the most richly appointed houses in their settlements, or both. As for the other variable, I know of only one case in the other lineages of a man who has no descendants bearing his surname. That man, a Li, has tablets for his Li ancestors in his home.

One wonders whether the lineages vary systematically in their tendency to remove tablets from the hall. Are Lous and Uis less likely to take tablets from the hall in the presence of the above factors than the Ongs are? Do the Uis, with a strong sense of unity and a well-developed lineage organization, opt to leave tablets in the hall, where the Ongs, less unified and less tied to the lineage by elaborate organization, choose to remove them? Perhaps. But there is no reliable way to measure this tendency. In Ch'inan, distance cannot be measured absolutely, but must reflect the view of the people who live there. That is, it is meaningless to point out that a Ui household 100 yards from the Ui hall has no domestic tablets, whereas an Ong household 100 yards from the Ong hall has them, because the same absolute distance may be perceived differently in each case. The same is true of economic distance. And, unfortunately, there are too few cases of broken descent lines to use that factor as a basis of comparison. All I can say, then, is that there do appear to be systematic differences, at least between the Ongs and the Uis. The Lis and Lous, between the two extremes, are even more difficult to scale.

We have seen that all seven Ong households outside the core area around the hall have domestic tablets. All seven are within an easy minute or two walk of the hall. In the Ui settlement, there are six households outside the core area: three just outside, two an uphill five-minute walk beyond these three, and the last some 15 minutes farther away up a steep mountain path. Yet none of these Ui households has Ui domestic tablets. I have seen the residents of the farthest Ui house struggle down the mountain bearing heavy tureens of soup and other dishes to be offered to the ancestors in the hall. They insist strongly that "the Ui tablets belong in the hall." Uis as well as Ongs can remove tablets whenever they like, for convenience or to adorn a rich house, but several Uis endure more inconvenience than any of the Ongs do in order to leave their hall tablets "where they belong." This difference correlates well with the other systematic variations between the lineages noted in Chapter 5. The Uis, solidly unified behind their single hall with its accompanying rich corporate lands, are reluctant to create internal nodes by means of domestic tablets. The Ongs, with less involvement in corporate lineage activities associated with the hall and more internal dissension, more readily remove tablets from the common hall and establish autonomous worship centers.

Still another comparison among the lineages is fruitful. When Ongs remove tablets from the hall, they sever their ritual connection with *pai-pais* held in the hall. Once they establish an altar in the home, they need no longer return to the hall for any reason. Worship of all the ancestors on all occasions can take place in front of the domestic altar. When Lis, Lous, or Uis remove tablets, however, they retain ritual ties to the hall. Whenever the responsibility for corporate feasts falls on them, they must carry out the necessary rites in the hall, not in the home. In this sense, one could say that those Lis, Lous, and Uis who have domestic tablets participate in both a domestic cult and a hall cult of ancestor worship, something like Freedman's scheme. Yet, there is no way for domestic tablets to be promoted to the hall, as Freedman would have it. Once tablets are set up outside the hall, according to my informants, they could never be returned to the hall. If the establishment of domestic tablets should prove to be the tendency of the future in Ch'inan, so that most households finally have domestic tablets for worship of all but the most remote ancestors, then two cults, domestic and hall, will have emerged. But as the Ch'inan case shows, the development from one cult to two need not always begin with a domestic cult from which the hall cult derives. Where a single location for all tablets is an important symbol of lineage unity, the hall cult may develop first and its domestic subdivisions later.

CHAPTER 8

Missing Tablets

In considering the location of tablets, I have not raised the possibility of a tablet's not being made for a person on his death. If the creation of a tablet depends on the obligation a living person feels toward the deceased, might there not be cases in which no one has a sense of obligation and consequently no tablet is made? To answer this question, we must first determine what factors create the obligation to make a tablet for a deceased person. When I asked informants about this, I was told repeatedly that such an obligation can be created if one inherits land from a person who is otherwise a stranger as long as no one else is more obligated to him. Some important implications of this question of degree of obligation will be taken up in the next chapter. Here I wish to focus solely on the importance of inherited land in creating an obligation on the part of the heir to make a tablet for his benefactor.

An exemplary case, which many people described, involves a Li man who served in the army. He made an agreement with his commanding officer, a mainlander with no wife or descendants, to make a tablet for the officer, to bury him, and to carry on the rites of ancestor worship in return for inheriting his property. In this case, there was no personal bond between the men other than that created by the transfer of property; the two were not close friends nor were they like father and son. In the absence of any personal tie, the debt created by inheriting property from another man was strong enough to require the making of a tablet and all the other duties of ancestor worship.

The question of the relation between inheritance and ancestral tablets became even more pertinent after I had copied the tablets in the hall boxes of the Li lineage. Before I had been given permission to do so, several Lis told me not to bother because "there is nothing inside the boxes anyway." At the time I assumed this was a diversionary tactic to dissuade me from the project. But when I saw the generation boards in the boxes, I realized my informants had been telling me the truth. In the box for the first *fang*, for example, there were names for the third generation of Lis. They were written in order of birth, not in order of death; each entry was in precisely the same form and order as the information in the Li genealogy. The boards for the members of the fourth generation, all of whom are deceased, for the fifth generation, most of whom are deceased, and for the sixth generation, some of whom are deceased, were empty. The records in the second *fang* box were in a similar state, except that a partial list of fourth generation names from the genealogy had been copied onto the appropriate board. I will not include the second *fang* in my discussion because a few of its members have tablets in their homes. Since I do not know what tablets they have there I cannot draw conclusions about which of their ancestors have tablets. The members of the first *fang*, however, have no domestic tablets, so that any tablets made for their deceased relatives must perforce be in the hall.

With this in mind, I was forced to conclude that three generations of ancestors in the first *fang* have had no tablets made for them. I was told that in the late 1950's the altar in the hall was very dirty and messy, laden with tablets of all sizes and shapes. To improve the appearance of the hall, the Lis burned all the old tablets without copying the names from them, and replaced them with the three *fang* boxes now in the hall. The names inside the boxes were copied out of the genealogy. When I asked about recent ancestors whose names are not in the box, I was told, "Nowadays we don't write the names of the dead." Some people added, "Writing the names of the dead is the way it is supposed to be. Anyone can write the names of his ancestors if he wants to, but no one does." Even more persistent questioning led people to insist that they did not know why there were names missing. They often simply summarized by saying, "We Lis don't write the names of our ancestors anymore."

In the absence of more than one case of this phenomenon and with no clear explanation of it from the Lis, I can only suggest an answer: I suspect that the failure of the Lis to make tablets for their ancestors is related to their lack of rice land. They do, of course, still own a small piece of corporate land whose income continues to rotate among the lineage *fang*. But the land originally cleared by the early settlers that would have been subdivided and handed down over the generations has been lost. This land, which I will call ancestral land, was sold in the early generations of the lineage. Lis often say, "Our ancestors gambled away all our land. Now we have nothing left at all." The Lis are alone among the lineages in this deprivation. They are also alone in their complete lack of ancestral tablets for recently deceased lineage members. R. F. Johnston, a British official who made acute observations about social life in the Shantung peninsula, cites a saying that supports this answer (1910: 285):

The fact is that the possession of property—especially landed property—is regarded in practice as an inseparable condition of the continuation of the ancestral rites. This theory is often expressed in the formula *mei-yu ch'an-yeh mei-yu shên-chu*—"no ancestral property, no ancestral tablets." If the spirits of the deceased ancestors have been so regardless of the interests of their descendants that they have allowed the family property to pass into the hands of strangers, it is thought that they have only themselves to blame if for them the smoke of incense no longer curls heavenward from the domestic altars.

Johnston concluded that when ancestors are responsible for the loss of family property they are no longer worshiped. After further discussion, I will return to this point, to see whether his conclusions or the milder consequences referred to in the phrase "no ancestral property, no ancestral tablets" are more accurate.

Although I never heard the exact phrase Johnston cites, I often heard Lis complain resentfully that they are deprived and poor because their ancestors lost their rice land. And occasionally I heard more revealing comments. Once during the death-day offerings to a Li ancestor, a tactless daughter-in-law said, "These ancestors didn't leave us anything; I don't see why we have to worship them at all." She was hushed by her mother-in-law, but I suspect that her statement expressed at least in part the Lis' true feelings in the matter. As the case of the army officer who was worshiped by his heir shows, inherited property creates the obligation to carry out rites for the dead. It is reasonable to expect that if no land is inherited, the obligation to carry out these rites might be weakened. In the Li case, the paddy land cleared and cultivated by the earliest ancestors was lost through carelessness; the rice land that can supply a family with its most important commodity has ceased to flow from father to son. Although most of the obligations of ancestor worship, such as death-day offerings and burial rites, continue to be fulfilled, one aspect of the cluster of acts that make up the cult of the dead has disappeared: Lis no longer make tablets for their ancestors. To be sure, the earliest ancestors have their names carved on the three large boxes. But these tablets were prepared as a community project, largely for the purpose of beautifying the hall and making it competitive with the other halls in Ch'inan; it was not a filial act done by sons soon after the death of their father. The filial act of making tablets for the dead has ceased to take place in at least the first *fang* of the Li lineage.

Given the rules that admit some tablets into the hall and exclude others, the Li development should not be too surprising. Those rules are based on the contribution made by the deceased to the lineage. As in the case of a man who marries uxorilocally, if he detracts from lineage wealth by taking his labor and offspring elsewhere, he loses the right to have his tablet in the hall. The Lis have not reached the point of saying that their ancestors have no right to have tablets in the hall, but they *have* reached the point of not giving them individualized places in the hall.

Curiously, the men who actually lost the ancestral land—most lineage members believe that the second- and third-generation Lis gambled it away—have tablets. Indeed, rather than being singled out for exclusion, these men were commemorated through a project organized by the whole lineage. (Of course, there are other reasons why men in the second generation should have tablets, for aside from their individual contributions to the lineage, they are focal ancestors, heads of the three *fang* that mark the internal divisions within the lineage. Their names, emblazoned on publicly visible boxes, are part of the outward-looking hall cult by which the lineage represents itself to the other lineages.) Meanwhile, the men who were in no way responsible for the loss of the Li ancestral lands, those in the succeeding generations, have not been given tablets. It is as though the entire institution of sons making tablets for their fathers is gone. It may be that one aspect of the cult of ancestor worship, the duty of making tablets for the deceased, is a reciprocal of the obligation of fathers to hand on ancestral property to their sons. If there is no property, no tablets are written.

At this point I will leave the Li case in order to consider tablets in the hall boxes of the other lineages. If we find there the same correlation between loss of ancestral land and lack of tablets, my interpretation of the Li case will be strengthened.

In order to measure unambiguously such a correlation, I have made some restrictions on the data. Since people who move out of Ch'inan often remove their ancestors' tablets from the hall, I have eliminated from the sample all *fang* or descent lines whose only living representatives are not resident in Ch'inan. I was able to copy the tablets from just a few altars outside Ch'inan, so I cannot be sure which ancestors have tablets there. I have also excluded lines of descent whose members have domestic tablets in Ch'inan, because I did not copy all of these. This restriction applies largely to the Ong lineage, which has the most domestic altars. As long as some members of a line of descent live in Ch'inan and do not have domestic altars, I can include them in the sample, for then the original tablet would be in the hall; those who move away or set up a domestic altar would have to make a copy.

In addition I have eliminated tablets of women from the sample. One reason is that there might be some explanation other than lack of property for a woman not to have a tablet. For example, if a wife failed to bear any children, the lack of direct descendants could account for the omission. Also, the ownership and care of land is usually men's business. Land is registered in men's names, cared for by them, and passed on by them to their sons. It seems appropriate that lack of land would be related to the omission of men's tablets rather than women's. The sample, then, is deceased men with some descendants who reside in Ch'inan and do not have domestic altars. Each man is counted as one case, involving one decision to make or not make a tablet. I begin with the generation below the last represented on the outside of the hall boxes, for those publicly visible names are the result of lineage action, not of action by a group of land-inheriting siblings. This eliminates the two earliest generations from the Lou and Ong samples and the three earliest from the Ui sample.

In the sample, as constructed, there are 33 deceased males in the Ong lineage who have tablets in the hall box, and eight deceased males who do not.* Since the descendants of the men without tablets in the hall are resident in Ch'inan and have no domestic tablets, and since there is no other place the tablets could possibly be, we can conclude that there are eight individuals whose direct descendants have failed to make tablets for them. Because none of them is recently deceased, it is likely that these men will never receive a tablet.

In every one of the eight cases in which a tablet is missing, the man's descendants told me that they had inherited no paddy land. True, some do own land, but it is land they purchased themselves. The ancestral paddy land, in all cases, had been lost long since, before or during the lifetime of the ancestor without a tablet. This

---

* There are three Ong ancestral tablets that I am unable to identify, either with the help of the household registration records or with the help of my informants. Conceivably, they represent one or other of the eight men whose tablets are missing, since Taiwanese sometimes follow the practice of writing a generation name on the ancestral tablet, which differs from the name the person was known by in life. This seems unlikely, however, because in other cases I found that the direct descendants knew about their ascendants' generation names, whereas none of the descendants of the eight men in question could identify the unknown tablets. It is my guess that these three tablets are for ancestors of Ongs who have moved out of Ch'inan.

TABLE 5
Correlation Between Lack of Ancestral Land and Lack of
Ancestral Tablets, Ong, Lou, and Ui Lineages

| Lineage | Tablet missing (11) | | Tablet present (64) | | Total in sample |
	No land	Land	No land	Land	
Ong	8	0	7	26	41
Lou	3	0	3	9	15
Ui	0	0	3	16	19
TOTAL	11	0	13	51	75

NOTE: By land I mean specifically ancestral rice land passed down from father to son.

part of the correlation is perfect; if there is no tablet for an ancestor, his descendants did not receive land from him (see Table 5).

One point about the figures should be clarified. Since each missing tablet has been counted as one case, two or more instances of missing tablets in the same line of descent have been treated as individual cases. In fact, this happened only once, as shown in Fig. 2. Although the land was lost just the one time (in C's day), there were two occasions on which no tablet was made, and on each occasion a different set of descendants was responsible for omitting the tablet: D and his brothers; E and his brothers.

Even though the absence of a tablet is always correlated with lost land, in seven instances Ong descendants made tablets despite the lack of land. This is not inconsistent with my earlier findings: if descendants do not inherit productive land, that is grounds for them to omit some aspects of the ancestral cult, in particular the making of one or more of their ancestors' tablets. But the lack of rice land does not always lead to the omission of tablets.

The data from the Lou lineage is consistent with the Ong material. The Lou sample is small because I copied the tablets in only two *fang* boxes and eliminated many lines of descent whose members have moved away. Just as in the Ong case, every instance of a missing tablet is correlated with missing ancestral land. There is no case of a missing tablet when the descent line has maintained its ancestral land.

The Ui case provides neither negative nor positive evidence

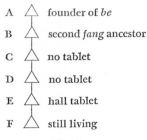

Fig. 2

simply because there are tablets for all the ancestors. But there are proportionately fewer cases of lost ancestral land than in the Ong and Lou cases, and so we could expect fewer tablets to be missing. Another factor in the Ui case is strong identification with the solidary lineage. Members may write tablets for their dead as representatives of the lineage rather than as individual forebears and owners of property. In that light, we would expect fewer cases of missing Ui tablets even if there were proportionately as many instances of lost land.

Taken together, the Li, Ong, Lou, and Ui cases lead to the conclusion that the points at which tablets are lacking are not distributed randomly but are correlated with the points at which ancestral land has been lost. But even though tablets are not made for some of the dead, the other rites in the cult are usually carried out for those forebears; certainly they are buried and worshiped regularly.

To understand the close association between this one aspect of the cult, the making of a tablet, and one social correlate, the inheritance of rice land, we can consider the nature of the tablet in other contexts. Giving a deceased person a tablet in the hall is like giving him a special seat on the corporate property of the lineage. His soul is thought to occupy the tablet at times; and at all times the tablet is reserved solely for his use. If a part of the rites for the dead is dropped because of a man's failure to pass on ancestral land, it is fitting that it should be the part involving a reserved place on the corporate property of the lineage. A man who wastes ancestral land, thus neglecting the interests of his descendants, is reciprocally neglected by his descendants when they deny him a special seat on lineage land. In addition, we have seen how the right to a seat in the hall is bestowed or denied on the basis of contribution to lineage resources. It is appropriate that the dead who have failed to preserve or hand on ancestral land, thus bringing loss to lineage members, would not be given a seat in the corporate hall.

To restate the proposition at its simplest: those who do not inherit rice land from their forebears feel to some extent relieved of their obligation to them; this weakened obligation may lead to the omission of certain rites for the dead; the particular part that is omitted, the making of a tablet, is dictated by the significance of the tablet itself in other contexts, as a concomitant of contribution to the lineage, and as a reserved seat on the corporate property of the lineage.

The fact that the cult of the dead is fragmented in such a way as to allow part of it to be omitted and part to be preserved may be related to the character of the ritual symbols that play an important role in the cult. V. W. Turner suggests (1968: 21, 44) that ritual symbols are multivocal, representing many things at once. Similarly, ancestral tablets are compact coding devices; every aspect of them is significant in some way. As we have seen, the form of the tablets marks them as representations of either focal ancestors or more recent ones. Their location is a guide to economic and social distinctions within the lineage. As we will see in the next chapter, the responsibility for their worship and the times at which they must be worshiped reflect other significant social variables involving obligation and debt. In a larger context, the entire cult of the dead is a bundle of acts and objects. Far from being a unitary institution such that all parts of it occur automatically according to simple rules, it can be fragmented into many distinct acts, each of which is significant in a different way. One part of the institution, making tablets for deceased persons, may be abandoned in the absence of inherited property; this does not mean that other parts of the institution will also disappear

where there is no property. R. F. Johnston says that when there
is no property, the ancestral rites as a whole vanish. But the Chinese phrase he quotes, *"mei-yu ch'an-yeh mei-yu shên-chu"*—"no
ancestral property, no ancestral tablets," says only that where there
is no property there is no *tablet*. It remains to be seen whether
the observation of other parts of the cult, such as worship on
death-day anniversaries or worship at graves, is conditional on
other things.

CHAPTER 9

Worshiping the Dead

THE DEAD who are not given tablets because they failed to pass on paddy land to the living may still receive offerings in the after-life, when they are dependent on the living for sustenance. The food offered to them and the mock money burned for them keep them fed and clothed. Otherwise they would lack the necessary creature comforts and suffer. Analysis of the obligation to worship the dead must account both for the conditions under which the obligation is created and for who falls under that obligation. Such analysis reveals, not a simple correlation with an obligation created by property inheritance, but a complex correlation with obligations created by other kinds of debts as well. One aspect of the cult of the dead, the making of tablets, is a concomitant of the inheritance of rice land. Another aspect, the worship of the dead with incense and food offerings, is a concomitant of a wider social dimension, the existence of many kinds of obligation and debt.

In my discussions with informants about actual cases of worship of the dead, I found they considered the obligation of worship to be present or absent on the basis of several generally accepted rules:

1. If X inherits property from Y, he must worship Y.
2. If X is a direct descendant of Y, he may or may not worship Y.
   a. If X is Y's only descendant, he must worship Y.
   b. If X is the most obligated descendant, he must worship Y.

An understanding of these regular patterns can best be obtained through a study of actual case histories. As Fredrick Barth has put it (1966: 2), "Explanation is not achieved by a description of the patterns of regularity, no matter how meticulous and adequate, nor by replacing this description by other abstractions congruent with it, but by exhibiting what *makes* the pattern, i.e. certain processes. To study social forms, it is certainly necessary but hardly sufficient to be able to describe them. To give an explanation of social forms, it is sufficient to describe the processes that generate the form." By looking at actual cases it is possible to see how people judge obligation to be present here or absent there as a result of their particular interests and goals.

To emphasize the importance of property inheritance as a creator of obligation, I will begin with instances in which property inheritance is more important than descent or is the only factor involved. Then I will turn to cases in which descent plays the dominant role, though property inheritance may also enter in.

One of my first clues to the importance of property inheritance in determining who must worship particular dead people came while I was examining the ancestral tablets on the domestic altar of a compound belonging to the Iap family on the outskirts of the main Ong settlement. The old man of the house told me that his Iap ancestors had come to Ch'inan long ago, at the same time as the Ong settlers, and had cleared land. As he was explaining this history, I noticed a dusty and barely legible tablet for an Ong woman to the left of the Iap tablets on his altar and behind it, several other Ong tablets on which the personal names were illegible. When I asked him about these tablets, he brushed the question aside, saying, "Oh, there was an Ong widow who had relations with my Iap grandfather and bore children by him. We worship her because of that, but we don't really have to, because the Ongs worship her, too." When I asked about the other Ong tablets on his altar he said, "I don't know why those tablets are there. We only worship that one Ong woman, not any other Ongs."

Later, when I questioned the Ongs about the Iaps, they did little to disguise their feelings of animosity and indignation. The accepted story among them was that a Iap man had wandered into the Ong settlement, alone and without resources, had been taken in and given a position as fieldhand, and eventually had been allowed to marry an Ong woman uxorilocally. Some of the children had not only been allowed to take the Iap surname, but thanks to the generosity of the Ongs, had even been given some Ong land as their inheritance. This story, told with a tone of considerable resentment, often ended with the summation, "Now just look at those Iaps. The descendants of the children named Iap are living on our land just as if it were theirs. They have built a fancy house on our land, too. But because they have our land they must worship *all* the Ong ancestors—not just the woman who married the Iap man originally, but the woman's parents, grandparents and so on all the way back to our original ancestor."

The Ongs claimed that the numerous Ong tablets on the Iap altar were for the direct ascendants of the woman who married the Iap man. As they see it, the Iaps are strongly indebted to the Ong ancestors because they possess some of the Ong ancestral land. This debt should be continually repaid by offering produce from the land to the Ong ancestors on the anniversaries of their deaths. The Iap man, realizing that if he admits he worships Ong ancestors he is admitting his own ancestors' dependence on the Ong lineage, denies that the land originally belonged to Ongs and hence that he is obligated to worship Ong ancestors. The question turns not on descent but on the obligation to worship that is automatically created by the inheritance of rice land. The question of obligation is important in this case because it is linked to the question of the Iaps' dependence on the Ongs. If the Iaps were to admit they owe all their land to the Ongs, they would then have to admit to a new status: as a satellite compound, a mere offshoot of uxorilocal marriage to an Ong woman, dependent on the Ongs' beneficence for their livelihood.

In the Ong-Iap case the controversy is largely over property inheritance. Descent, even if it were brought into the forefront of the quarrel, would only reinforce the claims of both parties. The Ongs, for instance, could claim that the Iaps were descended from an Ong woman and, through her, from the earlier Ong ancestors, thus forging a second link between the Ongs and the Iaps who got their property. In other cases, the line of direct descent does not follow the line of property inheritance. Yet the inheritance of property just as surely creates the obligation to worship the person who bequeathed it. For example, if a male lineage member who has reached old age has never married or produced direct descendants, he may name as his heir a member of the lineage in a collateral line of the next lowest generation, perhaps his brother's son. If the young man agrees to take the property, he must carry out all the proper ancestral rites for his benefactor in return.

If a man who foresees that he may die without descendants has no collateral kin, he may arrange to have a virtual stranger carry out the rites of worship for him after his death. The story the Lis often told about the agreement between the army officer and the Li man who served with him is one example. I heard other accounts of men without descendants who sold their land before death for a reduced price with the understanding that the buyer would make up the difference by financing their funerals and providing for them in the afterlife. The seller uses the obligation created by selling his land at a low rate to ensure his well-being after death. Thus, just as property inheritance accompanied by descent entails the obligation to worship, so also may property inheritance in the absence of descent require worship.

Weakening the relationship between the parties still more, we find that mere use of a deceased person's property may entail the obligation to worship him. Kim-bo, an old lady who is a member of the fifth *fang* of the Lou lineage, revealed the following story to me in bits and snatches during the course of several conversations. After the death of Kim-bo's father's brother, Lou Kau, his wife moved to the south of Taiwan with all her children. Finding no one who wanted to purchase the piece of paddy land that was her husband's share of the Lou ancestral lands, the wife, A-bi, had agreed to let Kim-bo's sons till it and use or sell the rice without paying any rent. In return, Kim-bo was to be responsible for regular worship of the original owner, her father's brother, Lou Kau. All went smoothly until A-bi arranged for the sale of the paddy land to someone outside the lineage. Kim-bo, no longer obligated to Lou Kau's family because she was no longer getting the produce from their land, stopped worshiping him. Meanwhile, A-bi fell ill, and the fortunes of the family business began to decline. She returned to Ch'inan to recuperate and to accuse Kim-bo of bringing on all her troubles because she had stopped worshiping Lou Kau. This interpretation was reinforced when a god, consulted about the reasons for A-bi's troubles, accused Kim-bo of negligence.

Thus condemned, Kim-bo did not accept the sentence, but reasserted her interpretation of where the obligation to worship the dead man lay. After burning incense in the lineage hall, she called on her father's brother, saying, "You can't come back here causing trouble because I don't worship you any more. The land I once used now belongs to others, and I get no benefit from it. You should only expect worship from A-bi and her sons, not from me." After this, so the story goes, Lou Kau, now clear about who was supposed to worship him, stopped making his wife sick and his sons suffer financially. It is plain from this tale that persons who receive the fruits of the land once belonging to a dead person may be obligated to offer part of those fruits to the former owner unless the obligation is repaid in some other way. If Kim-bo had paid rent to Lou Kau's family, she would not have been expected to worship him. The act of worshiping the dead is an accepted way of repaying an obligation or debt both in return for a gift of land and in return for use of the land.

As these examples show, the obligation to worship the dead is a flexible matter, open to interpretation by both the living and the dead. Some would even go so far as to turn all this around: instead of holding the use of land as the source of an obligation to worship the dead, they would make the act of worship a justification for its use. In one case a Li man had married a Ui woman uxorilocally. According to their agreement, two of the sons were named Ui and two Li. Also by the terms of the marriage, the Ui ancestral land was to be inherited only by the Ui boys. In time, however, both Ui brothers moved away from Ch'inan. One of the Li sons has been tilling the land inherited by his two Ui brothers for many years. He told me that one time the Uis returned and confronted him with the demand either to stop using their land or to pay rent. He had replied, "You two worship only your Ui mother and Li father. You make offerings to none of the higher Ui ancestors, whereas I have been making generous offerings to all my direct ascendants among the Uis even back to the founding ancestors. Doesn't that show that I am entitled to use of this land?" According to my informant, his two Ui brothers were effectively silenced by this argument. The implication is that the Li man, by paying his debt for the products of the land to his Ui ancestors, had earned the right to till the land, and that his Ui brothers, by failing to make the sacrifices, had lost it. The rule we began with, that if a man inherits land from another he must worship the other, can be rewritten in some cases to include *use* of land. In other cases it can be reversed to read that if a man worships a line of ancestors, he attains the right to use the land those ancestors once owned. Whether or not these revisions occur in any given instance depends on the persons involved and how they interpret their own and others' obligations to the dead.

I deliberately began this analysis of the obligation to worship the dead with those cases in which property inheritance plays a vital part in order to help overcome the common conception that ancestor worship among the Chinese is essentially a matter of obligations between agnates created by descent. But in so doing, I have underemphasized the part descent plays. Under considerable prompting, people in the village would eventually say that men must worship their parents, grandparents, and so on, up to the founding ancestor of the lineage, and that wives must worship only the ancestors of their husbands. Although they seemed uncomfortable making such broad generalizations, they were at ease and eager to offer opinions as soon as I filled in the outline of some specific situation. Then their answers quickly demonstrated that whether or not the pattern of descendants worshiping direct ancestors is followed depends on the particular circumstances in a given case. One situation in which a person almost invariably worships his or her direct ascendants is when he or she is the only living descendant. A parent must receive minimal rites of care in the afterlife from someone; if there is but one descendant, he or she is obligated to provide them. Hence a married woman, who would normally not be required to worship her own parents; an adopted-out son or daughter, who would normally worship only the adoptive parents, and leave the care of the natal parents to siblings; and a uxorilocally married man, who would normally expect his brothers at home to worship his parents, would all be bound to make offerings to their natural parents if there were no other offspring.

It is only in this circumstance that a person is obligated to worship his parents and grandparents whatever the nature of the relationship between himself and them. In every other situation, there is room for interpretation, contention, and debate about which descendants should be responsible for worshiping which forebears. The question often turns, as indicated by part two of rule two above, on who is most obligated to the deceased. To illustrate, if a man has more than one son and fails to leave one son any property, perhaps because of incompetence, the disinherited son need not worship his father in the afterlife. Most of the people I asked about this replied, "Why would that son want to worship his father if he didn't get any property?" Some added that though a son was justified in not making offerings to his father under these conditions, he still risked his father's anger; an angry deceased father could easily bring sickness or misfortune on him. No matter how strained a son's relations with his father, he may be held accountable to his father anyway simply for the gift of life. Still, if relations are so bad that the son is disinherited, he may resign the care of his father's spirit to his brothers and at least attempt to go his own way with impunity.

Between grandfather and grandson there is no such basic debt as this. Hence, some grandchildren may be strongly obligated to their grandparents for having received their property, and others not. In the latter case, the bond between the grandchildren and their grandparents is easily attenuated. For example, one time, as I was collecting lists of dates on which lineage members worshiped their dead, a Ui man, G (see Fig. 3), was unable to cite the dates on which he worshiped his grandmother and grandfather. Bit by bit, the story emerged. His father, E, married a Ui woman, D, uxorilocally. According to the terms of the marriage agreement,

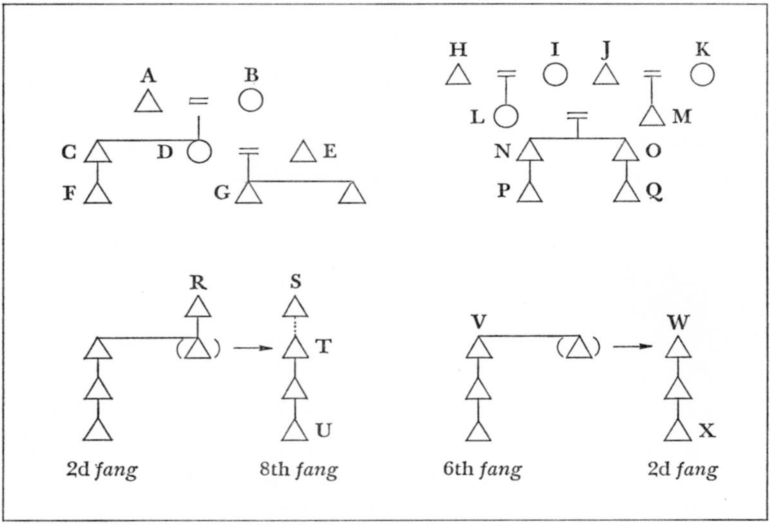

Fig. 3

all the children were named Ui. The agreement had also specified that each of the male children would receive some of the Ui ancestral lands through his mother. However, the woman's brother, C, broke the contract, keeping all the Ui property in his own hands and robbing the children of the uxorilocal match of any land. As a result, G explained, "Those Uis who got the land worship our common grandparents and other higher Ui ancestors. My brother and I worship only our parents." One of the grandchildren, F, is clearly more obligated to his grandparents, A and B, because he received Ui ancestral land. As long as someone is responsible for worshiping the grandparents, they will be satisfied in the afterlife. It is felt to be fitting that those with the heaviest obligation should carry out this duty.

In other instances, rather than some descendants being bypassed entirely in the distribution of property, as in the case just discussed, all descendants receive property but from different sources. Let us say, for example, that a man (M in Fig. 3) marries uxorilocally, gives one of his sons, O, his own surname, and bestows his own property on him. Meanwhile, the other son, N, takes his mother's surname and inherits her lineage's property. Both N and O may worship both parents, since the one is as obligated to them as the other for his upbringing and very existence. But if they wish, they may divide the responsibility, the child who inherited from his mother being responsible for worshiping her, the other being required to worship his father. This division of responsibility is more likely to occur in the next generation, however. Then P will be required to worship his grandmother, L, and her ascendants, H and I, and on up the line; and Q will be required to worship his grandfather, M, and his ascendants, J and K, etc. Of course, P and Q might both worship both lines, but the difference in their respective obligations is likely to lead them to worship following the line of transfer of property.

Two unusual cases I uncovered during my survey of days on which the dead are worshiped illustrate even more dramatically the delegation of responsibility for ancestral worship to the persons most obligated toward the dead. U, the manager of the Ui lineage, a member of the eighth *fang*, told me that he did not worship his grandfather, T, though he did make offerings to his father and great-grandfather, S. Repeatedly, he insisted that since his grandfather had been adopted into the eighth *fang* from the second Ui *fang*, the second *fang* was responsible for worshiping him. Upon further questioning, U explained that the second *fang* had kept the land earmarked for T because he was adopted out. Since they got his property, they should worship him. U held to this interpretation, even though he recognized that he and his *fang* were all descended from T.

Confronted with this information, the members of the second *fang* somewhat indignantly assured me that the eighth *fang* must certainly worship T. "Our ancestor gave a son to the eighth *fang* who fathered them and all their descendants. Of course they worship him." Some of the second-*fang* members added that T had in fact received a small piece of mountain land as part of his inheritance. Since this land had been handed down to the eighth *fang*, its members were all the more obligated to worship him. When I went back to U with this new information, he said, "Oh, yes, T brought along an insignificant piece of mountain land. But all his rice land stayed in the second *fang*. That's why the second *fang* has to worship him."

One member of the second *fang* was especially vituperative when I asked him for his opinion. "Certainly the eighth *fang* worships T. Just let them come over here and say they don't. In fact, they should also worship R, T's father. One time, to shame them into it, we invited them here on R's death-day anniversary. When they asked whose death day it was, we said, "*Our great-grandfather's.*" The issue of who must worship T turns on who is most obligated to him. The eighth *fang* holds that the second *fang* should worship him because it inherited the rice land that would have been his if he had remained in that *fang*. The second *fang* holds that the eighth *fang* is more obligated to T because its members are his descendants and moreover received a portion of second-*fang* mountain land.

After discovering this dispute, I set out to find someone else with an ancestor who had been adopted out from one *fang* to another in the same lineage. I was able to locate a man in the second *fang* of the Lou lineage, X, whose grandfather W had been adopted from the sixth Lou *fang*. He said there was no question about who worshiped W. Because the second *fang* was descended from him and had even received a portion of sixth-*fang* paddy land from him, the second *fang* was responsible for worshiping him. When the land was divided among W's brothers, he received a good portion of what would otherwise have been his normal share, including some paddy land. The inheritance of a portion of paddy land led X to judge himself and the rest of his *fang* more heavily obligated to his grandfather than the sixth *fang*. Consequently, he worshiped him without question. In the case of grandparents and ancestors in higher generations, ties created by descent may be insufficient to instill the obligation to worship. Whoever receives the property that belonged to them may be held more strongly obligated than a mere descendant. If the line of property transfer follows descent, there is no question of who is obligated to worship.

Under most circumstances, if someone is obligated to worship a deceased person, he and others so obligated will continue to do so indefinitely. There were seldom any gaps between the most recent ancestors and the founders of the lineage in the lists of death-day anniversaries people celebrated. This means that many people worship five to seven generations of ancestors; they foresee no possibility that some of them might ever be forgotten. As a rule, ancestors are worshiped indefinitely once a year on the anniversary of the day they died. In such cases, each ancestor is given a separate identity, a separate feast in his personal honor. But in some situations, as I shall outline below, a different pattern occurs.

In most instances, even the earliest ancestors, the lineage founders, are worshiped on their death-day anniversaries. In the case of the Lous, however, the earliest ancestor and his wife are worshiped together on a single date chosen by the lineage leaders, the fifteenth of the eighth month. Perhaps the Lous, most developed in lineage organization and power, have elevated their earliest ancestors beyond personally remembered forebears. Their character as focal ancestors representing the unity of the lineage is well demonstrated by the use of corporate funds for their worship; the calendrical date divorces them again from personal identity and makes them essentially abstract symbols of the lineage. The readjustment of dates in the Lou lineage applies only to the founders; all more recent ancestors are worshiped on their death days.

A few small groups in Ch'inan have made a readjustment of dates for the opposite reason. I discovered during my survey of death-day anniversaries that the Peqs, peripheral to the Li lineage settlement, and three non-Lou groups living in that settlement, did not remember dates for their ancestors beyond two generations above the oldest living member. The higher ancestors were all said to be worshiped together on the ninth of the ninth month. None of these groups has a lineage organization, a hall, or any common property. In contrast, most lineage members claimed that no one who belonged to a lineage could possibly worship all the ancestors on one day. Where there is a strong lineage organization buttressed by corporate property, the identity of the early ancestors is a vital matter. Most important, they are one of the means by which living members emphasize their relationships with one another; when all members of a *fang* worship the *fang* ancestor on his death day they reaffirm their agnatic relationship as his descendants. Where relationships focused on distant ancestors are not important, as in the Peq group, the early ancestors are not worshiped individually.

Regardless of whether the earliest ancestors are worshiped together or singly, the dead of the immediate past are normally worshiped on their death-day anniversaries. Celebration of that day is a sign that the deceased has living descendants who personally remember him. Only those of the recently dead who produced no direct descendants are worshiped on a day other than their death day—along with some other ancestor, perhaps, or on some calendrical holiday, such as New Year, when all the other ancestors are worshiped as well. The same is true of men whose heirs were adopted late in life so that there was no strong tie of common experience; for example, the mainland officer who gave his land to the Li soldier. In contrast, a man who adopts a young child to be his heir will probably be worshiped on his death day because the experience of the adopted child is in most respects like a natural son's. He will have lived for many years in the same household with his adoptive father.

Just as making a tablet is a concomitant of inheriting land, so worshiping a dead person on his death-day anniversary is a concomitant of being his descendant. This correlation is appropriate for two reasons. First, the dead man is more likely to be personally remembered if he begot or adopted a son who lived in the same household with him until his death. If he is well remembered as a distinct individual he would properly be given his own separate offerings on a special day. Second, the separate stream of incense that floats upward from a death-day offering for one person corresponds to the separate line of descent that extends from him to his descendants. If a man has descendants who are uniquely his, he is ensured a line of descent that passes through him alone. If a man dies without descendants, whoever is appointed to wor-

TABLE 6
Reciprocal Obligations Between the Living and the Dead

	The living must:		
	Worship on a calendrical holiday	Worship on death-day anniversary	Make an ancestral tablet
If the dead:			
Leave property to a collateral relative or to a nonrelative	x		
Leave direct descendants	x	x	
Leave property to a direct descendant	x	x	x

ship him will still be principally obligated to his natural father. The merging of the two descent lines corresponds to the merging of the offerings for the man without descendants with the offerings for another ancestor.

From all this, and with what was determined in the last chapter, we can compile a simple set of reciprocal obligations that sort out some of the constituents of the cult of the dead. The list of reciprocal acts in Table 6 deals only with minimum obligations the living owe the dead under various conditions. It bypasses the problem, already discussed in this chapter and the last, of *which* persons among the living must carry out these minimum obligations. The table shows that the cult is a bundle of distinct and separable acts that depend on various relations between the living and the dead. When the dead leave property, whoever inherits it must reciprocate with worship; when the dead leave descendants, they must reciprocate with worship in return for the gift of life and in return for support during childhood.

Considering the cult of the dead in this way alone, however, gives us an incomplete picture. Although it is true that the living carry out services for the dead as a means of repaying their debts to them, it is also true that the dead have the power to demand, if need be, the care they require. As we have discussed them so far, the obligations and debts of the living to the dead are modeled on ordinary relationships of reciprocity similar to those that hold among the living. To move beyond the misleading idea that relations between the living and the dead are but an extension of relations between the living requires an analysis of the powers of the dead and how they use them. This, in turn, requires consideration of the activities of the dead in another guise, how they behave as corpses soon after death and in their graves still later.

CHAPTER 10

Worship at the Grave

WHAT HAS concerned us to this point is how the cult of the dead reflects and codes social and political relations: the corporate lineage hall as a symbol of the political and territorial relationships among lineage communities; the placement of the tablets as a code for the extent of lineage membership and for economic and social distinctions within the lineage; the delegation of responsibility for worship of the tablets and the times at which worship must be carried out as expressions of different kinds of obligation and debt and the conditions that create them. At this juncture, an examination of the cult leads to a different complex of relations. The aspects of the cult I have thus far considered reflect ties among the living as much as between the living and the dead. Even the obligation to worship the ancestors turns on which of the living is the most obligated to the dead rather than solely on relationships between alive and deceased persons. The following chapters deal less with interpersonal relations in the ordinary, mundane world (the *iong* world), and more with ties and breaches between living persons and the dead in their *im* world. In this direction lie the parts of the cult of the dead that express, reaffirm, and readjust the villagers' world view. Here can be seen their hopes for an ideal life and their attempts to face and correct one that is less than ideal.

Interment of the dead and worship at the grave thereafter differ radically from the relatively simple rites that take place in the hall or home. The sequence begins as soon as it seems apparent that a person is dying. At that point he or she is placed on a bed of boards supported by benches, which is set up in the ancestral hall directly in front of the ancestral tablets. Sometimes the move is premature. A Li man became so sick that he was unable to rise from his bed, and his relatives, thinking that he would die soon, moved him into the ancestral hall. But three days later he was still living, and they moved him out again. It is said to be good to let a person die in the hall "so that he will be close to the ancestors." It is also considered dangerous to move a corpse into the hall, so every effort is made to allow the dying to expire in the hall, avoiding the necessity of moving the body in after death.

After a person has died, his lineage relatives are exceedingly busy for the next few days making mourning clothes and preparing food for guests. The earliest guests to arrive are usually lineage members living away from the village. They make every effort to arrive by the evening of the day of the death in order to witness the coffining. The first part of this procedure, which takes about two hours, is carried out by Taoist priests hired for the occasion, who play an ensemble of bells and gongs while standing around the body chanting. These activities are considered best left in the hands of experts; most relatives sit on the sidelines chatting or attend to food preparation behind the scenes. When the priests have finished playing and chanting, the lineage members who are present begin the tasks that are their responsibility: transfer of the body to the coffin and continuous vigil during the night and the next few days until the funeral.

The family of the deceased hires a geomancer to choose a day on which the deceased and his relatives can safely experience a funeral. Careful selection of a time is necessary because on certain days of the year dangerous monsters are thought to be abroad. Known as *iau-kuai,* these monsters are created when some man or animal is improperly buried. If a funeral took place when a *iau-kuai* was around, the corpse, perhaps because of its transitional state, would be vulnerable to attack. Harm, such as many deaths in a short period of time or drastic loss of wealth, would then result for the descendants. Other days are generally safe for funerals but unlucky for certain persons. To warn them, a list of dates is always posted at funerals; anyone whose birthday is on the list simply stays away from the burial ground.

The funeral ceremonies are long and complex, usually lasting four or five hours. On the morning of the funeral, the coffined body is moved out of the hall to rest on a spot, again chosen by the geomancer, somewhere in front of the hall. Some of the women, garbed in the appropriate mourning dress, gather around the coffin to wail. As guests arrive they offer incense before the coffin, standing in front of a long line of tables laden with food offerings for the deceased. After both affines and descendants have paid their respects to the dead and the coffin has been symbolically nailed shut, the funeral procession forms. Traditional Chinese bands, a Western-style brass band, the coffin with its bearers, and most of the deceased's direct descendants file through the village and across the Hengch'i River until they reach the public grave-yard on the hill behind Ch'ipei.

At the grave the coffin is placed in a shallow trench and care-fully oriented by a geomancer, who aligns it in the most beneficial direction. Then it is covered with a mound of earth. Three days later, some of the descendants return "to see that everything is all right." This done, they need not return again until the spring grave-cleaning festival, when they weed the grave and offer food to the deceased. Thereafter the grave is visited yearly for six or seven years. Then, on a propitious day, the coffin is disinterred, and, if the flesh has sufficiently rotted from the bones, they are removed, rubbed clean, and arranged in a ceramic pot, which is placed in the hole left by the coffin. After this, the grave is still visited without fail every spring. Some people improve the site of the bones simply by covering the pot over with earth and erect-ing a carved gravestone. Others build elaborate concrete housings for the pot with a gravestone in front and a concrete platform surrounding it on three sides. These improvements may accom-pany a change in location for the bones or may be made while they are in their original location.

The responsibility for the regular cleaning of ancestral graves below those of the founders of the lineage is not systematically delegated; anyone who has free time goes to weed and set the graves in order, acting as a representative of the ancestor's other descendants. In the case of the Li, Lou, and Ui founding ancestors, however, graveside worship is a lineage affair, assigned to the particular sub-*fang* that is in charge of the corporate feasts for the year; as in the case of other corporate worship occasions, the offerings are paid for out of lineage funds. In this sense worship at the graves is like worship of the ancestors in the hall: the recently dead are cared for by their descendants on a private basis, whereas the most remote dead, being representatives of the lineage, receive offerings paid for with corporate lineage funds.

Similarly, graves, like hall tablets, ordinarily never cease to be worshiped. Virtually all lineage members could cite the location of each of their direct ascendants' graves up to the founding ancestor. On the day of the spring grave-cleaning I accompanied several different parties; in each case they were able to find all of their ancestors' graves. This was true even though many graves had never been improved since the bones had been placed in the pot. By cutting away the year's overgrowth around the approximate site of the pot, they were invariably able to find it. Only one family told me they had "lost" an ascendant's grave. After looking in vain for hours, they resorted to more ambitious methods. On the one hand, they burned prodigious amounts of paper money for Tho-te-kong, asking him as overseer of the things of the earth to help in the search. On the other, they enlisted the help of over a dozen fellow lineage members. Only after extended and repeated searching did they give up. Freedman submits that bone pots that are not given elaborate second burial are neglected and forgotten after a generation (1966: 120), but to this point in Ch'inan, they are remembered and preserved indefinitely.

Despite these few similarities, grave worship on the whole differs radically from hall worship. The most obvious difference is the sort of food that is offered at the grave as opposed to that presented in the hall.* The food offered for ordinary death-day

* The importance of the difference in food offered to supernatural beings was suggested to me in an unpublished paper by Arthur P. Wolf, "Gods, Ghosts and Ancestors."

sacrifices before the tablets in the lineage hall or on a domestic altar is essentially the same as the common fare of the villagers, though it may be richer in meat and other delicacies. Typical offerings are half a chicken, cleaned, cooked, seasoned, and chopped into bite-sized pieces; a pork liver, boiled, seasoned, and sliced; stir-fried eggs; various soups, with a selection of cooked and seasoned ingredients cut into small pieces; and cooked rice. Chopsticks and bowls are always provided. After these offerings are made, the food is eaten without further cooking by the members of the family and their guests.

In stark contrast, foods presented at the graves, though potentially edible, are not soaked, seasoned, or cooked; most of them are dry and unpalatable. These offerings, consisting basically of 12 small bowls of foodstuffs, commonly include dried mushrooms of various sorts, dried fish and meat, dried noodles, and dried bean curd.

The difference between these offerings, taken together with other data about the kinds of food offered to the gods, leads me to suggest that the kind of food offered to a supernatural being is an index of the difference between that being and the living beings making the offerings. The scale along which the offerings differ is one of transformation from potential food in its natural state to edible food. At the end of the scale, farthest from edible food, is the live animal. After the animal is killed, it may be further transformed by being skinned (or plucked) and cleaned. Moving still closer to edible food, the meat might be dried to preserve it for later use. Alternatively, the full transition to edible food is made, with the meat being cooked, seasoned, and cut into small pieces. The vegetable equivalent proceeds from a growing plant to a vegetable or fruit just plucked to the removal of inedible parts, washing, cooking, seasoning, and cutting.

Supernatural beings are offered food that is less transformed, and therefore less like human food, according to their difference from the humans making the offerings. For example, of all the supernaturals, the ancestors are probably the most like those who offer them food. As ancestors in halls or domestic shrines they are well-known kinsmen with distinctive, individual identities; they can be spoken to, apologized to, thanked, and so on. They are generally accessible and familiar beings. Consequently, they are offered food that is precisely like the food consumed by those who offer it.

The gods, on a more distant level, receive different offerings according to their rank. The lowest god in the supernatural hierarchy, Tho-te-kong, the earth god, receives food like the fare of humans except that it is unseasoned and uncut. Usually he is offered three meat items—a chicken, plucked and cleaned but still whole; a scaled, cleaned fish; and a slab of pork—that have been boiled until fully cooked but have not been otherwise transformed. In addition he may be given cooked rice or noodles that have been soaked but not cooked. Chopsticks and bowls are not provided. Tho-te-kong is only somewhat different from humans. Although he is more powerful and less accessible than the ancestors, his images show him looking like a man, and he can be cajoled and influenced when he is impersonated at funeral ceremonies. The difference between him and the ancestors (and thus the greater distance between him and the people making the offerings) is like the difference between a kinsman and a local policeman: a kinsman is known, trusted, and accessible; a policeman is less well known, less trusted, and less accessible.

Moving to the top of the hierarchy, the highest god, Thi:-kong, receives the most untransformed food on the occasion of elaborate *pai-pais*: raw fowl with a few tail feathers left unplucked and the entrails hanging about their necks; a live fish; a whole raw pig with its entrails hanging about its neck; and sometimes two stalks of sugarcane, uprooted whole from the ground with roots and leaves still intact, constituting the vegetable equivalent of the whole, raw animal offerings.* For less extravagant *pai-pais*, Thi:-kong receives six or twelve kinds of dry food in small bowls, precisely like the offerings made at the grave. I suggest Thi:-kong is offered food that differs markedly from human food because he himself is so different from human beings and human-like beings

* Co-su-kong, who ranks just below Thi:-kong, also receives these offerings at his major *pai-pai*. Both gods are usually also offered fruit and steamed cakes.

TABLE 7
Food Offerings Made to Supernatural Beings

Recipient	Plant	Animal
Thi:-kong (highest ranking god)	Whole; untrimmed	Live; or if dead, only skinned (plucked) and cleaned
Ancestor in grave	Dried	Dried
Tho-te-kong (lowest ranking god)	Cooked or soaked	Cooked but uncut and unseasoned
Ancestor in hall	Cooked, cut, and seasoned	Cooked, cut, and seasoned

such as the hall and domestic ancestors. Unlike the ancestors, Thi:-kong is seldom communicated with or propitiated. Only at New Year and at birthday celebrations for elderly people is he beseeched for wealth and long life; these are infrequent rituals in comparison with those for lesser gods. Unlike Tho-te-kong, Thi:-kong is not represented by any image or any temple. Some people say that the term Thi:-kong designates not a particular god but an office that is occupied by various gods in turn; most contend that Thi:-kong is the highest and most powerful god yet cannot explain why he is given no physical representation. All these factors—his inaccessibility, his great power, his lack of a physical image—set Thi:-kong off from ordinary people and lesser gods. His great distance from the ordinary and familiar makes it appropriate that his offerings should be far from the commonplace.

Looking at the difference between the offerings to the ancestors in the hall and the offerings to them at the grave in the light of the scaling of the offerings to the gods (see Table 7), we are led to investigate the nature of the difference between the ancestors in those two locations. The raw, live or dry food offered to Thi:-kong marks distance in power and accessibility from human beings; the dry food offered at the grave may mark an equally great distance between the ancestor as resident of the hall and the ancestor as resident of the grave. When I asked informants why they took dry food to the grave, I was usually told, "because the grave is too far away." On further questioning, it became clear they meant only that it would be inconvenient to carry heavy bowls of soup up the mountainside where most of the graves are located. Others said, "We take dry food because taking regular food would be too dirty." They usually went on to point out that food taken to the graves had to be carried outside in the open air, whereas food taken to the hall was carried only a short distance, often under the cover of the settlement's interconnected roofs. On the surface these explanations are plausible; dry food is lighter and easier to haul long distances, and, because it will be cooked after it is brought back, its exposure to unhygienic conditions is not particularly important. Yet I noticed that even when a grave was located just on the fringe of a settlement, scarcely farther away than the hall, dry food was still offered there. And even when lineage members lived long distances from the hall, they still brought heavy bowls of soup and other fully prepared dishes when they came to worship the ancestors in the hall.

Still more striking, the two kinds of offerings cannot be combined or substituted for each other. Lou Kim-bo told me that her husband had died years ago on the day of the spring grave-cleaning festival. Hence that day is both his death-day anniversary and the day when his grave should be cleaned. But she would have to prepare the dry food for the grave the day before the grave festival, she said, because the two offerings were "not at all the same." Offerings could not be made to her husband at his grave on the same day that he received regular anniversary offerings in the hall. If informants' statements about the distance to the grave are inadequate on their face to account for the sharp distinction maintained between offerings made there and in the hall, we must look for other ways in which the two settings differ.

The most fundamental difference between the hall and the grave is that the grave is where the corpse of the dead person is located. Although an ancestor's soul is said to be present sometimes at the hall and sometimes at the grave, his corpse is permanently present only at the grave. By looking at actions and attitudes that apply to the corpse alone, we may come to understand why the grave offerings are so different from those of the hall. The time when people are most directly exposed to the corpse is the short period before the coffining. One ritual that takes place in this period shows clearly the fear and dread people feel toward the corpse. This ritual, called "the cutting" (*kuaq-tng*), is the last rite before the actual transfer of the body to the coffin.

I witnessed this ritual only once, at a coffining in the Li settlement. The body of the deceased, a fifty-five-year-old woman, was lying on a wide board placed on benches outside of the hall. Because she had died in Taipei, several hours had elapsed between the time of her death and the return of the body to the settlement. This made it dangerous to move the corpse into the hall, so it was displayed just outside. By about 10:00 P.M. the Taoist priests had finished their chanting and packed away their instruments. The large crowd milling around were mostly Lis of the first *fang*, the *fang* of the deceased woman. Except for the body, which was illuminated by bright, naked electric bulbs, everything was dark. Everyone was busy and seemed to be gripped by a kind of noisy hysteria. Women stood about the body keening and wailing; men and other women dashed about carrying food and objects for the rituals to come. But then the tempo of the action began to increase and the wailing grew louder and louder. Suddenly, order began to emerge out of the confusion around the body. The oldest lady in the lineage moved to stand next to the corpse, weeping, keening, and rocking back and forth. She was followed by the deceased's direct descendants, who lined up next to her. Finally, all the other Lis present, regardless of what *fang* they belonged to, formed into a long line stretching away from the corpse, down the cement courtyard and into the darkness on the steps leading away from the hall.

At this point, an assistant priest brought out a length of string, which he tied to the wrist of the corpse and fed out so that it passed through the hands of everyone in the line. Next he gave everyone a slip of the mock paper money ordinarily burned at funerals and a stick of incense. Each person folded the paper money and held it in one hand so the string passed through the fold and did not touch his hands. The incense was held with the money. While everyone stood there silently except for several women who continued to wail, a Taoist priest faced the corpse, banging together two cleavers and reciting incantations. After a time he moved down the line of Lis followed by his assistant, and stopping in front of each person, cut the string, leaving everyone holding a separate piece. This they then placed, along with the paper money and incense stick, in a basket held by the priest's assistant. Finally, when all the pieces of string were in the basket, it was taken away from the hall and burned to ashes.

Some informants told me that the string-cutting ritual signifies separation between the living and the dead. "The rope that stretches between the corpse and the living is cut to keep the dead away from his descendants so he will not come back and cause trouble for them later on." Others said the meaning of the ritual is expressed by the saying "When you weed, get out the roots"— that the intent is to eradicate as completely as possible the connection between the living and the corpse. The corpse is thought to be inherently dangerous; anyone who has come into contact with it will seek ways to prevent further contact in the future. Not only descendants of the deceased, but anyone who cares to, can stand in the line at the coffining and be finally cut off from the corpse. Several Lis told me later that I, too, should have stood in the line.

It is partly the capacity of the corpse to turn into a dangerous and powerful monster, or *iau-kuai*, that is feared at the coffining. While the corpse is in an indeterminate state between a living man and a buried ancestor it is relatively less predictable and controllable. If insufficient precautions are taken, and the corpse does become a monster, it will harm anyone it meets; hence anyone present at the coffining, descendant or not, may receive ritual protection against the corpse. Many of my informants had heard stories of corpses that were not protected as they should have been. The most common incident was said to have occurred in a neighboring town, where for some reason the burial of a dead man had been delayed for more than a year. His relatives had built a shed next to the house to cover the coffin but had left chinks in the roof so that the sun and moon were able to shine on it. Because of this the corpse was able to turn into a *iau-kuai* with long white hair, huge fangs, and a long tongue. The dead man's soul was able to leave the corpse and cause sickness and other troubles for the people in the area.

The continued presence of the corpse in the grave may well account for the difference in food offerings there. Although the corpse is less liable to escape its normal form when it is safely buried, as we shall see, it is still capable of autonomous changes that threaten those around it. The aura surrounding the ancestor in the hall is that of the known and familiar; descendants often prepare special dishes that were favorites of the deceased. But at the grave, 12 fairly standard dry substances are offered because "We have to be sure to include something he will like." The implication is that the descendants do not know which foods the ancestor as buried corpse will eat. Nor can they explain how he is able to consume dry, uncooked food.

The fact that the hall can only be occupied by those who have a right to be there, namely, ancestors, also helps to explain the difference in food offerings at the two sites and the sense of uncertainty about the ancestor in the grave. Unlike the hall, the grave is a place to which all manner of spirits, including *kui* (ghosts) who are not ancestors, have access.* "At the hall only the ancestor comes to eat, though he might bring along a friend; it is like the feast that the living have after the offerings. But at the grave there might be flocks of ghosts around trying to eat the offerings we make to our ancestor." Accordingly, many of the activities at the grave are directed against any uninvited ghosts who might be on hand. To ensure that the ancestor receives the offerings made to him, for example, the smoldering ashes of the paper money burnt for him are doused with a cup of wine to "mark" this and all the rest of the offerings as his alone and to prevent other ghosts from

---

* *Kui* is a term used generally for all the souls of the dead. Ancestors, those dead to whom one is obligated as a kinsman, are usually referred to by a more polite term, commonly *co-kong*, but if pressed most informants will concede that *co-kong* are *kui*, albeit more approachable and better known than the *kui* of dead strangers.

taking them. The living who are present also need to be protected. The most common measure taken to this end is to pass out red steamed cakes to everyone who comes to the grave, the red color acting as a prophylactic to ward off any danger from lingering contact with ghosts. Another common precaution is to warn children against urinating anywhere near a grave. Everyone knew what had befallen one small boy who had urinated at a grave near Ch'inan. A ghost who happened to be at that spot had thereupon followed the boy home and had plagued him with illness until the child was exorcised of his tormentor by a god.

In sum, the grave, located outside of the settlement, is very different from the hall in that access to it cannot be controlled; it is freely haunted by the souls of the dead. These dead persons, like the ancestor buried there, are living but are no longer part of the familiar, observable *iong* world. When someone visits the grave he is exposing himself to one of the gates of the *im* world and must deal with dangerous ghosts on their terms. In contrast, when the souls of the ancestors visit the hall they rejoin the *iong* world; living people can relate to them as known, familiar ascendants. This difference, which begins to make the contrast between edible food offered in the hall and inedible substances offered at the grave intelligible, only partially describes the character of the ancestor in the grave. To describe it more fully, we must turn to the ways the ancestor in the grave continues to interact with the living long after his burial is over.

CHAPTER 11

The Geomancy of the Grave

The most perceptive and complete analysis of Chinese geomancy has been written by Maurice Freedman. His material, gathered in the New Territories, relies more on professional geomancers than on laymen (1966: 126), and perhaps for this reason he emphasizes the mechanistic aspect of geomancy, that is, the geomancer's manipulation of abstract forces around the gravesite to produce a desired result. Freedman is acutely aware, however, that the professional geomancer's views may differ from the views of the peasantry he serves, affirming that "in popular religion a reverse transformation is worked by which the disembodied forces of the geomancer are turned into personal entities" (1969: 10). As he would perhaps predict, when we turn to the villagers of Ch'inan, we find that they see the ancestor in the grave rather than abstract forces as the source of geomantic benefits. Hence, geomancy as they regard it is a most fruitful place to begin looking for the activities of ancestors after they are buried.

Before exploring the implications of the popular view of geomancy in Ch'inan, however, I must clarify the differences between that view, as it was explained to me by my informants, and the view of the professional geomancers, as it was explained to Freedman. According to Freedman's analysis, the geomancy of graves principally involves the site of second burial, after the corpse has been disinterred and its bones arranged in a ceramic pot. Those who can afford to do so go to great lengths and some expense to find a choice site for the second burial of an ancestor's bones, for if a good location is found the descendants of the deceased will reap various rewards, notably many offspring, wealth, or outstanding success. To discover such a site one hires a professional geomancer, a man who has the required technical knowledge to point out the spot that will best ensure the flow of geomantic benefits to the descendants. The geomancer must consider, among other things, whether the height and shape of the hills surrounding the site will guarantee the concentration of "Cosmic Breaths" thereby protecting them against wind and water. To further guarantee the presence of the Breaths, he must also see to it that two opposite and complementary forces, known as the white tiger and the azure dragon, are present on either side of the gravesite (Freedman 1966: 122–23). The geomancer operates like a technician arranging materials in the right order, not like a shaman propitiating powerful forces. If he follows the principles of his trade correctly, the benefits of geomancy will automatically follow.

Although the bones of the ancestor must be at the site in order for geomantic benefits to flow to the descendants, the dead cannot affect the outcome of the geomancy. Says Freedman (1966: 126): "I concluded that in this context the dead were passive agents, pawns in a kind of ritual game played by their descendants with the help of geomancers. The accumulation of Breaths followed automatically from the correct siting of the grave. The dead themselves could choose neither to confer nor to withhold the blessings that flowed through their bones." Acknowledging that there is some ambiguity on this matter, and that some sources feel the comfort of the ancestor is important in determining whether or not the benefits will accrue to the descendants, Freedman still concludes (1966: 127), that "in the end the dead can do little to thwart the process set going by geomantic technique."

In a later discussion (1967: 89–90), he moves beyond this position to suggest that "where . . . the authority of the past generations, as represented in the cult of the ancestors, weighs heaviest, there men redress the balance by recourse to the geomancy of the tomb. They take a kind of geomantic revenge, using as things what are otherwise symbols of autonomous virtue. As *yang* the ancestors are revered, as *yin* manipulated." Far from playing an active part in the operation of geomancy, the ancestors are prey to the manipulations of their descendants. After their bones are cleaned and in a pot, they can be moved at will in accordance with the demands of geomancy. They are passive objects whose sole function is to serve as the transmitting medium for the independently operating forces of geomancy.

When control of the bones of the dead is seen as a matter of technique based on sound mechanistic principles, fierce competition is likely to arise among those who are in a position to benefit from good geomancy. This was certainly what J. J. M. DeGroot (1897) found in Amoy, where the geomancer uses the markings on the face of a compass to align the grave. As DeGroot describes it, the innermost ring around the magnetic needle of the compass is composed of the eight trigrams, or *pa kwa*, each of which is associated with several things: directions, such as north, northeast, east, and southeast; elements of nature, such as fire, wood, earth, metal, and water; zodiacal animals, such as the dragon, the bird, and the tiger; stems and branches (combinations of two characters used to represent moments in time); and family positions, such as father, mother, eldest son, eldest daughter, middle son, middle daughter, and so forth. Characters representing each of these are ranged by category in concentric circles around the ring of trigrams (pp. 959–70).

After consulting the compass, the geomancer attempts to find a correspondence between the shapes and directions indicated thereon and the configurations in the surrounding landscape. The ideal location of a grave might require certain shapes in the surrounding hills, for instance, a dragon to the east, a tiger to the west, a bird to the south, and a tortoise to the north (p. 949), as well as certain topographical features, like stony ground and peaked, rounded, or steep mountains, in the proper combination to represent the elements wood, fire, earth, and so on (p. 956). With a perfect configuration, all descendants of the deceased would benefit equally; but if the configuration is not perfect on all sides, then the descendants, and brothers especially, will almost certainly wrangle over the alignment of the axis of the grave, each hoping to have the character representing him facing a favorable direction.

Since the maintenance of a geomantic prospect is so delicate that it can be upset by the slightest change in the environment, we can see that a person might easily explain his loss of good fortune by charging that someone had tampered with the geomantically beneficial site; and conversely, he might expect that to deprive someone of his fortune, he need only meddle with the surroundings of the source of that person's good geomancy. There is evidence that conflict over geomancy was widespread in China, and that it involved people less closely related than brothers. Hsien-chin Hu, writing of Shantung and Kiangsu provinces (1948: 38), states that "disputes within the *tsu* [patrilineage] are frequent, the poorer families endeavoring to bury their dead near the graves of luckier *tsu* relatives." Indeed, such disputes often even crossed surname lines. A typical case is that of the Lo and Chang families of Szechwan province, cited by David Crockett Graham (1961: 115). Jealous of the success of the Lo family, the Changs hired stonemasons to hack up a large rock located on Chang land that was said to be the source of the Los' good geomancy. In the subsequent lawsuit, the lawyers prolonged the case without reaching a decision, so the two families agreed to settle out of court. The settlement was to be reached by seeing which of the two could throw the most silver into the Yangtze River, which ran between their property. In the process both families were financially ruined; the poverty of the Los was attributed to the damage done to their lucky stone. According to the view of geomancy we have been discussing, because the flow of benefits depends on a fine balance between configurations around the grave, the least change in the important surrounding land can ruin the geomancy. Bringing about such a change would be an easy way to confound one's enemies.

This account of geomancy, which is representative of the core of Freedman's analysis and is consistent with other published descriptions, differs markedly from what I was taught about the geomancy of graves (*hong-cui*) by the residents of Ch'inan.* The first intimation I had that there might be a central difference on this point came from a ritual performed at burials, which seemed to suggest that the people of Ch'inan see the ancestor himself, not an abstract, geomantic force, as the agent responsible for fortune or misfortune. In preparation for this ritual, the temporary paper tablet of the deceased is transported to the grave inside a cylindrical wooden container called a *tau*. This container, once the standard measure for rice, continues to be associated by the villagers with that basic, most important foodstuff. In the bottom of the *tau* are several handfuls of a curious mixture: five or more kinds of grain or seeds, such as beans and unmilled rice; several Taiwanese coins; and a number of nails. According to the villagers, the grain stands for the crops that are planted and reaped, and more generally for food itself, the coins for wealth and financial success, and the nails, or *tieng*, for male offspring. (*Tieng* and another word meaning male are homophones.) Together, these elements represent the most fundamental and axiomatic goals of Taiwanese life. A man or woman who dies having achieved a measure of material security and leaving male descendants has lived a full life. During life most people's pursuits and endeavors are directed toward attaining these goals. To plant and reap the crops, to earn enough cash to provide other necessities and some luxuries, to produce sons who will carry on one's line are the tasks that fill and fulfill most people's lives.

At the grave, after the coffin is buried, aligned and covered with earth, the geomancer stands at the front of the coffin with the descendants of the dead man gathered around him. Holding the *tau* in one hand, he takes a handful of the grain-coin-nail mixture with the other and throws it out over the grave. Three times he does this, each time calling out, "May this family have high officials, wealth, and many sons!" The descendants chorus "Yes!" in

---

* Unless otherwise noted, the information in the following discussion was obtained from Ch'inan residents, and in good part from those most knowledgeable about ritual affairs in general. I will discuss separately what I learned from a professional geomancer in Sanhsia.

reply. Precisely the same ritual will be repeated later if an elaborate concrete grave is made after the bones are cleaned. The villagers assume that this request is directed specifically to the ancestor. "We tell him how we have taken proper care of him so
that his gravesite will be comfortable. In return we hope he will
protect us, bringing us the benefits we ask for."

To follow up this hint that the ancestor plays an active role in
dispensing geomantic benefits, I asked many people to tell me
what they could about *hong-cui*. The reply of one old Lou lady
is typical. "If the *hong-cui* of a grave is poor, it means the ancestor is living in a house with a bad feeling. Since his house is uncomfortable (*bo-hou-ce*), he will come back and make trouble. The
households of his descendants will be filled with problems—sickness, bad crops, and so on. If the *hong-cui* is good, then the ancestor is comfortable and won't bother people." Her reply, and those
I was given by others, definitely focused on the condition of the
ancestor rather than the condition of the geomantic forces, i.e.,
the Cosmic Breaths.

To be sure, speaking of the ancestor's "comfort" could be simply
a metaphorical expression of the effect of geomantic forces on the
ancestor. And it is also possible (as Freedman allows may be the
case) that the ancestor is seen as simply a transmitting medium
for geomantic forces, permitting them to operate through him
when he is comfortable, blocking them when he is uncomfortable.
But after I questioned the villagers more closely on this subject it
seemed to me that this is not the case. In fact, I put the specific
question to informants, asking, "Does the ancestor himself bring
about the good benefits?" The answer was invariably yes, that the
ancestor himself is indeed what makes things happen. Further, I
was told that the word *hong-cui* refers precisely to the ancestor's
state of comfort; good *hong-cui* means that he is happy and at
ease, bad *hong-cui* that he is uncomfortable and unsatisfied. Few
used the words for "geomantic force" and "Cosmic Breaths" in
their responses, and many of those I questioned did not even
know what the words meant. Nor, as we shall see, were such forces
said to play any part in determining the comfort of the ancestor.

If the concept of geomantic Breaths is simply missing from the villagers' view, one then must ask whether the ancestors were thought to be powerful enough to bring about real benefit or harm to their descendants. Everyone I asked said that they were. One man, Lou Kim-hue, said, "If the ancestor in the grave is happy, he will help us. If he is uncomfortable, he will punish us with sickness or trouble so that we fix what is wrong. If the grave is not especially comfortable, but not seriously lacking either, then he may or may not help us."

If the ancestor is the sole source of geomantic benefits, then we might expect that care would be taken to ensure his comfort in the grave beginning with the first moment of burial. This is exactly the case in Ch'inan. Among those holding the view of geomancy Freedman presents, second burial marks the beginning of most concern with the placement of the bones; it is then that benefits are most likely to start flowing from the grave. In Ch'inan, however, benefits can begin with first burial if the ancestor is pleased. Hence a propitious time is selected for burial to protect the deceased from being accosted by wandering spirits. And propitious times are also selected for other changes in the grave: when the bones are cleaned, and when the bone pot is moved. If the fortunes of the family are good between the burial and the bone-cleaning, it is assumed that the ancestor is fairly satisfied with his burial place; the bone pot will probably be kept in the same spot. If the family should suffer misfortune at some later date, the bones might then be moved to another place to improve the ancestor's condition. Benefits can flow from the ancestor at all times after the first burial if the ancestor is sufficiently satisfied.

Whether or not the ancestor will protect his descendants is determined, among other things, by how comfortable his grave is. By this my informants meant not that a site chosen according to the dictates of geomancy was somehow mysteriously pleasant for the ancestor, but that the site was literally comfortable in much the same way that residences of the living are comfortable and pleasant to live in. The geomantic prospect (the surrounding landscape) became, in my informants' terms, the view—the scenery from the vantage point of the grave. Very few informants knew anything about the desirability of specific configurations of hills surrounding the grave. For them the issue was whether the view was beautiful and pleasing for them, and, by extension, for the ancestor.

At one point I thought I had found an informant who held a different view. Hou-a, the *tang-ki* in the Li lineage, remarked that his grandmother's grave, located behind the Ong settlement, had been ruined—"hit"—by the chimney of the Ong brick kiln. I thought perhaps he held something like the same view described by Freedman and others, and meant that the kiln had spoiled the configuration in front of the grave, or that its foundations had struck at one of the forces working to concentrate the Breaths, so I asked him if a geomancer had told him the kiln was bad for the grave, or if he knew it on his own. He replied, "No one told me it is bad. Anyone can tell just by looking that it's bad." I asked why the chimney was bad. "Because the ancestor is uncomfortable with it there," he answered. Pressing further, I pointed out that the chimney was not very close to the grave, so it was not clear to me how it could affect the ancestor. "Oh," he said, "it's because of the heavy, black smoke that pours down from the chimney onto the grave. No one would like living in a place like that at all." When Hou-a spoke of comfort, he meant it literally. For him and others in the village, *hong-cui* deals with the suitability of the grave as a dwelling-place. Good *hong-cui* means, among other things, that the view is pleasant, and that the air is not spoiled by ashes and soot.

A similar case involves a grave for an early Lou ancestress, which is located adjacent to several houses in the Ui settlement. The Lous said the grave had been built there long before, when the land had not yet been rented to the Uis. The Uis contended that the Lous had built the grave there deliberately to deprive the Uis of a piece of valuable land. A high barbed wire fence surrounds the grave as evidence of the Lous' claim to that piece of land; drying wash belonging to Uis is nearly always hung on the fence as evidence of the Uis' rejection of that claim. If the villagers held a mechanistic view of geomancy based on the importance of configurations in the surrounding landscape, the Lous could easily complain that the Ui houses next to the grave had spoiled the concentration of geomantic forces at the grave. But though I often heard them complain that the grave's *hong-cui* was ruined, I never heard them blame it on the existence of nearby construction. The *hong-cui* was spoiled, they said, because the Uis had built a toilet near the grave; the objectionable odor was making the grave an unfit place to live. The ancestors' comfort is analogous to ordinary people's comfort. Whatever makes a place bad for people to live in makes it bad for the ancestors too.

After the bones of the deceased have been cleaned and placed in a pot, much, if not most, of the effort to secure good *hong-cui* centers on the pot itself—its condition as well as its location. One man, Ong Ho-cui, who occasionally came to the Ong settlement to hold séances with the gods to determine the cause of someone's sickness or misfortune, told me, "Saying that the *hong-cui* is bad just means that the ancestor is uncomfortable. Sometimes it is bad because water or ants get into the pot containing the bones." At one of these sessions, a *tang-ki* had entered a trance, possessed by the spirit of Co-su-kong. An Ong woman who is poor and is neglected by her promiscuous husband asked the *tang-ki* why her home was full of trouble. He replied that her mother-in-law's grave had bad *hong-cui*. "There is a roof tile in the pot with the bones, and so the ancestor cannot stand living there. That is why she is returning to cause trouble." Another man told me that in a dream shortly after the spring grave-cleaning festival he had seen rain falling in through the roof onto his father. Returning to his father's gravesite, he had discovered that the boards placed over the bone pot had become dislodged, allowing rain to drip onto the pot. At the grave festival, whoever cleans the graves must open all accessible pots to inspect the condition of the bones. The presence of ants or excess moisture may be reason for moving the pot to another place with better *hong-cui*, that is, to a drier spot or one with fewer ants.

In general, whatever material surrounds the corpse or bones is regarded as the house of the ancestor. If the house is in disrepair, the ancestor is ill-tempered and will cause trouble. As a preventive measure, whenever the grave is visited yellow slips of paper are placed at intervals over and around the coffin or bone pot. This is said to be "like patching holes in the roof." The best way to keep the pot safe from insects and the elements is to build a final grave of brick and concrete. In these permanent graves, the pot, resting on a concrete foundation, is enclosed in a small brick room, which is sealed with mortar and covered with a mound of earth. A hefty gravestone stands in front, along with a semicircular porch of poured concrete for people to stand on while making offerings. This type of grave was often described to me as "a house with brick walls and a roof just like our houses."

At times informants do move away from an explicitly literal interpretation of the ancestor's comfort, though they stay with that view in its essentials. People know, for example, that the grave should be carefully oriented according to the geomancer's directions, and say that this somehow affects the ancestor's comfort. But they do not know exactly what the effects are or how the system operates. They are satisfied to believe the orientation has meaning without being able to explain why in terms of an analogy to human comfort. They do not, moreover, resort to explaining the effect of the alignment of the grave in mechanistic terms of geomantic forces or Cosmic Breaths; the orientation of the grave is important for them only to the extent that it somehow increases the ancestor's comfort.

No matter how many precautions are taken to ensure the ancestor's happiness in the grave, they may still prove inadequate. The grave for the *be* ancestor of the Ongs is finished with a concrete housing, but the foundation has slipped over the years, and the gravestone is now quite visibly tilted forward. The disabilities of three members of the *be*—a child who is unable to walk, another who is unable to talk, and a middle-aged woman who occasionally becomes violent—are laid to the discomfort of the ancestor in the tilted grave. Less visible faults in the grave are more often the focus of concern. Sickness, financial trouble, infertility, and crop failure are commonly attributed to trouble with the grave: the pot has a leak, ants have invaded it, or a foreign body has found its way there. Ordinarily, the pot is not moved but is merely repaired or made more secure. However, if ants or water continue to be a problem, the pot may be moved to a drier or less ant-infested location. Reasons given for moving a pot are inevitably concerned with increasing the ancestor's comfort in a literal sense, not with attaining a better concentration of geomantic forces.

The picture of geomancy one gets from the Ch'inan villagers thus differs strikingly from the picture drawn by Freedman and others. In Ch'inan, the crucial consideration is the comfort of the ancestor. Geomantic arranging and grave offerings are both directed to that end. If these are effective, the ancestor himself, not the *hong-cui* of the gravesite, will bring one good fortune. As I pointed out, one consequence of the mechanistic view of geomancy is that brothers and strangers compete keenly for the benefits of a site or seek to destroy them for others. Does the Ch'inan villagers' view of geomancy have the same effect? My impression is that it does not, that competition exists in substantially lesser degree than the literature describes in other places. Many people told me that there is no differentiation in the distribution of geomantic benefits: "The ancestor cares for all his descendants equally so if the grave is comfortable, the descendants will all prosper." Others believe that the *hong-cui* is not the same for all brothers, but that it is equally good in different ways; one brother may be blessed with wealth, another with many offspring. The expectation is that the grave will be equally good for all if the ancestor is satisfied, and that, conversely, things will be difficult for all if he is not. In the second case, all the descendants would have an interest in changing the grave to improve the ancestor's lot.

There are of course obvious cases of inequity between brothers. This prompts some to deny completely the efficacy of the ancestor in the grave. As one informant said, "I don't believe that *hong-cui* works. You just have to look around to see that brothers aren't equal—one is rich, one poor, one has many sons, one none. If the ancestor were helping them, he would help them all equally."

Others find various explanations for the misfortunes of some of
the brothers. Occasionally, brothers will wrangle over the siting
of the grave, those who are prospering wanting the grave to stay
where it is, those who are suffering wanting it to be changed. But
the usual expectation is that brothers will prosper in the same degree, each being the equal recipient of the ancestor's help.

Because of this expectation, the people of Ch'inan are less prone
than others to individualize geomantic fortune by burying each
ancestor in a separate grave. Where the mechanistic view of geomantic forces prevails, a person would feel that the more graves
he has a share in, the more chance he would have of receiving
benefit from at least one of them. But where the emphasis is on
the attitude of the ancestor, the separation of graves does not matter as long as the ancestors buried there are comfortable. Consequently, as an economy measure the villagers bury more than one
ancestor in the same finished grave whenever they can. Whether
or not two ancestors can be buried together depends on the com-
patibility of their horoscopes as analyzed by a professional geomancer. According to my survey, husband and wife are most commonly buried together, and now and then a father and son. Often
the final burial of one ancestor will be postponed until the bones
of another, compatible ancestor have been cleaned so the two
graves can be combined. The most extreme extension of this practice is the provision of one burial vault for an entire lineage. None
of the Ch'inan lineages follow this practice, but I found three
vaults in the Hengch'i public graveyard that were marked "The
collective grave of the X family" and were large enough to hold
a great many bone pots. My Ch'inan informants found this idea
altogether distasteful. "How could you put all the dead of your
lineage in the same grave? Not everyone can get along while alive,
so how could they live together after death?" The objections were
grounded not in a concern for the maximization of geomantic
benefits, but in a concern for the comfort and happiness of the
ancestors.

I have tried to deemphasize the competitive aspects of geomancy
in Ch'inan because the rivalry for benefits seems to be less intense

there than elsewhere, but it would be misleading to imply that such struggles do not take place. All the same, as we shall see, the nature and consequences of those struggles fit in with the villagers' nonmechanistic view of *hong-cui*. The one case I discovered of a fight between siblings over a grave siting involved four brothers in the Lou lineage, two of whom do not live in the village. The pair in Ch'inan planned to build a joint grave for their parents without consulting their brothers, but the other two heard about it and arranged to steal their mother's bone pot. The Ch'inan brothers went ahead anyway, building the grave with only the bones of their father. Then, in a year or so, things began to go wrong for them: the wife of one brother fell sick and did not improve, and all the chickens in the other's poultry farm became diseased and died. The Lous' interpretation of this ill-fortune was that the deceased couple were unhappy at not having been buried together and so were punishing those responsible. The two brothers who built the grave had hoped to disadvantage the other brothers by leaving them out of the calculations to find a site. If their horoscopes were not considered, the site might not "fit" them. Their plan back-fired because the stealing of the bone pot interfered with the comfort of the ancestors. Once again, the emphasis is on operation of the personal force of the deceased as determined by their comfort in the grave. The likelihood of conflict between brothers is lessened when the burial takes place normally, because they all expect to benefit equally. If a person wants to rob his siblings of geomantic benefits, he must trick them by carrying out the entire grave-building process without their knowledge, an extreme measure and one not likely to succeed.

The likelihood of conflict between those less closely related than siblings is similarly reduced in Ch'inan, since the functioning of geomancy is not seen as conditional on the delicate balance of the configuration of land surrounding the grave. Those who hold the mechanistic view could be expected to fear any disturbance in the land near a gravesite. But for most Ch'inan residents, only the condition of the bones and the state of the grave itself are of critical importance. While I was in the village, a new house was constructed on the edge of the Lou settlement, not 20 feet from two graves. When I asked whether the excavation would have any effect on the gravesite, the reply was, "No, as long as the grave itself is not disturbed, it won't matter." Even more dramatic, several large buildings were constructed on the hill behind Ch'ipei. Not only was considerable earth moving necessary to build a road up to the construction site, but the road itself brushed past several graves, though it did not actually touch them. None of this mattered either, I was told. Furthermore, though I asked time and again about the public graveyard where most Ch'inan residents bury their ancestors, which is extremely crowded, with graves practically on top of one another, I never heard any complaints about the congestion. Sometimes, when I was present at a grave ceremony, another grave was being constructed nearby. No one seemed upset by this at all. In order to harm one's enemies in Ch'inan, one would have to attack the grave or the bone pot directly. But such a step would be just as likely to turn misfortune on the attacker. The only cases of grave-robbing or destruction I heard of were said to have been the work of city gangsters, seeking bones to carry out sorcery. My informants felt the gangsters were sure to suffer dire consequences because the souls of the dead men present in the bones would punish them.

These views—that good geomancy means the comfort of the ancestor, that the ancestor is the agent responsible for fortune or misfortune, that brothers need not compete for the ancestor's favor because he will help them all equally, and that the land surrounding a grave is less important than the grave itself—were expressed by almost all the villagers I questioned. One informant, however, did have further things to say on the subject. This was a young Lou man with many business contacts in the city, one of a small party of young men from the fifth *fang* I accompanied on a visit to the grave of the *fang*'s founder. He said, of the site:

The grave has good *hong-cui* because it faces three mountain peaks. This has led to three famous people in the *fang*—a doctor, a school principal, and a lawyer. The fact that the gravestone is dry and has no moss growing on it is also a sign of good *hong-cui*. It means that the grave is "bright" because the sun gets to it. The absence of moss on the stone is an indication of wealth, and in fact, our fifth *fang* is the wealthiest in the Lou lineage. To the left of the grave as you look out with your back to it is the dragon and to the right is the tiger. The dragon should be higher than the tiger.

When it came to a fuller explanation of the dragon and tiger, or of the meaning of "brightness," the young man could go no further. Like most of his fellow villagers, he still insisted that good *hong-cui* basically meant the comfort of the ancestor, so the grave's dryness and brightness probably meant that the ancestor had a warm, dry place to rest. In one respect, however, he did hold a different interpretation: in his remark that the three mountain peaks were responsible for the three famous people, he did not directly relate their success to the comfort of the ancestor. This remark moves toward the kind of analysis given by the professional geomancers in Sanhsia, and I presume in Taipei as well. Chances are that he had acquired this information through his business dealings in the city.

Unfortunately, I did not have time to canvass the professional geomancers of Sanhsia. However, I did manage to spend a number of evenings with one man who was said to be the best geomancer in town and who was hired regularly by residents of all four *chu*. It was clear from the start that his assumptions contrasted with those held by the villagers. He was full of talk about the forces of the azure dragon and the white tiger and about the necessity of specific configurations around the grave. Although I cannot say whether his views agree in every particular with those presented in the beginning of this chapter, they plainly agree in their emphasis on the automatic operation of the force of *hong-cui*. While conceding that the ancestor would be comfortable in a site with good *hong-cui*, the geomancer did not agree that the ancestor was the source of the fortunes or misfortunes of the descendants; if the *hong-cui* were good so that the ancestor was comfortable, the good benefits would flow automatically from the forces balanced at the grave. Not unlike the villagers, this man played down the competitive possibilities of geomantic striving, remarking that unless a grave was equally good for the eldest three sons of the deceased, he would not recommend it. The positions of the professional geomancer and the villagers in Ch'inan are not so much incompatible as different in emphasis. He stresses the operation of forces that he can manipulate at will. They stress the operation of beings that must be propitiated, appeased, and ultimately satisfied in every demand. The question of why geomancy has been given this interpretation in the village cannot be answered until it has been related to the more general question of the level, extent, and kind of ancestral activity in Ch'inan.

CHAPTER 12

Ancestral Interference

BEFORE WE consider why ancestors in Ch'inan behave as they do, let us take a brief look at how other anthropologists would account for the particular character of a society's ancestors. Those who attempt to explain cross-cultural variation in the attribution of benevolence or malevolence to ancestors fall into two broad camps. In one camp are those who see childhood experiences in socialization as the source of a later attribution of aggression to supernatural beings. (See Lambert et al. 1959; Whiting and Child 1953: 273–304.) In the other camp are those who look to later experiences of inheritance and succession for the source of the fear of deceased ascendants. I will return to the socialization hypothesis later. Here I want to discuss only the theory that focuses on inheritance, concentrating not so much on whether the theory itself is sound as on whether it can be applied at all to the Chinese case. Investigation of this question will lead us to examine the Ch'inan variants of Chinese inheritance, transfer of authority, and ancestral activity.

The inheritance theory is perhaps most concisely stated by Jack Goody (1962: 410). The argument runs as follows. When one person inherits property and jural authority from another, he has an ambivalent attitude toward his benefactor's death, being at once happy because he has come into his inheritance and sad because of the death of the loved one. In consequence, the heir feels guilty; he senses that his desire to inherit makes him in some way responsible for the death that must precede his inheritance. Since he feels he has brought harm to his benefactor, he fears the retaliation of that benefactor, now turned ancestor. As a result, if harm befalls him he is likely to see the ancestor as the agent responsible. As Goody puts it, "In the main, it is those from whose death one benefits that one fears as ancestors" (*ibid.*). Let us state the argument in terms of three conditionals:

1. If A, an heir waits for his benefactor to die before he can inherit property and jural authority, then B, after the benefactor dies the heir feels guilty for having had some part in the benefactor's death.

2. If B, then C, he fears the retaliation of the benefactor-turned-ancestor.

3. If C, then D, he attributes misfortune to the hostile acts of his ancestor.

In order to decide whether this argument can be legitimately applied to the Chinese case, I want to examine the way Maurice Freedman uses it. In the course of his stimulating and insightful discussions of ancestor worship, Freedman makes two claims: first, that A does not hold for China because an heir need not wait until his benefactor dies before inheriting property and jural authority, and second, that D does not hold for China because Chinese ancestors are benevolent, and misfortune is not ordinarily attributed to them. Freedman seems to imply a third claim: that the absence of A in China can explain the absence of D, in short, that not-D follows from not-A.

To establish his first claim, Freedman presents an analysis of the transfer of power and property in the Chinese case. He suggests that in modern China no one son is able to wrest property and authority from his father at the moment of his death, thereafter exerting that authority in his own right. Although sons usually inherit most of their share of the family property at the death of their father, a man who falters because of illness or old age may readily hand over domestic authority and even his property to his sons in advance of his death. Further, sons usually marry before the death of their fathers, thus attaining full status as mature men. Far from trying to prevent this, Chinese fathers attempt to marry off their sons as soon as possible. Accordingly, says Freedman (1967: 95), they "do not look upon him as a serious barrier to the attainment of their economic and ritual maturity." Beyond this, even when a son inherits authority and property at his father's death, he cannot exert that authority in the same manner or over the same people as his father. In the absence of primogeniture, "no one son can step effectively into his father's shoes to exercise authority over the same range of people" (*ibid.*). Hence, sons do not necessarily wait for their father's death to inherit property and authority; nor, when they do inherit, does any one of them rule by virtue of succession.

Freedman's second claim, that ancestors in China are generally benevolent, is summarized in his statement that "while they will certainly punish their descendants if they suffer neglect or are offended by an act or omission which affects them directly (chiefly, the failure to secure for them a firm line of descent), they are essentially benign and considerate of their issue. Before taking action against their descendants they need to be provoked; capricious behavior is certainly alien to their benevolent and protective nature" (pp. 92–93). Freedman also points out that ancestral wrath cannot be directed by descendants against those they wish to control. A household head, for example, cannot use the ancestors' power to hurt as a sanction to uphold his own authority (p. 95).

It is more difficult to see whether Freedman intends to make the third claim, that the possibility of inheriting from the living is causally related to the benevolence of ancestors. First of all, it is clear that Freedman wants to posit some kind of connection between the form of inheritance he describes and the benevolence of the ancestors. He says (p. 93), "We may ask whether Chinese ancestors are kindly *because*, in making them ancestors, their descendants are not conscious of having displaced them from coveted positions of power" (my emphasis). Later (p. 98) he reiterates this point (again, the emphasis is mine): "For modern China, then, we may argue that ancestors are kindly ... *because*, in the absence of a corporate family, in the turnover of the generations a new head does not effectively displace his predecessor." Freedman plainly sees the Chinese form of inheritance as causally related to the benevolence of Chinese ancestors, but he does not make clear just how they are linked.

"The weight of the ethnographic evidence on ancestor worship," Freedman suggests (p. 93), "seems to be in favor of the hypothesis that, by being displaced, a man-become-ancestor is thought at once to resent his successor and to endow that successor with the authority to rule in his place." Here Freedman is speaking from the point of view of the ancestor rather than the descendant: the ancestor is thought to resent his successor if he has been removed from a desired place of power. Is not Freedman thus assuming the same connections between A and D that Goody does? To say that the ancestor resents having been removed is surely to imply that the heirs have taken away power and possessions he coveted. It is not unreasonable, then, that they would feel the guilt and fear described by Goody.

Other evidence that Freedman wishes to depend on Goody's explanation can be found in his book *Chinese Lineage and Society* (1966), where he attributes both the benevolence of Chinese ancestors and the absence of guilt among heirs to the fact that the inheritance of ritual authority need not wait on the father's death (p. 151): "Men do not stand as intermediaries between the ancestors and their sons, and the emancipation of the sons by their father's death is not an entry into ritual majority. From this fundamental characteristic of the Chinese family flows what, in the light of the comparative ethnographic evidence, appears to be the relative ineffectiveness of Chinese ancestors, their general air of benevolence, and doubtless too the lack of strong feelings of hatred or guilt towards them on the part of their descendants." In summary, Freedman's position appears to be that since A does not hold in China, neither do B, C, and D. This is taken as an explanation for the relative benevolence of Chinese ancestors.

Let us examine each of Freedman's three claims to see whether his argument can, as it were, be turned on its head. First we must ask whether Goody's argument can legitimately be used to account for the connection between the form of inheritance and the nature of the ancestors Freedman describes. Note that the argument proceeds if A, then B; if B, then C; if C, then D. Since the series does not start with "If and only if . . . ," there remains the possibility that other factors besides A could bring about B, operating either along with A or independently, even without A. For this reason, one cannot move from an "If A, then B" statement to an "If not A, then not B" statement. To illustrate in simple terms, the statement "if it rains the streets get wet" is true. But it obviously does not follow that "if it does not rain, the streets will not get wet," since the streets might get wet in some other way. Likewise, one cannot argue:

1'. If A', an heir does not wait for his benefactor to die before he inherits property and jural authority, then B', after the benefactor dies, the heir does not feel guilty for having had some part in the benefactor's death . . . and so forth.

In order to do so, one would have to demonstrate that no other factor besides A could bring about B, that no other factor besides B could bring about C, and so forth. This would transfer the entire sequence from "If, then" conditionals to "If and only if" conditionals. It would also allow us to argue from A' to B', etc. Otherwise, one cannot conclude that where A does not hold, B, C, and D will not hold either. In the Chinese case, for example, in the absence of A, some other factor, such as worry over having provided adequate medical care for one's father, might lead to guilt over his death.

This leads to the paradoxical conclusion that if Freedman is right in saying that A does not hold for the Chinese case, he cannot use Goody's argument to explain the allegedly benevolent ancestors. But in fact, I do not think he is right either in that claim or in his claim that D does not hold true for China. If I can show that both A and D are true for at least some part of China, then I can legitimately use Goody's argument. First, I must make the point that A and hence conditional 1 can be applied even if all property and jural authority are not obtained on the death of the benefactor. In other words, a man may grant some jural authority to his heir while still alive; as long as something is left to be inherited at his death, conditional 1 can be used in the argument.

As we have seen, Freedman points out that sons may obtain some authority before their father's death. Moreover, the authority a father holds is not transferred on undiminished to a single heir. If married brothers inherit from their father, each will probably set up a household independent of the others. Neither the eldest son nor any other son rules over his siblings as his father did. In China, in sum, the transfer of authority from one generation to another is a more diffuse process than in other societies: it is more gradual because sons may obtain part of their inheritance before their father dies; it is more dispersed because no one son takes over the full authority of his father. One might expect, then, that the guilt felt will be less since there is less to be obtained on the holder's death. Still, conditional 1 can be applied as long as some property or jural authority is inherited only at the father's death.

It seems clear, as Freedman himself indicates, that much does remain to be inherited at the death of a Chinese father. In Ch'i-nan, for example, I found a very strong feeling against sons' dividing the property of their father before his death. In fact, the separation of a son's household from that of his parents often takes place in two distinct stages. In many cases, shortly after a young man marries he and his wife set up their own economically separate household. Usually this means that they provide themselves with a new stove, either building a large brick one or purchasing a small, charcoal-burning hibachi, and that from then on, the wife will cook only for her husband and their children. Any money earned by the son or his wife thereafter becomes part of their private funds, though they may turn part of it over to the son's parents.

This initial separation is usually allowed as a matter of course; it is not marked by any ritual, such as a division of embers from the original stove. The land, meanwhile, is still legally owned by the father and is not divided until his death. The sons may till it jointly and divide the proceeds, or they may divide the land informally and till it separately. When I asked why sons do not divide the land before their father's death, I was told, "The land belongs to the father and mother [*chan si lau-pe lau-bu e*]; how can the

TABLE 8

Time of Division of Household and Land by Sons with Respect to
Father's Death, Lou Lineage, Ch'inan

Male sibling set	Division of household		Division of property	
	Before father's death	After father's death	Before father's death	After father's death
1		x		x
2		x		x
3		x		x
4		x		x
5		x		
6		x		
7	x			x
8	x			x
9	x			x
10	x		x	

NOTE: In the case of sibling sets 5 and 6 the land and property have not yet been divided because the mother is still living.

sons take it away from them?" It is evident from Table 8, which covers the ten male sibling sets in the Lou lineage still residing in Ch'inan (all the fathers are deceased), that in most cases, sons do not divide their father's property until after his death, and in some cases, not until after their mother's death as well. Even if sons set up separate households while their father is living, they usually wait until he has died before dividing the land. This is not to say that sons attain no jural authority before their fathers die; they simply add to what they already have when he dies. The father's death may mark the point at which a son sets up a separate household, economically independent from his brothers, or it may mean the formal separation of his share of his father's property from that of his siblings, along with the right to dispose of the land (sell it or rent it) as he pleases.

The transfer of property at death is strikingly expressed in the ritual of coffining. Before the coffining, a rice measure (*tau*) of the sort used at the burial is obtained and filled with the same mixture of grains, coins, and nails, the symbols of plenty and off-spring. Just before the corpse is placed in the coffin, the descendants gather around the body in their mourning dress, keening and wailing. Someone reaches under the coverlet over the corpse and brings out the stiffened arm. Then the hand of the corpse is placed in the rice measure and stirred around and around while the descendants wail more and more stridently. As soon as this ritual is over the body is sealed in its coffin. I was told that the ritual expresses the transfer of whatever property the deceased still possessed to the living. "It is to let the dead willingly give away the property to the heirs so that they won't have to steal it from him." Simultaneously, another ritual with a similar import takes place. First, someone prepares a small bowl of cooked rice and cooked chicken parts—the head, the feet, and the wings. Then, standing in front of the hall, a lineage member dumps the rice and the chicken head on the ground while someone else calls a dog and directs him to the food. As soon as the dog has taken the chicken head in his mouth, he is beaten with a long, whiplike plant until he dashes away in a frenzy. It was explained to me that the dog represents the dead man, the chicken head the prop-erty of the family held *first* by the deceased (*thau* means both head and first), the wings and feet of the chicken the property held later by the descendants, and the bowl of rice one meal out of the usual three consumed in a day. The head is given to the dead person to eat but the rest is kept for the descendants. Similarly, one meal is given to the deceased, and the others are saved for the descen-dants. "The dog, which stands for the dead man, is beaten so that he will run far away and not return. He has enjoyed his share of the property, so he should not come back and bother the living."

Although in most instances sons begin to attain their adult re-sponsibilities before the death of their parents, these rituals clearly state that something has been held back, which is to be passed on only at the death of the parents and not before. In most instances, this is the property hitherto held in the name of the deceased. Whether the death of the parents means that the sons can acquire rights over property, or independent economic households, or both, A in the argument is fulfilled. In Ch'inan, most heirs do acquire property or jural authority when their benefactors die.

Besides the authority inherent in the retention of property,

Ch'inan parents can hold lifelong control over their sons in another way: as long as one parent or the other is alive, a son is denied full participation in the ancestral rites. In the rotation governing corporate lineage ancestral sacrifices, the responsibility devolves only on those household heads who have no living parent.
Otherwise, the rotation is *i-lau ui-ci,* or "oldest as reference point."
This means that the responsibility falls on the unit of living parent and his or her sons, even though the sons may have economically separate households. In this sense, not until both parents die
does a man attain his own turn in the rotation, the right to full
responsibility in carrying out the corporate ancestral rites.

If, in Ch'inan, sons gain a significant measure of authority at
the death of their fathers and mothers, then the first premise of
the Goody argument holds here. Does his conclusion—that misfortune will be laid to the hostile acts of ancestors—also hold in this
instance? As we have seen, Freedman characterizes the behavior
expected of Chinese ancestors as "essentially benign." But it is my
impression that ancestors in Ch'inan are much more active and
interfering than this. Unfortunately, I am unable to say to the exact percentage point how many misfortunes are attributed to the
ancestors, for I have no record of the advice people received on
their frequent trips to consult professionals in Sanhsia or Pan-
ch'iao (near Taipei). In the village itself, I attended almost every
session at which a shaman attempted to determine the cause of
some ill. Six of them were prolonged sessions, some lasting over
several days, and involved cases of serious or intractable illness.
Two of these cases were diagnosed as instances of ancestral interference; one was held to be the work of an ancestor in the hall,
the other the work of an ancestor in the grave. But the frequency
with which ancestors are blamed for misfortune is surely much
higher than this suggests, because many out-of-town shamans tend
to blame misfortune on the ancestors, and geomancers, who are
resorted to very often, inevitably relate their interpretations to the
personal activities of ancestors.

Moreover, whatever the extent of the ancestors' activity, it is
clear that for the people of Ch'inan they are not as benign as

Freedman suggests. For example, by one of the characteristics commonly used to measure the relative malevolence of ancestors—capriciousness—the ancestors in Ch'inan are closer to those of the Lovedu of Africa, who are cited by Freedman (1967: 92–93) as examples of ancestors who cause misfortune even in the absence of neglect on the part of their descendants, than to those of the Chinese, who he says must be provoked before they will cause harm. It is true that the people of Ch'inan will always posit some reason for the ancestors' punitive actions (usually that the offerings have been insufficient), but this is not to deny that they feel the ancestors to be unreasonable to the point of capriciousness. After all, since there is no clear rule about what constitutes a sufficient offering, descendants are always open to the charge that they have not offered enough. As Ong Ciouq-kim put it, "You can make lavish offerings on all the proper occasions, but you never know that the ancestors won't come back and make trouble." I heard this sort of remark very often. One old Peq lady told me several times, "The ancestors are always coming back to make trouble. If your eight characters are low [vulnerable to supernatural attack], they will always be coming around to mess with you."

In general, it was difficult to get people to speak of the harm their ancestors had done to them. And it was more difficult still to get them to accuse an ancestor of acting wantonly. In one case in the Ong settlement, however, involving an elderly man whose back had been badly crippled for many years, most Ongs who would talk about it agreed that the man's trouble was caused by a malicious ancestor in his grandfather's generation. All attempts at propitiation had failed. "That ancestor just has a bad heart. That's why the man has that trouble with his back. The ancestor is causing it out of meanness." Here is a case in which we find an ancestor inflicting misfortune for no apparent reason. With respect to the characteristic of capriciousness, ancestors in Ch'inan rank rather high. Even when all appropriate sacrifices have been made to them, one still has no guarantee that they will not return and make trouble. Sometimes, as in the case of the crippled Ong man, they act without any provocation and continue to afflict even when treated especially well.

Another measure of ancestral malevolency is the extent of harm they are capable of causing their descendants. Most accounts indicate that Chinese ancestors do little more than make descendants mildly sick (e.g., Freedman 1966: 151). But in Ch'inan I encountered cases in which ancestors were said to have brought about serious debility or even death. In one instance the ancestors of the Uis and Lous have visited their wrath on three couples for breaking the oath that the two lineages should never intermarry. The punishments have been severe: one couple has remained infertile, all of the children of another couple have died, and the only child of the third couple is crippled. Similarly, the ancestors of the Ongs had barred their descendants from marrying any people named Ngo, because a Ngo woman once put poison in an Ong well. The one Ong-Ngo marriage in the settlement produced a daughter who has had periodic spells of insanity. Her affliction is attributed to the anger of the ancestors at the breaking of the oath. The most severe punishment I heard of was supposed to have been meted out by the Ui ancestors. "Several years ago a Ui man accidentally bumped and moved the incense pot for the ancestors in the hall. As a result, another man in the lineage died shortly afterward. When they opened the tablet box to insert that man's tablet, two more people died." Usually ancestors do not bring about serious infirmity without being seriously provoked (by having their oath broken, for example). Still, people do find it plausible that ancestors will inflict death as punishment even for simple carelessness.

Are the ancestors capable of such extreme interference only when directly provoked or irritated, or can they be encouraged to punish an affront to some living person? In other words, can they be invoked? It is a touchy subject, but two informants finally confirmed that ancestors in Ch'inan can indeed be called down on the living. One case, confided to me by the Li *tang-ki*, involved the wife of a man in the Li lineage. When, after her husband died, she began to sleep with his elder brother, the rest of the family became very upset by her unseemly behavior. Shortly thereafter, she lost her senses and tried to commit suicide by jumping into the river. At this point, the *tang-ki* was called in to determine the cause of her insanity. He discovered that some member of the family had burned a charm in the Li ancestral incense pot, asking the ancestors to punish the woman. After the *tang-ki* burned another charm in the pot, one designed to "talk peace" with the ancestors, the woman recovered.

In the second case, my informant, Ong A-cui, admitted that he himself had attempted to invoke the aid of the ancestors in his running battle with Ong A-iong. He told me that he had burned incense before the tablets, had explained to the ancestors that A-iong's house protruding in front of the hall had a bad influence on the hall, the ancestors, and the lineage members, and then had implored them to return and cause trouble for A-iong, making his household full of discord and sickness. According to A-cui, other Ongs had attempted the same sort of invocation. Although nothing striking had happened to A-iong, A-cui assured me that he was not in good health and that things could get worse. It is important to note that since anyone, apparently, is free to try his hand at invoking the ancestors, this practice does not systematically buttress any particular social position, such as household head.

As the guilt-inheritance-fear argument would lead us to expect, acquisition of jural authority on the death of parents is correlated in Ch'inan with a strong tendency to attribute misfortune, mild or severe, to the acts of ancestors. Because both A and D hold for this case, the argument can legitimately be used to posit a causal connection between them. It is possible that the extent to which one gains from a parent's death is directly correlated with the extent to which ancestors are credited with causing harm. If so, there may be considerable local variation among Chinese communities, depending on whether or not sons are kept from full jural majority until their parents' death. In Ch'inan, where division of the family property is almost always delayed until after the parents'

Ancestral Interference 203

death and where control over lineage ancestral rites is in the hands of the oldest people, ancestors are fierce, often capricious, and occasionally malicious.

The inheritance-guilt-fear hypothesis may go part way toward explaining how the ancestors are seen in Ch'inan, but to give it the last word would be to ignore its inadequacies and to pass over whatever explanation the people of Ch'inan themselves might have for the behavior of the ancestors. I will attempt to convey their view by analyzing one of their legends, the story of the yellow tails. It may be that in the indigenous view of how the ancestors have come to be the way they are we shall find evidence of the attitudes on which the inheritance-guilt-fear theory depends, something that cannot be observed directly. Alternatively, the legend may raise questions the theory cannot answer, leading us to consider a different hypothesis, the one that relates childhood experience rather than adult inheritance to the nature of the ancestors.

Before discussing the legend itself, however, I want to return to a part of the cult of the dead mentioned earlier, second burial, because some of the themes in the story are expressed in those rites as well. In order to explain to me why the Taiwanese must open the graves of their ancestors six or seven years after death to "pick up the bones" (*khioq-kut*) and arrange them in a ceramic pot, one old Lou man told me this story:

A long time ago an emperor wanted to build a great wall around his kingdom. To provide a labor force, he conscripted thousands of young men. Conditions were so terrible for the workers that many men died and were buried under or within the wall. When one young worker had not returned home for some time, his wife set out to find him. When she learned that he was dead, she cried until the entire wall fell down. Then in order to find her husband's bones, she bit off her finger tip and let the blood flow onto the ground. Whenever the blood hit one of her husband's bones, that bone came up and joined together with the others until the skeleton was complete. People told her to carry the skeleton in her arms so that her tears would fall on it, making veins of blood on the bones, and resulting perhaps in a return to life. Just then, Tho-te-ma [the wife of Tho-te-kong, the earth god] offered different advice. She said it would be better if the woman were to carry the skeleton on her back. But as soon as the wife did this, for she readily accepted the advice

of a goddess, the skeleton fell apart. Tho-te-ma gave this bad advice because she was feeling evil-hearted and thought that there were enough
people in the world already. After the bones fell apart, the woman put
them in a pot and buried them, marking the place with a stone. Thereafter, people continued doing this. Today, our picking up of the bones
is equivalent to the wife's using her bleeding finger to find her husband's
bones. We pick up the bones in order to let the dead live again.

Not everyone told me this story in response to my questions about
picking up the bones, but most people echoed its sentiments. As
Lou Kim-bo told me, "The ancestors' bones will mingle with the
earth unless we put them safely in a pot. There would be nothing
left. Putting them in a pot ensures that the bones will still be
there even 10,000 years from now." Similarly, an old man explained, "Our parents have raised us and cared for us. Now that
they are in need of it, it is our duty to save their bones from dis-
integrating in the earth by picking them up and placing them in
an urn. That way they will exist forever." The picking up of the
bones of the dead is said to be an unquestioned duty owed to the
dead. Their plight is viewed compassionately; without help from
the living they would cease to exist altogether.

Yet it is just the bones that are to be preserved. There is horror
in the possibility that the flesh of the dead might also be preserved.
Sometimes, I was told, when the coffin is opened for second burial,
the body has not decayed at all. When people described this to
me they evinced disgust and dread. Ong A-bi said, "When they
opened the coffin of my aunt, there she was just like a living person. All her clothes and skin were there. She looked just like a
person sleeping." In cases like this, where there is little or no de-
composition, it is assumed that the person has been mistakenly
buried in "covered corpse land" (*kai-su-te*). Something about the
surrounding earth has prevented the body from decaying. In this
event, the body will probably be moved and reburied. "When
there is flesh left, it is good for the dead man but bad for the
living. The dead are supposed to be reduced to bones." Sometimes
a corpse can undergo an undesirable transformation (becoming a
dangerous monster, or *iau-kuai*); at other times a desirable transformation (decay) does not occur. In the second case, no less than
in the first, the corpse is seen as a threat to the living.

If there is only a little flesh left on the body when the coffin is opened, it need not be moved. Someone will blow a mouthful of wine into the coffin, or throw some dirt into it, or merely expose the body to the open sky. Any of these measures is said to be sufficient to accomplish the complete decay of the flesh in another year or so. In no case can the descendants scrape off the remaining flesh. They must wait until it has decayed naturally, because "cutting off the flesh would be just like killing the ancestor."

All this implies that the dead person is expected to give up the form he possessed while among the living; his earthly flesh must decay. Otherwise, he would continue "just like a living man forever." It also presages one of the central motifs of the story of the yellow tails. As we shall see, the relinquishment of flesh may correspond to the deceased's abdication of some of his earthly powers. Just as the deceased must give up his flesh, so also must he give up his property and much of his domestic authority to his descendants. But descendants cannot take matters into their own hands, cannot bring about the disappearance of the earthly form of the deceased by cutting off the flesh of his corpse. They must wait patiently for their elder to die and the flesh on his body to rot on its own, for to hurry the process along is to kill their elder.

However long the wait, decay inevitably does its work and the deceased, reduced to a bare skeleton, is finally "dead." Yet, as we have seen, descendants are extremely careful to save these bones from extinction. Is it, then, that though something of the ancestor must die, something else must live on? To answer this question we must turn to the legend of the yellow tails, and specifically to those aspects of it that are relevant to the themes of inheritance, authority, and replacement.

When I set about trying to get people to tell me the legend, I found there were four different versions. The most commonly repeated and most complete version, 1, goes like this:

A long time ago when men lived in trees and still had tails, it was the custom to kill old men when their tails turned yellow and afterward to eat their flesh. One old man knew that his tail would soon turn yellow. In order to escape being killed he slipped down from his tree at night and ran away to the mountains. But since there was no food there, he soon died. In the meantime, his descendants set off to look for him so that they could perform the last act of eating his flesh. They took along with them a piece of cloth in which to wrap the body if they found it. But no matter how long and hard they looked, they could not find the body. Giving up, they cried in sorrow. Since it began to rain, they covered their heads with the cloth they had planned to use to bring the body back, and came home. This is why we cover our heads with cloth at funerals today.

Version 2 differs slightly:

In early times men had tails. When they got old, their tails turned yellow. As soon as this happened, their descendants killed them and ate their flesh. One time, however, an old man knew his tail was about to turn yellow. So he ran away to the mountains to avoid being killed. His son followed him there with a coarse hemp bag, hoping to find him and bring his body back to eat. But when he arrived at the place where his father was, the old man had already killed himself. In addition, his flesh had already rotted so that it was unfit to eat. Because he had nothing to eat, the son cried, put the bag over his head, and came home down the mountain.

Version 3 is still less elaborate:

A long time ago, men had tails. When their tails turned yellow they had to be killed by their sons, who would then eat their flesh. Since one particular man was very old, it was about time for his tail to turn yellow and for his descendants to kill him. One day, when he was up on the roof fixing some tiles, his son told him to come down, saying it was time to be killed. But then an immortal told the son he would have to bury the father and leave his body in the ground for three days before he could eat the meat. The son, realizing that the flesh would be rotten and unfit to eat by then, cried because he would have no meat to eat. Just then it began to rain, so the son put a piece of cloth over his head. This is the story of why we wear cloth on our heads at funerals.

And, finally, there was this version, 4:

A long time ago, men had tails. When the tails of old men turned yellow, their grandsons killed them and ate their flesh. One time there was a grandfather up on the roof fixing some tiles that had come loose in a typhoon. Meanwhile, the grandson was preparing to kill him. He heated a large pot of water like that used to skin slaughtered pigs. When the water was boiling, the grandson called up to his grandfather, "A-kong [grandfather], the water's boiled." A-kong knew what this meant and delayed, saying, "Just a minute; let me finish fixing this." But in the end they killed him anyway.

It is possible that this story is no more than a pedagogic device, intended to show what society is by giving a shocking picture of what society is not. In describing a time when the unheard-of practices of murder and cannibalism of elders took place, that is to say, a radically different, nonexistent situation, the story could be meant to draw attention to the existing situation, the realities of Taiwanese life that might otherwise be taken for granted. Yet, the manner in which the story was told to me suggests that it should not be viewed so simply.

After I first heard the story, I asked many people if they knew it or some variant of it. Some said they had heard the story, but refused to tell it to me. Others finally gave me their version, reluctantly, attempting to avoid telling it as long as possible. I asked one old man, Li A-chan, about the story many times because he was extremely knowledgeable about tales and legends. For many months he denied ever hearing of it. Then, practically on the eve of my departure from the village, he said, "There is a story that you ought to hear before you go," and proceeded to tell me version 4 of the story he had denied ever hearing. Of course, people might be hesitant to tell the story simply because it describes events they find shameful, even though those events have no relevance to society as they know it. On the other hand, the extreme reluctance to describe the murder and cannibalism of elders may indicate that far from being a simple description of a now deplorable past, the story reflects people's deeply felt desires, desires that they would as soon not admit exist.

To find what it is that makes the story shameful to tell, we must first understand what the story means. In the following I will discuss all four versions, though 4 appears to be the story only half-told, for it does not include the radical change from the killing and eating of elders to their flight and death by other means. All versions begin by describing a time when men had tails that turned yellow in old age. In other contexts, yellow is a color of high rank and accomplishment. For example, in mourning dress, yellow is worn by the fifth generation below the ancestor being mourned; the production of great-great-great grandsons is a rare and valuable achievement. Similarly, yellow is reserved for the Emperor and his descendants, those with the highest political rank in the land (A. Wolf 1970: 191). Consequently, the yellow tails may indicate the old men have reached the apex of their power and authority over their descendants. This interpretation is buttressed by the physical position of the old man of the story when he is introduced. In three of the four versions he is high up—in one case up in a tree, in two cases atop the house—a position commensurate with the high rank implied by the color of his tail.

In two versions the old man is on the roof fixing tiles. This implies even more, for the roof of a house is a kind of barometer for good or ill of the house and its inhabitants. Often, a house roof is the focus of rites to correct misfortune. Sometimes sickness or lack of harmony is attributed to roof tiles being in need of repair. Once, I was told, an old Lou man was very sick and Co-su-kong was asked to diagnose his illness. After the young man through whom the god spoke ran quickly to the old man's house and fixed a loose tile on the roof, the old man's health improved. Also, the water in which people boil the charms they obtain on routine visits to temples for general good luck is thrown up on the roof of the house, "to make things go right." The old man on top of the roof fixing tiles in the story is in a position of control over the people in the house. He is in charge of the affairs of his household, looking after them, setting them right when they go wrong.

From his position of height and authority, the old man then comes down to escape being killed and eaten by his subordinates. In versions 2 and 3 the sons specifically are to carry out the killing, whereas in 1 and 4, it is the descendants in general and the grandson, respectively, who are responsible. What is being emphasized is that subordinates in lower generations are to remove their elder. As Li A-chan, who told me version 4, said, "It does not have to be the grandson; anyone in a lower generation can do the killing." Sons are perhaps emphasized in two versions because they are the most exposed to the raw authority of their fathers. A man wields considerably less authority over collateral relatives; and affection between alternate generations eases his authority when he faces his grandchildren.

In every version but one, the old man successfully escapes his sons or descendants; his body rots before they are able to eat him. This part of the story seems clearly parallel to the rites of second burial in that there, too, the father's flesh rots away naturally, without being cut off by the sons. I wish to suggest, though it may only be clear why later in the discussion, that the flesh of the deceased represents some aspects of the authority and control he held while alive. Just as the flesh of the deceased disappears through decay, so certain parts of his authority are lost when he dies. Both processes must be allowed to occur in their own time, without encouragement from the sons. As we have seen, when the father dies, he loses certain kinds of control; the sons will acquire what authority he has to give up over land and ancestral rites, but they cannot take it away from him prematurely. Similarly, the hand of the deceased is stirred in the rice measure before the coffining so that the descendants will not have to steal his property from him.

The flesh rots without interference from the sons; they will gain authority in some areas where their father once had it. Yet even after death, descendants are not entirely free of the authority of their elders. Just as the dissipation of the flesh represents the authority the father gives up, the retention of the bones represents the authority he never loses. Unfortunately, the story of the yellow tails does not comment on the preservation of bones. The rites of second burial tell us, however, that the bones of the dead will last forever. They represent the residual authority the ancestors always retain over their descendants. Their demands that they be worshiped at both tablet and grave, that their standards of comfort be met through geomancy, that their oaths be kept, all buttressed by their ability to inflict sickness, misfortune, and even death, will continue forever.

The use of the distinction between flesh and bones to express acquisition of partial but not complete authority seems to occur in marriage rites as well. When the groom travels to his bride's house on the day of the wedding, he carries with him, among other things, a leg of pork. The bride's family immediately cuts all the meat off it and sends the bare bones back with the groom.

This practice is said to be mandatory; people contend that it is all right for the bride's family to keep the meat and eat it, but that to keep the bones as well would be too much. When a family accepts the gift of a bride from another family it incurs a heavy obligation toward the wife-giving family. Because of this obligation, which the groom's relatives are never entirely able to cancel, they must pay great respect and deference to the bride's family. In turn, the bride's relatives display a superior attitude toward the groom's family. As part of their superior stance, they are able to exercise considerable authority over the members of his family, demanding respect, criticizing them when they wish, even disciplining them. (See Ahern 1974.) It seems likely that the flesh the bride's family retains represents the authority it gains over the groom's family; and that not being allowed to keep the bones means this authority is not total. Although the bride's relatives possess considerable ritual power to harm or help the groom's family, there are customary limits on their use of it. They will not ordinarily interfere in the affairs of their affines except for a few special occasions, nor will they interfere too much.

Similarly, in the cult of the dead the decay of the flesh and the preservation of the bones suggests that the descendants attain only partial authority. Yet there is a fundamental difference between the two cases, for the bride's family is able to keep and *eat* the pork flesh, whereas sons are unable to eat the flesh of their father.*
The consumption of the pork flesh indicates that the bride's family attains authority over the groom's; the groom's family, however, has no authority over the bride's. If the sons were able to consume their father's flesh and leave his bones to disintegrate, the father would be absorbed and destroyed by the sons; so, like the groom's family, he would have no authority over them. This is what does not happen in the story and what stands in contrast to the situation today. The son fails to consume the flesh of his father and

---

* To do so would in fact be the exact reverse of the filial behavior expected of sons under certain circumstances. J. J. M. DeGroot (1901: 387) cites cases of sons giving their parents pieces of their own flesh to eat in an effort to cure them of some illness.

cries because he has no food to eat. He is sad, if I have read the
story correctly, because he has not rid himself of the authority his
father has over him, which has now become the control exercised
by the ancestors.

The son's intent was to place the father in his hempen sack
(version 2) and then to consume him. Instead the old man goes
untouched, and the bag goes on the son's own head. This leads to
the "just so" part of the story, the explanation that this is why
people now wear cloth on their heads at funerals. Just as some of
my informants explicitly named sons in their versions and others
only descendants in general, so some explicitly stated that the
cloth worn on the head was hemp, and others specified only cloth
of some kind. This accords with present-day practice: sons alone
wear rough hemp (*mua:-po*) on their heads in mourning; all other
mourners wear some other cloth, such as muslin (*te-a:-po*) (A. Wolf
1970: 190).

In any case the wearing of cloth on the head at funerals is an
overt sign of the obligation to mourn the dead. Because the descendants have failed to consume the flesh of the elder, to take his sub-
stance into themselves, they cannot attain full independence of
him. This is why, as I read the story, they must wear the cloth
badge of mourning. The wearing of mourning implies that they
are obligated to the dead in many ways, ways that differ, of course,
among descendants. Sons are obligated to provide burial and the
rites for the recently deceased, as well as regular worship, so long
as they live. Descendants in lower generations are obligated to
carry on that worship thereafter. All those subordinate to the deceased owe him respect and honor. He who must mourn as a son
and others who are related to the deceased in different ways are
all under the yoke of the dead man, obligated to serve and please
him in the grave, in the tablet, and in the underworld. These demands never cease, but are made on and met by generation after
generation; there are few forgotten ancestors in Ch'inan. The ancestors' control, exercised over the living by inflicting sickness
or misfortunes for a variety of offenses, is never relinquished.
Although sons gain in authority after their father's death, in the

end father still reigns supreme. At the end of the myth in version
1 the old man is still high on the mountain, untouched by his son.

The motion of the characters in the story up and down through
space reinforces my analysis of it. In the most elaborate version, 1,
the elder begins spatially high, comes down, and then proceeds to
a final high position on the mountain. He was highest in life, exercising authority over his descendants. At death he comes down
a notch, giving up his property and control over most domestic
affairs. But in the end he is reinstated to a superordinant position
with a different but impressively powerful authority. The descendants, for their part, start out the story in a low position relative
to the elder, move upward attempting to gain control in the mountains, but fail and come down again; in the end they are again
lower than the elder. As if to doubly reinforce the casting down
of the descendants, two other elements enter the story at this point
that echo the high-low movement: tears fall from the descendants'
eyes, and rain falls from the sky.

The foregoing analysis uses two techniques: first, it seeks for
analogies between objects and acts in the story and objects and
acts in the villagers' life today, and then it attempts to show how
patterns of movement in the story give force to those analogies.
All of this is to the end I set out earlier, namely, explaining what
import the story has for the villagers by making explicit the connections and assumptions they implicitly understand to lie behind
it.*

If the story can be taken as a key to the attitudes most of the
people have toward their ancestors, then the inheritance-guilt-
fear hypothesis breaks down in one important respect. Rather
than expressing descendants' guilt over having taken *some* authority from the dead, the story reveals a concern over the inability
of the living to wrest *all* authority from the dead. The central
focus is not that the dead have given up something of value, but
rather that they have not given up everything of value. The son

* A similar approach has been followed by Burridge 1967. Compare his views
with Lévi-Strauss 1963.

weeps because he has no flesh to eat; though sons inherit control over property and domestic affairs, they never fully escape the authority of the ancestors. The death of every ascendant means both a liberation from some kinds of control and a continuation of other kinds of control; the old truly never die. The story reveals not people's guilt over what they receive from the dead and fear because of that guilt, but people's regret at their inability to wrest all control from the dead.

One could contend, of course, that the villagers feel guilt even though they do not express it in the story. But we have seen that guilt is not expressed in any of the rituals surrounding the recently dead either; the emphasis there is on transferring goods from the deceased to the living while avoiding further contact with the corpse. It seems reasonable to expect that if guilt over having robbed or caused the death of an ascendant were a serious concern, it would be discernible in some rite or myth surrounding death or in people's statements about inheritance and succession. Having found no evidence of guilt here, I find the inheritance-guilt-fear theory less appealing. Even if one were to object that guilt need not be openly expressed at all (thus asserting that the inheritance-guilt-fear theory could still apply), one still needs to account in some way for the attitudes that are evident in the story of the yellow tails, namely, that the living never escape the hold of their dead ascendants.

Perhaps, then, it would be more fruitful to look in a different direction for an explanation of the ancestors' activity in Ch'inan. As noted, other theorists suggest that childhood experiences are related to the malevolence or benevolence of ancestors. For example, Lambert, Triandis, and Wolf (1959: 164) believe "there is a general tendency for less indulgent treatment in infancy to be related to predominantly aggressive deities in the cultural belief system, and for more indulgent treatment to be related to benevolent deities." Without analyzing their theories in detail and without being able to offer data that could prove or disprove them, I want to suggest tentatively that a peculiarity of child-training customs in Ch'inan may be related to the unusually high

degree of ancestral activity there. The suggestions I present below
are only that—suggestions—because I did not collect any systematic data on child rearing; I can merely offer observations that
were made casually during my rounds in the village, incidental
to other concerns.

The disciplinary practice that I have in mind seemed to be used
whenever children committed a fairly serious offense or annoyed
their parents beyond patience. The most common infractions invoking it, I was told, are going to a place that has been put off-
limits, whining constantly for attention, and fighting with other
children. In any of these circumstances, the adult who intends to
discipline the child picks up a dry, thin switch of bamboo, herds
him or her into an exposed place, usually an outside courtyard
in the midst of several houses, and there harshly commands the
child to "kneel!" (*kui*). In one incident, which took place just outside my house, the grandfather of the two small boys who lived
next door (aged one-and-a-half and three) forced them to kneel
on the ground because they had been fighting with each other.
When they saw their grandfather pick up his switch, they had
started to run away, but at his command to kneel they stopped
running and burst into tears. From this point, their dismay and
fright became more and more evident. After ordering them to
kneel, the grandfather circled around them, hitting them with
the switch and shouting accusations: "You don't behave at all.
All you do is fight, hurt each other, and bother me." Meanwhile,
the uproar had brought a crowd of several adults and many children, who had rushed out of the surrounding houses. They stood
around the small kneeling boys, alternately laughing openly at
them and joining in on the scolding. The boys sobbed desper-
ately and occasionally tried to escape by starting to rise to their
feet. Another shout of "kneel!" sent them down again. This treatment continued for about five minutes, and then the younger
child, still a toddler, was allowed to leave. A few minutes later
the three-year-old was released also.

To my certain knowledge these two boys received this kind of
punishment at least once a month, meted out variously by their

mother, father, grandfather, and grandmother. Beyond that, I cannot say how frequently such measures are applied or which adults carry them out most often. It seemed clear that direct ascendants (especially fathers) are most likely to start the process, but other relatives inevitably take part in the berating and ridiculing.

I was told, and my observations confirm, that this is the primary way in which children are disciplined. For less serious offenses, children may be shouted at or swatted, but they seemed little affected by these measures. By the time children are six or seven years old and ready to start school, almost none of them need to be punished by being forced to kneel and suffer abuse. They are said to have learned to stop doing the things that would prompt punishment. Only very rarely will an older child misbehave. Then a more severe penalty, such as making him kneel and hold a pan of water over his head for a considerable period of time, is exacted.

It is clear that this pattern is not typical of all Taiwanese villages, even those in the same area. In at least one other village in the Taipei basin, children are spoiled and indulged for their first six or seven years. Only after that are they disciplined, and then harshly, often with severe physical punishment (M. Wolf 1970: 40–41, 43–44). Possibly this difference in child training is related to the varying perceptions of the ancestors in Ch'inan and other places. According to Lambert, Triandis, and Wolf (1959: 168),

the frequent hurt and pain in infancy [defined as the first year of life and as long as treatment characteristic of that first year persists, with childhood being put at approximately five through twelve years old] in societies with aggressive deities causes anxiety in the child because of his conflicting anticipations of hurt and of nurture. His conflict is reduced by a conception of the deity as aggressive and thus compatible with human anticipations of hurt.

Perhaps the early inception of punishment in Ch'inan (in infancy rather than childhood, as in other villages), together with the villagers' use of both systematic ridicule and physical punishment, make being disciplined a more intensely painful experience and produce a more extreme conflict between the expectation of being nurtured and that of being rejected. If so, one would expect supernatural beings (perhaps including ancestors) to be more aggressive in the Ch'inan case.

I would also like to explore, equally tentatively, a different possibility. Perhaps the way the ancestors are expected to behave is a direct extension of the way they acted while alive. More specifically, it may be that those experiences people have of their ascendants which are most vividly impressed on them are what carry over to the time when their ascendants are deceased, shaping their expectations of them as ancestors. Say, for example, that a man remembers his mother and father best as they were when they were close to death; their character at that stage of their lives might be the character they would be expected to have as ancestors. By this view, one would expect the relative inactivity of very aged men and women to be reflected in relatively inactive ancestors.

Considering the Ch'inan case in this light, one might be led to suspect that people would remember most intensely their early experiences of their ascendants, rather than those undergone as mature adults watching their elders grow old. As I have suggested, extremely young children are subjected to a kind of excruciating discipline that seems to instill in them a deep respect for the authority of their elders. In the case of fathers and sons, at least, this childhood experience is not replaced by another type of interaction. In most cases, as far as I was able to observe, when a boy reaches six or seven years of age a formal distance springs up between him and his father. They seem to avoid interacting whenever possible; what verbal contact they have deals with pressing household or business matters. This lack of interaction between father and son is especially apparent when groups of people sit around chatting. In this sort of casual situation, fathers and sons seldom, if ever, speak directly to each other, and indeed do not even respond to one another's general remarks. In the case of sons, the intense experience of being disciplined in childhood is never replaced later by a different, less fearsome but equally influential interaction with their fathers. Even though this same formal distance in later life is not typical of the relations between sons and their mothers or grandparents, it is still possible that the early experience of their discipline could overshadow all later experience of them.

Meyer Fortes (1949) has found something like this pattern in an African case, the Tallensi, where ancestors are "a standardized and highly elaborated picture of the parents as they might appear to a young child in real life—mystically omnipotent, capricious, vindictive, and yet beneficent and long-suffering; but the emphasis is far more on the persecuting than on the protecting attributes" (p. 235). While one may accept Fortes's description of the similarity between ancestors and parents as they appear to young children, one would wish for some independent evidence that the similarity is a result of the way people remember their parents. That is, before we can attribute the punitive nature of the ancestors in Ch'inan to people's childhood experiences, we need to know which aspects of deceased parents stand out most in people's memories.

For a long time in the field I was at a loss about how to obtain evidence, separate and apart from the ancestors' punitive role, that people in fact feel the ancestors to be much like their parents as they knew them in childhood. Finally I found confirmation of this in people's view of the ancestor as resident of the underworld. As we shall see in the next chapter, the dead are often visited while they are in the underworld. Are they described there as they were just before death, perhaps old, feeble, and incapacitated? Or are they described as they were in some other period of their life cycle? In the main, those who are sought in the underworld died in old age, at sixty-five or over. In some cases these people were active right up to their deaths, earning money by planting fields or picking tea; but in the majority of cases they had ceased to contribute economically to their households for some time, having grown weak and sick at the approach of death. Yet my informants, without exception, pictured the dead as active, wage-earning adults in the underworld. One son, on his visits to his father in the underworld, repeatedly asked him about his jobs there, how he earned money, how much he earned, and so forth, though the man had died at age seventy-four, feeble and bedridden. Another man visited by his son had been an electrician during his youth and middle years, but had retired many years before his death. Yet when he was asked what he did in the underworld, the reply was that he earned money by being an electrician. A woman who was old and helpless before her death reported that she was "busy managing the household and gambling a lot" in the underworld. The dead in the underworld retain the personalities and characters they had while alive, but they are remembered as they were during their active middle years, not as helpless old men and women awaiting death.

In line with their active role in the underworld, the dead there are often sought out for advice and information. One woman visited her mother to ask what to do about her son's inability to control his urination. Another time she requested her mother's opinion about whether or not to return to her natal family for a visit. Sometimes the dead give unsolicited advice, telling the visitor not to go on a long trip, or not to go in a certain direction, for example. In this sense also, they continue an active life, directing the affairs of the living. In short, when people visit their ancestors in the underworld, they regard them from the vantage point of a child rather than from the vantage point of a mature adult. It is as if, in the Ch'inan case, childhood memories of one's ascendants overwhelm all later experience of them; when the ascendants die, the most intense memories take precedence.

In this light the active character of the ancestors in Ch'inan makes sense. Their tendency toward capriciousness; their meting out of harsh punishment; their control over geomantic benefits; their demands that they be worshiped indefinitely: all these characteristics could emanate from people's propensity for remembering them chiefly as they were in their disciplinary, authoritarian role. To be sure, as was discussed, one's ascendants do not entirely stop exerting authority as they grow old; their authority is perhaps less intense and obvious, but it is present nonetheless. As I have suggested, it is this authority, which is most severe in childhood but which is maintained in some form until the ascendant's death, that is the central focus of the story of the yellow tails. The story is an expression of the cumulative weight of that authority extended over a lifetime; its gist is that the living can never get entirely rid of the authority of the dead. One could say that in a sense the living are victims of their own memories. They are saddled with the expectation that their ascendants must act in death as in life; descendants expect no less than that the ancestors will act as they did during the period of their life when they could exert the most control over their subordinates. We are now in a position to understand why people were so reluctant to tell the story of the yellow tails. They believe, on the one hand, that respecting their ascendants is right and good; indeed, they expend untold effort transforming that respect into action both while their ascendants are alive and after they are dead. On the other hand, they are admitting in the story (if they can be persuaded to tell it and if the hearer can interpret the message) that caring for one's dead ascendants is an onerous and often unwelcome task.

CHAPTER 13

The Underworld

So HEAVILY does the burden of worshiping the ancestors seem to weigh on the people of Ch'inan that one might easily have the impression that the cult of the dead is made up wholly of portions of calculated duty and helpless fear. Certainly, many aspects of the cult do arise out of the necessity of repaying obligations to the dead; and many others out of fear of their reprisal. But to view the cult as a dual composite of duty and fear is to omit one of its most important elements. The dead, besides manifesting themselves in hall tablets and in their bones at the graves, appear in yet another guise, as residents of the underworld.

Although many of the rites that occur before burial are not directed to the ancestor in any particular form or place, several rites and offerings made after the funeral are directed specifically to the ancestor in the underworld. Whereas he is not expected to behave much differently there from the way he behaves in the grave or the tablet, his descendants show a markedly different facet of their relationship to the dead in this context. Care of the ancestor in the underworld is characterized by solicitous concern and affectionate remembrance. After the funeral and burial rites are over, the ancestor is contacted in the underworld not out of fear that his dissatisfaction there may lead to trouble for the living but rather out of a desire to perpetuate cherished relationships.

The first of the rites directed unambiguously toward the dead in the underworld takes place on the evening of the funeral. At some point after death the soul, or one of the souls, of the deceased is said to proceed to the world of *im*, the underworld. There he is judged by the rulers of the underworld: if he is found guilty of any serious crimes, such as murder, theft, or unfilial behavior, he is sentenced to punishment; and if he is judged extraordinarily worthy, he is allowed to go to heaven (*thi:*), to live forever in comfort and plenty. In fact, however, neither prospect is a real possibility for the ordinary person. Only an extremely exceptional man would have a chance of going to *thi:*, I was told, and nowadays, no one is that exceptional. Failing this, the deceased must wait the allotted time for his reincarnation, when, depending on the quality of his life, he will be reborn as a rich man, a poor man, an animal, or even a plant. The chance of being punished for crimes is as unlikely as the possibility of going to *thi:*. The punishments the rulers of the underworld can mete out are graphically depicted on scrolls that Taoist priests bring to funerals. On them one can see a full range of punishments, from a tormented man with knives protruding from every part of his body because he was a thief, to a man being lowered into boiling liquid because he was unfilial. In spite of the detail of these tortures, most people insisted that none of their ancestors would suffer them. Although they admit that everyone has committed some wrong or other, they assert that the performance of certain rites on the eve of the funeral will cancel out all misdemeanors and "make it as though they had never been committed."

The performance of these rites, known as *kong-tiek*, requires the services of a Taoist priest and several assistants; these last may double as musicians and acrobats if necessary. In the following descriptions, I focus on the events that were most important to the people of Ch'inan, events that they could explain to me as the rites were in progress or when they were over. They did not understand many of the details of the rites, and claimed that these were secrets and understood only by the Taoist priests. Consequently, I can describe only a small fraction of the rituals that make up a *kong-tiek*. Still, my description is fairly representative of the villagers' perceptions. Although they realize that the priest carries out many rites in which they do not directly take part, they are content to feel that "he knows what he is doing," and that "it will somehow help the dead." The events I describe serve at the least to demonstrate that the deceased is cared for in the underworld, one other context besides the grave and the hall.

The ceremonies of *kong-tiek* are intended specifically to benefit the person who has just died, though ancestors who died earlier and have not yet received a *kong-tiek* may also benefit. The rites are focused on the individual by the use of a paper figure to represent the deceased.* This figure, which is purchased, depicts a young or old man or woman, depending on the person's sex and the age at death. As the rites progress, the figure is moved around the scene of action to illustrate the deceased's role in the events in process. In the first event of the evening a square table is set up in an open area in front of the hall with its legs resting on four benches so as to elevate it about three feet above its normal height. The priest and his assistants, in colorful yellow or purple robes, begin to weave slowly in and out around it. One assistant holds the paper figure of the ancestor, another the paper figure of a horse. The men increase their speed, dodging in and out, some running in one direction, some in another. The strident noise of horns and a furious drumbeat urge them on to a frenzied pace. They maintain this furious pace until their strength gives out, then run out of the cleared area. Immediately they are replaced by some men (or on occasion just one man) who execute a series of acrobatic and balancing acts. Many different stunts are performed depending on the talents of the performers. Some balance chairs and tables on their clenched teeth, others do tumbling and cartwheels. All performances, however, include several acts with burning implements. In one, kerosene-soaked rags on the end of a long bamboo pole are set afire, and the pole is then twirled around with great speed. In another, rags are lit at both ends of a rope, which the performer holds in his mouth. Thereupon he twists his head back and forth so that the rope ends spin about his head very rapidly, the flames making a loud roar. The onlooking crowd is

---

* Though in the following discussion I refer to a single paper figure, there are often several paper figures for other ancestors when they are included in the ceremonies.

alternately frightened by flying sparks (and an occasional flying rope or pole) and delighted by an especially daring act.

All of these performances are said to act out the travels of the dead person to the underworld. The chase around the table represents the first stages of the trip, when the deceased rides a horse that carries paper money for him to spend when he needs it. The spinning torches are to "open the gate" (*khui-mng*) for him. Because the road to the underworld is beset by dangerous monsters and unknown obstacles, the deceased might succumb to some fatal disaster long before arriving unless he receives help.

The next event marks the arrival of the deceased at the gates of the underworld. The paper figure of the deceased is moved to the central, elevated table. Then someone, usually the priest, stands on a bench alongside the table, and in a loud, commanding voice reads out from a document prepared beforehand the deceased's name and address, and then the names of his or her ascendants and descendants. People said the information was read out so the underworld officials would be able to identify the new arrival. In this way the reading of this document ties the performance of the *kong-tiek* to the individual it is to benefit. Hence, the people say that this moment marks one of the most essential points in all the ceremonies. After this, it is assured that any crimes or wrongs committed by the deceased will be erased.

The final major performance of the *kong-tiek* both completes the travels of the dead person into the underworld and establishes firmly that he will be secure from any harm. To set the stage, two tables are now placed about 15 feet apart in the open area in front of the hall, and a single length of cloth, of the sort commonly used to tie a small child to its mother's back, is stretched between them. The paper figure of the deceased is moved onto the table farthest from the hall along with an incense pot. When all is arranged, a musician plays a jaunty tune on a stringed instrument while one of the priest's assistants hobbles in, dressed like an old man. With his white beard, staff, and bent frame, he is immediately recognized by everyone as Tho-te-kong, the earth god. At first, the god simply wanders around the audience, making jokes and delighting the children, but eventually, the priest, who acts as the descendants' emissary, tells him that someone needs help crossing the bridge into the underworld. At this the cloth stretched between the two tables becomes the center of attention as a representation of the bridge. Tho-te-kong begins to circle the bridge, followed by a line of the deceased's direct descendants. As they circle, Tho-te-kong talks about how difficult it is to cross the bridge without the help of a god because of the terrible monsters and demons waiting below to snatch up anyone who takes a wrong step. The descendants, knowing that the god must be paid for such an invaluable service, drop coins into a bowl under the table every time they complete a circle. Tho-te-kong leads them on and on, until the amount of money collected satisfies him. He often urges them to make more donations by exclaiming that the prices of food and medicine have gone up recently, and that a person needs more money to live on today. Occasionally, the priest interrupts to plead that there is enough money in the pot and to ask that Tho-te-kong consent to lead the deceased across. Finally, the god agrees, collects his money, and hobbles off stage. Then, after one of the descendants takes up the paper figure and another the incense pot, they slowly walk the length of the cloth bridge, sliding the figure along until they reach the other side. Once there, the descendants kneel before the figure. Directed by the priest, the eldest son throws a pair of coins used to divine the will of the recently deceased. When at last both coins land up, all is well with the deceased; he has arrived in the underworld safely and has found conditions good there.

Once the coins land up, whether on the first or tenth try, everyone present helps carry a great many piles of thick, white, paper money, which is said to be the principal currency of the underworld, to a suitable place for burning. The descendants stand in a circle around the money, and, after the pile has been lit, they join hands. They must maintain unbroken contact around the fire until the last ash has burned down; otherwise, the money would not be able to reach their ancestor because ghosts, the souls of other dead people, would be able to snatch it. This act completes the *kong-tiek* and ensures the dead a comfortable place in the underworld for a time. He has been safely guided across the dangerous outskirts of the underworld and has been given ample funds to provide himself with food and protection while he is there.

After the *kong-tiek* is over, the dead person is still not left to his own resources in the underworld. Beginning with the seventh day after the funeral, seven offerings are made for him at seven-day intervals. The first of these is said to help the deceased make the emotional adjustment to his new life in the underworld. Early in the morning of the seventh day, Tho-te-kong leads the ancestor to a lake in the underworld where he must wash his hands. When he sees that the water has made his fingernails turn black (i.e., begin to rot), he knows for the first time that he is dead. From there he is led to a mountain from which he is allowed one last glimpse of his living relatives. In anticipation of the terrible grief and sorrow the ancestor must feel on that day, the descendants rise very early to make offerings and to weep for him. They say, "If we get up early enough to wail before the ancestor finds out he is really dead, then his own sorrow will be lessened. The more we weep, the less he must."

Weeping and wailing take place at the other six offerings as well. Here, in contrast to the perfunctory offerings made at the hall on an ancestor's death-day anniversary, emphasis is on the emotional state of the deceased, not just on whether or not he has enough to eat. Accordingly, the food presented in these offerings is for the rulers of the underworld in the hope that they will not be harsh in their judgment of the deceased. Some people believe that during the 49 days after a man's funeral he moves through seven (some say ten) halls or palaces in the underworld, being judged by a different official in each one. Whether or not everyone in the village has so clear an idea of what happens in the underworld, they all believe that the dead need the help of the living to escape punishment. The *kong-tiek*, the vast quantities of paper money, and the seven offerings are all designed to keep the deceased from suffering. It is as though people were empathizing with the dead through these offerings; they imagine what it is like to realize that one is dead or to be held accountable for all one's past deeds. The rites of the first 49 days after the funeral express the preoccupation of the living with the experiences of the dead.

The final series of rites during these 49 days even more explicitly expresses the concern of the living with the comfort and ease of the deceased. At the time of the funeral the sons of the deceased order a number of small-scale replicas of everyday necessities and coveted luxuries made of bamboo splints and paper. At the least a modest house is included, perhaps with only one square room. If the sons decide to spend more, they may order a house with three rooms or even one with two stories. The houses, normally about five feet tall, stand at about table height on a scaffolding of bamboo splints. Their roofs have curved eaves like the roofs of the Ui and Lou halls; their outer walls are decorated with multicolored bits of paper, foil, and mirrors, producing a dazzling effect. Inside, paper is used to simulate elaborate furnishings, such as beds with comforters and pillows, windows, chests, dressers with mirrors, sofas, and chairs.

The most elaborate array of paper objects I saw was for a woman in the Li lineage. Outside of her large, three-room house stood representations of two armed door guards. Inside the front gate, in the open courtyard, were replicas of an electric fan, two television sets, an electric rice pot, a washing machine, a car with large tail fins, a radio, lawn furniture, and a refrigerator, along with several servants wielding mops and brooms. The entire display was arranged in the Li ancestral hall; on an adjacent table stood a paper figure representing the deceased woman. Just as the rites at seven-day intervals express concern with the experiences of the deceased, so the purchase of paper houses and domestic furnishings show concern with the minutiae of the ancestor's daily existence. Relatives sometimes carry on long discussions while gazing at the paper house, enumerating all the comforts provided for the dead. Those close to the deceased are clearly anxious about the precise conditions of the ancestor's existence in the underworld.

At some propitious day and hour within the 49-day period, the deceased is "moved in" (*zip-chu*) to his new house in the underworld. This event parallels closely the same event, moving into a new house, in the *iong* world. In both instances a propitious day must be chosen; in both cases a kind of sweet soup made of red and white balls of ground glutinous rice is served. The most complicated *zip-chu* ceremony I saw involved two paper houses, one of which was for an old man, the most recently deceased member of the family. Because several people who died before him had not had a *kong-tiek* or paper houses made for them, these were provided for them along with his. Paper images representing seven people were made for the *kong-tiek*. The same seven—the old man, his mother and father, his adopted daughter, his elder brother and sister-in-law, and his younger brother—were moved into paper houses on the chosen day. At the beginning of the ceremony, paper images of the elder brother and his wife, who reportedly had not gotten along with the rest of the family, were moved into a one-room paper house. The other five images were moved into a larger, three-room house. Following this, several bowls of sweet rice-ball soup and an appropriate number of chopsticks were arranged in front of the houses. Three cups of wine and a pack of cigarettes were added for the pleasure of the recently deceased man because "he drank wine and smoked cigarettes every night. Unless we provide those things for him, he will not be happy." To see whether or not he and the others were satisfied, a pair of divining coins was thrown. Since both landed up, indicating that all was well, the ceremony was at once concluded by serving everyone a bowl of sweet rice-ball soup.

The paper ménage remains in the hall until about the forty-ninth day after the funeral. At whatever hour the geomancer determines is most propitious, the house and all inside it are burned in order to transfer the goods entirely to the underworld. After various offerings have been made to the deceased, the pair of divining coins is thrown to see that he is satisfied with the preparations. A slip of paper giving the dimensions of the paper house and a list of its contents is burned so the waiting ancestor will know what to expect and can be sure to collect everything. The burning itself takes place outdoors. While the house is being moved outside, great care must be exercised to avoid damaging the delicate structure. (The Li *tang-ki* told me that a family once inadvertently knocked off part of the roof of a house before burning it. Immediately afterward, people fell sick and things went wrong in the household. The accepted explanation was that the ancestor was unhappy because his house had arrived with a hole in the roof, allowing rain to come in. After the family burned a paper replica of the part of the roof that was damaged, their problems ended.) Once the house is transferred safely outside, it is carefully arranged so that the floor is level, lest the ancestor receive a crooked house, be uncomfortable, and return to cause trouble. When the house is finally arranged, bags of wood shavings and paper money are piled in the empty spaces under the floor, a match is touched to the shavings, and the whole edifice is consumed in a tower of flames.

Although the burning of the house marks the end of a sequence of acts for the dead in the underworld (by the forty-ninth day the deceased has been judged, redeemed, and safely ensconced in his new house), it does not mark the end of contact between the residents of the *im* and *iong* worlds. At times, with the help of an appropriate ritual specialist, people are able to descend into the underworld in hopes of catching a glimpse of a deceased relative or of finding an explanation of misfortune in the *iong* world.

I witnessed seven such "excursions" in Ch'inan, all in the Ong settlement. They occurred whenever Tiu: Ho-cui, a resident of Sanhsia who was a friend of many of the Ongs, came to visit. Referred to by the villagers as the *tang-ki*, he possessed the necessary knowledge of incantations that make "looking around the underworld" (*kuan-louq-im*) possible. People in the other settlements had less access to a *tang-ki* who was able to lead them to the underworld; to make a visit, they had to attend a session in the Ong settlement or travel to a *tang-ki* in T'aoyüan, a market town to the west of Sanhsia. Consequently, the Ongs were far more knowledgeable about the underworld than the other villagers. Although almost everyone in the other settlements had heard of trips to the underworld, not everyone had witnessed one.

Talk of a trip to the underworld usually began whenever the *tang-ki* arrived. But before he would arrange a trip he made sure there was sufficient interest among the Ongs. For each inquiry directed to a resident of the underworld he charged NT $10, and he told me it was not worth the trouble unless he could earn over NT $100 an evening. To ensure that sum he needed at least five or six people who would agree to ask questions. In addition, he needed the services of Ong Bieng-tiek, a young man who acted as his informal assistant.

Since this practice has not been adequately described in the literature, I shall go into considerable detail on one trip I saw while in Ch'inan. On this occasion, as on most, Ong Bieng-tiek circulated through the settlement at dusk after people had finished eating dinner, announcing that a trip to the underworld would be starting soon. On the way he stopped at the small local store to buy several packs of paper money and incense. Meanwhile, the *tang-ki* made his ritual preparations in a small house on the outskirts of the settlement, which the residents had vacated for the evening. First, he arranged bowls of fruit and candy on a table to serve as offerings to whichever god came to lead people to the underworld. This done, he wrote out several name and address forms, leaving blank spaces for a name and house number but filling in "Ong settlement, Ch'inan Li, Sanhsia Chen, Taipei Hsien" on each. These he would complete later when he learned which relatives the participants wished to contact. A few early arrivals stood around chatting as they folded paper money in half or rolled it into funnels for easy burning.

After a while, when about ten adults and twice as many children had arrived, the *tang-ki* announced that only those who wished to attempt to go to the underworld could have their feet on the floor. All but four of those present scrambled up on one of the two platform beds in the room while the would-be travelers, two middle-aged men, a young man, and a young woman, took seats on tall stools alongside the offering table. The atmosphere was excited, very like the feeling at the start of an excursion: children giggled and shrieked at each other, adults chattered loudly. When the four candidates for the trip were seated, perched straight-backed on the stools, blindfolded and hands resting on their knees, Ong

Bieng-tiek, the *tang-ki's* assistant, began to beat a wooden clapper loudly and steadily on the table, making a strident, piercing "Clap, clap, clap." The *tang-ki* lit incense and offered it, facing out the open door. Then returning to the center of the room, he chanted the names of several gods (among them Co-su-kong), burned several slips of paper with these names written on them, and placed the ashes in a small bowl of water, attempting to entreat some god to come and possess the body of one of the candidates in order to lead him to the underworld. Although everyone was sure that a god's presence was necessary for the trip, it actually seemed to be of little account. The *tang-ki* chanted the gods' names frequently during the first part of the session and kept people away from the open door so the gods could enter, but after one of the candidates had entered a trance, it was taken that he had been possessed by a god, and nothing more was mentioned on the subject. The man in the trance was treated not like a god but like himself; he was ordered to go or not to go to various places at the will of the *tang-ki*.

While the clapper beat continuously, the *tang-ki* repeated the names of the gods and burned incense and paper money under the noses of the four candidates. Occasionally, he would sprinkle them with water from the bowl in which he had placed the ashes of paper with the gods' names written on them, stamping his foot and shouting "Go! Go!" After about an hour of this treatment, three of the four were shaking periodically but were jerking "awake" in between spells. The fourth, the young woman, an Ong daughter-in-law, got up, declaring that she was giving up because it was too uncomfortable sitting on the stool. Now the *tang-ki* concentrated all his attention on one of the middle-aged men, Ong Kim-ci:, filling the air around his head with smoke, shouting at him to "Go!" and feeling his hands to see if they were cold. (The *tang-ki* explained later that he could always tell when someone was beginning the trip because his hands would grow icy cold.) Kim-ci: responded to the extra attention and began to shake more and more steadily, his hands lightly patting his knees. Finally, he said quietly, in a low voice, "There's no road." At that everyone knew he had entered the underworld; the other men were shaken awake so they could watch the proceedings.

The next series of events were concerned with helping the traveler over the hurdles at the entrance to the underworld, much as the *kong-tiek* is designed to help the deceased find his way there. When Kim-ci: repeated that he could not find the road, the *tang-ki* decided that the problem must be Tho-te-kong, wanting money. Accordingly, he began to burn paper money on the floor in front of Kim-ci:. "No, no," said Kim-ci:. "He won't let me through. The people here won't put down the bridge and let me over." The *tang-ki* kept on burning money, saying that it was perfectly good money, and that Kim-ci: should just go on across the bridge. "No," Kim-ci: repeated. "They won't let me over. They say to find another road." "All right," replied the *tang-ki*, "find another one, but hurry up."

Once Kim-ci: was on the move again, he began to shake more vigorously. His feet jogged up and down, and his head moved slowly from side to side as if he were looking for something. His travels were punctuated by frequent remarks, such as "No road at all" and "Have to climb these mountains." Finally, he found another bridge, and after the *tang-ki* burned some money, the black-faced man who guarded it allowed Kim-ci: to cross. Still, his adventures were far from finished. He described himself as climbing laboriously up mountains without end. When he said he saw horses, the *tang-ki* urged him to mount one so as to make better speed. "No," Kim-ci: said. "They won't let me get on." Soon after, he said that he saw Tho-te-kong. "Ask him if you have arrived yet," said the *tang-ki*. "He says I'm not there yet," replied Kim-ci:. Then, seeing terrible animals with the heads of horses or pigs and the bodies of other animals, he said urgently, "I'm frightened; I don't want to go on." The *tang-ki* tried to reassure him and urged him to continue. "How can it be so far?" Kim-ci: asked. "I've been walking so far, and I'm not there yet." At this, one of the other men asked if he saw any cars he could ride in. In response, Kim-ci: stopped jogging his feet and moved his head around and around, looking, but he was unable to find a car. Eventually, after more walking and looking, he said he could see some houses ahead. This seemed to be a cue for everyone in the room to relax: Kim-ci: was out of the wild, mountainous border zone between the *iong* and *im* worlds, and had arrived at a different, but ordered, place.

According to the *tang-ki*, the underworld is organized into ten kingdoms or palaces, each ruled by one of the officials of the underworld. Each kingdom is a replica of the *iong* world, containing the same cities, towns, and villages in the same relationship to each other as in the *iong* world. After judgment, each person is sent to one of the kingdoms, depending on the date of his birth and hence the animal sign under which he was born. Most of the villagers have a simpler picture. For them, there is only one kingdom, which is a complete replica of the *iong* world. When people die they go to live in the area of the underworld that corresponds to the *iong*-world town or village they lived in. This disparity of views accounts for some of the confusion in the rest of Ong Kim-ci:'s narration of his trip through the underworld.

As soon as Kim-ci: said he could see houses ahead, the *tang-ki* took up one of the address forms he had made and filled in the name and house number of one of the relatives Kim-ci: wanted to visit. Burning the paper, he then instructed Kim-ci: to travel to the second kingdom. Kim-ci: obediently walked on awhile, then cried out that he saw his grandfather off in the distance. "He's too far away, he doesn't see me. Why won't my grandfather turn and look at me?" The *tang-ki* told him to call out to his grandfather, but Kim-ci: just kept repeating that his grandfather did not see him. "Grandfather does have a house, though, and it looks fine," he added.

At this point, one of the onlookers told the *tang-ki* he wanted to contact his mother, who, I learned later, had hanged herself at the age of forty-nine. The *tang-ki* consulted a book to see what kingdom the woman should be in, then sent the traveler there. Shortly, Kim-ci: announced that he could see the woman he was seeking, together with her father-in-law. The *tang-ki* consulted his book again to see whether or not both should be in the same kingdom. According to his calculations they should not have been, but Kim-ci: was not deterred. He went on trying to talk to the woman, who ignored him or did not realize he was there.

Walking on a bit, Kim-ci: said he could see his elder brother sleeping in bed. Throughout the following episode, Kim-ci: leaned forward, his head stretched out and inclined to one side, just as if he were scrutinizing the face of a sleeping person. He spoke to his brother, calling out, "Elder brother! Elder brother!," but received no response. The *tang-ki* burned money to encourage him to answer. Soon Kim-ci: reported that his brother had received the money and had placed it on his bed, but still showed no sign of recognition. He only covered his eyes with his arm and lay there smiling. The *tang-ki* burned more money and told Kim-ci: to call his brother again. But Kim-ci: reported, "He is getting out of bed and going away." Burying his face in his hands, Kim-ci: began to cry, saying, "My brother won't talk to me. My own brother won't talk to me." After a few minutes of sobbing, he raised his head and looked around, commenting that his brother's house looked fine and was staffed with two servants. Trying to divert him from the loss of his brother, the *tang-ki* asked him who lived next door. Kim-ci: looked over that way and said, "I thought I knew who that was, but he turned his back on me before I could see. What is the use of my coming here if no one will talk to me? I'm going home."

The *tang-ki* suggested that Kim-ci: travel around a bit more, but he was adamant about wanting to return. The trip back was not as difficult as the arrival. The *tang-ki* simply read an incantation from a sheet of paper, ending with the command, "Come back! Come back!" And several people called out Kim-ci:'s name. He slowly stopped shaking and became still. In a few minutes, he removed his blindfold and dazedly wiped the tears from his eyes. He apparently remembered what had happened because he kept repeating that his brother would not talk to him. The experience must have been exhausting, for he promptly went to one of the beds, and making room for himself, stretched out and fell asleep.

No sooner had Kim-ci: stepped down from his stool than Ong

Bieng-tiek, the *tang-ki*'s assistant, took it, saying he wanted to go for a tour of the underworld. This young man, as always, went into a trance very quickly, after about ten minutes of clapper-beating and chanting by the *tang-ki,* and then crossed the border of the *im* world in a few minutes. The *tang-ki* at once sent him to see the garden of the underworld. There he described the flowers, their marvelous shapes and unusual colors and scents. The onlookers questioned him freely, often laughing at his responses. Next directed to one of the prisons where wrong-doers are punished, he reported seeing a man being crushed in a rice-grinder, his blood flowing out in a constant stream. After describing another man, who was tied to a red-hot iron pillar, Bieng-tiek turned away in disgust.

Here let me interrupt briefly to say that every person in the *iong* world is believed to have a house in the underworld, which along with its garden and the tree growing there, represents him or her in the *im* world. In the case of women the tree in the garden is a flowering one. On trips to the underworld, people often request the traveler to visit their houses and trees, hoping that the condition of one or the other may be the cause of some trouble in the *iong* world, and that they can arrange to have the problem fixed so the *iong* world will right itself.

To resume my narrative, the *tang-ki,* allowing that young Bieng-tiek had seen enough torture, now instructed him to go to the second kingdom and see his tree. When he arrived there, he reported that the kitchen was very dirty, and that, moreover, the roots of his tree were sickly, and one of its branches had been eaten away by bugs. Hearing this, the *tang-ki* burned a packet of paper money, telling Bieng-tiek to hire some workmen to come clean the house where it was dirty and fix the tree where it was damaged. As we shall see later, the condition of the tree and the house usually reflects the physical condition of the person they represent.

After Bieng-tiek had arranged for his tree to be repaired, he set off on his own to "tour around." On the way he saw many paddy fields, which like those in the *iong* world were ready for planting. He also saw shops selling noodles, fruit, and medicine, much like a street scene in any small town. As soon as he began to describe a group of girls walking along the street, the *tang-ki* began to read an incantation that brought the young man back into the *iong* world. The *tang-ki* said later that if Bieng-tiek had been attracted to one of the girls, he might have refused to leave the underworld, remaining there forever. On other occasions, Bieng-tiek has stayed in the underworld longer, touring more extensively and describing such things as motion-picture theaters and houses of prostitution. In most cases, his descriptions prompted both great hilarity and great amazement: hilarity at his youthful enjoyment of girls and movies, and amazement at how similar the underworld is to the *iong* world.

It is plain that there is a very different emphasis when the dead are contacted in the underworld as compared with the hall or the grave. There, they are not sought out just because they are ascendants or because they left property behind; nor are they regarded as dangerously powerful creatures, as at the grave. Descendants are under no avowed obligation to visit their ancestors regularly in the underworld; when they have a chance to do so, they tend to seek out those they remember especially vividly or with whom they have some special business. By far the most frequently met relatives are the parents, who are usually the most recently dead relatives and probably the most clearly remembered. Kim-ci:'s contact with his grandfather was the only instance I know of in which an ancestor in the second ascending generation was seen in the underworld.

The second most frequently met people in the underworld share the characteristic of having died prematurely under unusual circumstances. Often people who die young do not receive the full complement of rites for the dead; they will be buried properly, but the large expenditure involved in the *kong-tiek* may not be made for them. Perhaps because these omissions directly affect their comfort in the underworld, their relatives worry about the conditions they are living under there. Sometimes this worry extends beyond the immediate relatives: a visitor will announce that he sees a person who has died prematurely or violently even though the close relatives have not asked him to seek that person out. For example, one time a traveler in the underworld said he could see a group of young men who had been killed in a coal mine accident. They refused to talk to him because they were naked, having no clothes to wear. Finally, they agreed to answer his questions if he would turn his back. The rest of the report described the dreadful conditions under which the men had to live out their time in the underworld. In another case, the traveler spotted a woman who had died at thirty years of age. In dying so young she was considered to have committed an unfilial act, and in consequence, even though she had borne children for her husband's family, they refused to burn a paper house for her. According to the traveler, she had no house to live in, and having been given no money to spend, had to engage in hard labor to earn enough to buy food.

The living also seem preoccupied with those among the dead whose dreams or lives were unfulfilled at death. The best example of this involves a girl who died at age eighteen, before marriage. Virtually every time a trip was made to the underworld in the Ong settlement, her relatives would try to communicate with her. When sickness in the family was attributed to the girl's desire to be married posthumously, several attempts were made to determine her choice of a marriage partner. One time, she was asked if she still wanted a marriage arranged. After she replied affirmatively, her sister-in-law asked her whom she wanted to marry. She replied that it was a Li man who had died at the age of twenty-six. Although they plied her with further questions about who the man was, she would reply only that he would somehow identify himself. When I left the village, negotiations were still going on over the girl's marriage.

What of the dead whose personalities are no longer distinctly remembered? The answer seems to be that they are neither seen nor visited in the underworld. For one thing, as the memory of an individual fades, he ceases to exist in the underworld for the living; and for another, as time passes, a dead person moves closer and closer to the point when he will leave the underworld by means of reincarnation. That the dimly remembered dead cease to be visited in the underworld and that rebirth takes place from the underworld is an entirely appropriate conjunction. Regarded in this way, the apparent inconsistency between the concept of the reincarnation of the dead into another personality or form of life and the concept of their continued existence on ancestral altars and in their graves is lessened. The ancestors live on in the underworld as intimately remembered loved ones. When that facet of their existence is lost, they disappear from the underworld both by reincarnation and by relegation to oblivion. This disappearance does not conflict with their continued worship at altars and graves, for, as we have discussed, other aspects of the ancestors' personalities are reflected in those places.

Now that we have traveled to the underworld, so to speak, we are in a better position to relate that world to the wider world view of the Taiwanese. As we have seen, the *im* world is not conceived as a direct opposite of the everyday *iong* world. Indeed, quite the contrary, the two worlds are precisely alike in many ways: the crops are planted at the same time, and the stores and houses in the *im* world are replicas of their *iong* counterparts. Moreover, even the aspects of the underworld that are different, such as the places of punishment for wrongs committed during life, are but extensions of *iong* institutions, in this case, earthly courts of law. To understand how the two worlds complement each other, let us take a closer look at the *im* house and its tree as representations of the bodies of living men and women.

Together the house and tree are capable of representing every part of the human body. Ordinarily, the tree roots stand for the feet and the tree itself for reproductive functions. If the *im* roots are pushed up out of the ground, for example, or are bug-infested, workmen will be hired to fix them so the *iong* feet can recover. Similarly, the flowers on a woman's tree are given the greatest attention, for they stand for the children she has borne or will bear. There is a bud for each child the woman is to bear; as soon as she bears one, a flower opens and drops off. A stillborn child or one who dies at birth is represented by a sick, damaged-looking

flower that remains on the tree. Most often, a traveler who is sent
to view the tree of a woman finds nothing wrong with the flowers.
He simply describes how many flowers have bloomed and dropped
off, and how many buds are still on the tree. Occasionally, a woman
who has had trouble bearing children asks about her tree. In one
instance, a young Ong woman who had had several early miscar-
riages asked a traveler to check hers. He reported that he saw no
sign of flowers there, either in bud or on the ground, and that,
further, there was a white tiger sitting in wait below the tree; it
was the source of all of her trouble because it had been eating any
flowers that grew on the tree, i.e., any fetuses she had carried. He
advised her to make special offerings to the white tiger to appease
it and encourage it to leave her flowers alone. I was told that if all
else fails, an extreme measure that will correct childlessness is to
hire workmen to uproot and remove a woman's tree, planting
another in its place.

The house alongside the tree continues the analogy with the
human body. According to the *tang-ki,* the roof of the house corresponds to the head; the walls to the outer layer of the body, the
skin; the stove top to the face; the door of the stove to the mouth;
the electric light (a modern touch) to the eyes; the bricks at the
bottom of the stove to the intestines; the floor of the house to the
urinary system; and the well to the organs of the body, such as the
heart and liver. Hence, when a traveler tells someone that his well
water is muddy or that the walls of his house are dirty, the person
knows that something is wrong with his organs or his skin, as the
case may be. By this scheme, if the house and tree are visualized
on top of one another (see Fig. 4), the parts of the body they represent fall roughly in the same order as in the human body. This
arrangement also shows that all the "dirty" or unmentionable
things—the functions of urination and reproduction, and the feet,
which the villagers think of as inherently filthy and smelly—are
grouped together.

Although only the *tang-ki* was able to give me such a detailed
analysis, almost everyone knew something about correspondences
between the body and its house and tree, most commonly those

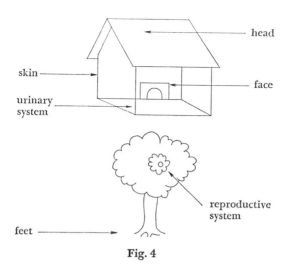

Fig. 4

linking the roof to the head, a woman's flowers to her children, and
the roots to the feet. There is some individual variation in how
other parts of the body are said to correspond to parts of the tree
or house. This leaves room for the person with a dirty well, say, to
assume that the well stands for whichever internal organ is causing
him discomfort. At the least it is clear that a great many villagers
engage in speculation about the relation of the body to its tree and
house; it is not an esoteric matter restricted to ritual experts.

Although the underworld house and tree are usually linked to
the body and its physical state, the condition of the house may also
reflect a social ill on occasion. Once, A-iong, the stubborn old man
who refuses to vacate the abandoned Ong hall, asked a traveler to
look at his house. His health had been poor recently, and he
thought something in his house might need repair. But when the
traveler arrived there, he reported, "The whole house is bad and
should be knocked down." A-iong's refusal to move from his offending house was the source of his social trouble, the hostility
toward him in the community. It was this fault, rather than some
physical trouble, that was reflected in his underworld house.

In some ways the relationship between the underworld house
and the body it represents seems like that between the *te-li* and the

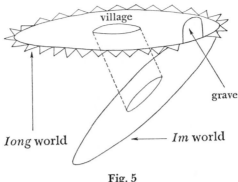

Fig. 5

social groups they represent. It is not clear whether a trouble in the *iong* body brings about a corresponding trouble in the *im* tree, or vice versa. It may be that like *te-li* and social groups, the two are not so much causally related as associated with each other. A fault in one corresponds to a fault in the other; fixing one implies that the other is also fixed. One can both act to change conditions in the *im* world with some prospect of changing the situation in the *iong* world and remedy some physical ill with the expectation of automatically righting a corresponding fault in the underworld tree or house. In the sense that acting on the *im* world is a route by which people can correct trouble in the *iong* world, the two worlds are complementary.

This relationship between the two worlds extends to other contexts as well. Represented graphically, the villagers' view of the relationship between the *iong* and *im* worlds would look something like the diagram in Fig. 5. The grave, located in the mountains of the *iong* world, is one gateway to the *im* world. Here *iong* and *im* come close to overlapping; the ancestor in the grave is said to be *im*, and *im* spirits of the unknown dead are said to hover about graves. There are other routes to the underworld, such as the ones used when the *tang-ki* leads a person in trance across mountains and wild lands to those parts of the underworld that correspond to the *iong* world (dotted lines in the figure). Many of the important aspects of the *im* world are related to trouble, sickness, or injury in the *iong* world. We have seen earlier how the ancestor in his grave is often seen as the source of sickness and trouble in families. This is true also of the ancestor occupying his paper house in the underworld. And then there are the ghosts, or spirits of the unknown dead (*kui*), which the people blame for many, if not most, of their illnesses. All these troubles can be ameliorated by acting on the inhabitants of the *im* world or taking steps in their behalf: the grave or house of the ancestor can be repaired; food and money can be offered to ghosts to encourage them to return to the *im* world. Likewise, if the source of trouble is one's own *im* house or tree, steps can be taken to correct the problem.

It is as though when the expected and hoped-for order of good health and plenty in the *iong* world is disrupted, the source of the trouble can almost automatically be sought in the *im* world. The *iong* and *im* are not opposed to each other as order and chaos, but rather complement each other, the possibility of modifying the *im* world leading to the possibility of increasing the desired conditions in the *iong* world. When there is trouble in the *iong* world, it is most often said to be a result of an intrusion of the *im*: an ancestor or ghost is making trouble; one's house or tree needs repair. Paradoxically, identification of trouble with *im* agents both pins the blame on them and provides a way for the living to try to clear up the trouble by propitiating or modifying them. In this sense, when the fabric of order in the *iong* world is rent, the *im* world acts like a patch, allowing people to take action that may correct the defect.

Although the two worlds are complementary rather than antithetical, they cannot freely intermix. In many respects, as we have seen, the *iong* and *im* worlds are very similar. Yet despite this continuity, they are kept very separate. The villagers often told me, for example, that the spirits or souls of the dead (*kui*) cannot leave the *im* world at will. Those ghosts that are abroad in the *iong* world have been given permission to leave the *im* world by the king of the underworld. A spirit may be granted such permission if it receives no offerings from the living and needs to return to the *iong* world in the guise of a hungry ghost to snatch what it can from them. A hungry ghost almost by definition has no relatives because presumably no one would neglect a deceased relative entirely. Other *kui* may occasionally be allowed to leave the *im* world simply to visit their old home or to travel around the *iong* world, but as a rule the number of *kui* that are allowed to leave is limited. Only on the occasion of the ghost festival, which falls on the fifteenth of the seventh month, is the restriction on travel to the *iong* world lifted. On this day, the king of the underworld to said to throw open the gates of the *im* world and allow ghosts to leave as they wish. Consequently, the villagers make extensive offerings to the dead on this day, both to those dead to whom they owe an obligation (mostly their ancestors) and, separately, to hungry ghosts and other *kui* that may be in their vicinity. Except for this unique situation, in which *im* personages fully penetrate the *iong* world, the inhabitants of the underworld are kept carefully apart from the world of the living.

The separation between the two worlds is carried over to the occasions when communication is established between inhabitants of the *im* and *iong* worlds. At those times, as I have described, a resident of the *iong* world must enter a state of trance and, with the help of a god, undergo frightening travels through wild, mountainous country before he reaches his destination. Although communication with the gods is also conducted through a person in trance, the two forms of contact differ greatly. In the one case the god possesses the person, expressing his own words and personality through another's body and voice. A *tang-ki* possessed by Co-su-kong, for example, will become arrogant and insist that those around him accord him the respect due a god. In contrast, the traveler to the underworld shows no marked change in behavior except for the characteristic shaking of the trance state. In no sense is he possessed by the spirits of those he speaks with in the *im* world. When he relays a message, he always prefaces it with "he [or she] says." The tranced traveler retains his own identity. When someone wishes to visit a dead relative, to speak with him directly and observe him, he must himself cross the difficult border between the *iong* and *im* worlds. Because the dead cannot come directly to the living, possessing someone and speaking through him, the distance between the two worlds is emphasized.

In a similar way, communication with the dead in the under-world seems to allow people to express or act out the inevitable consequence of death—the division of the dead from the living and the inability of the two to interact as they once did. In another society in which second burials are the practice, the realization that the dead are irretrievably gone seems to come at that point. Maurice Bloch (1971) suggests that when the Merina of Madagascar practice ritually sacrilegious acts on the corpse of a relative (throwing it about and dancing with it), they are forced to realize that the dead relative is completely dead, "nothing but a pile of dry bones." "The ritually sacrilegious attitude which is forced on the living is one which makes them consider their relatives as irreversibly dead, and consequently separates the dead from them in a definitive manner" (p. 169). In Ch'inan the rites of second burial seem to have the opposite import; there the stress is on the obligation to ensure the continued existence of the deceased. The collecting and cleaning of the bones of the dead is regarded as the utmost in filial behavior, not a shocking sacrilege.

But when we turn to the incidents in the underworld, we do find people expressing a kind of separation between the living and the dead. When the dead are visited, they are often observed to be at a great emotional distance from the living. In the episode I recounted, Ong Kim-ci:'s brother refused to speak with him, though clearly aware of his presence, which he acknowledged by smiling. Nor was this particularly unusual. The dead in the underworld very often refuse to speak with the living, and those who do speak usually break off the conversation abruptly, leaving the questioner upset at how easily the dead can walk away from a once-beloved relative.

In seeking some explanation for this difficulty in communication, I asked several people why the dead in the underworld so often refuse to talk to the living or fail to notice them. Some responded that the dead are afraid to speak lest a visitor become too concerned with their troubles and refuse to return to the *iong* world. Others stressed that people undergo a change in personality at death, becoming "very solitary." These replies seem to reflect two ways of accommodating the loss of familiar, two-way interaction with relatives after death: the dead do still care for us but cannot show it because we would suffer; the dead change beyond recognition and no longer have the same personalities. It is not necessarily that in face of this unresponsiveness people suddenly feel more separated from the dead. Rather, when a living person sees a loved one in the underworld at such a distance and describes the experience to the others present (sometimes expressing his own dismay by weeping), he is outwardly and publicly admitting what he has known inwardly since the death: the close, emotion-laden ties of dependence and support between kin can never be renewed.

Outside the Circle of Bamboo

S O F A R, I have restricted this essay to data gathered in Ch'inan, describing variations in the cult of the dead and lineage organization in one community and emphasizing how coherent the elements of the system are when viewed as parts of a single setting. It is time now to see if some characteristics of the cult occur elsewhere.

Early in my stay in Ch'inan, I encountered a difficult case that I despaired of ever understanding. This involved a family living in a village called Chulun, located several miles farther up the Hengch'i River toward the mountains. Although surnamed Ong, these people are not related to the Ch'inan Ongs. Still, their ancestors are said to have come from Anch'i on the mainland; also, they have affinal ties with the Lous in Ch'inan. Earlier, I suggested that certain historical peculiarities of settlement in Ch'inan account for some characteristics of the cult of the dead and lineage organization there. In particular, I held that settling in an area set off by natural barriers, confronting the aborigines together, and cooperating in the building of an irrigation network led the four agnatic settlements to see themselves as separate parts of a single political and territorial system. All the same, it is clear that historical development alone cannot account for the form of the cult of the dead, since some of the same characteristics I found in Ch'inan mark the cult as it is practiced by the Ongs of Chulun.

I first became aware of this unusual case while visiting an old lady who acts as a go-between for many marriages in Hengch'i. She and her family live in an isolated, U-shaped compound in the midst of paddy fields in Chulun. All the tablets for their ancestors are kept in a central room, set aside for common use. As we sat in this room, another old lady came in carrying a tray loaded with rice and three kinds of cooked food—a whole chicken, a fish, and a slab of pork. Because these are the offerings that are usually reserved for Tho-te-kong, I was astonished when she presented them, not in front of his image on the right side of the altar, but in front of a small ancestral tablet on a separate shelf to the left of the altar. The go-between explained that the ancestor in the tablet was the man who had originally cleared and settled the land. After he was killed by aborigines, the land had been taken over by some people named Lim. Still later, the Ongs' ancestors had begun to till the land as tenants of the Lims. Finally, under the land reform carried out in 1949, the Ongs became the legal owners. The Lims had worshiped, and the Ongs continue to worship, the original settler, who at his death had declared his intention to remain in the area eating the produce of the land he had cleared. The Ongs worship him on all major feasts, such as New Year and the Winter Solstice, and before each rice crop is harvested.

Comparing this case with what we found in Ch'inan, we immediately see one familiar theme: the obligation to worship a dead person, related or not, where some strong debt exists. In this case, the original settler expended much effort to clear and defend the land. Because he died before selling the land, and so never was repaid for his efforts while alive, all those who use the land after him are obliged to reimburse him after his death. Since his efforts involved clearing the land, it is appropriate that he be repaid with rice, a direct product of the land, and meat, an indirect product of the land.

To account for the existence of a tablet for the original settler, let us recall the previous analysis of which lineage members receive a tablet. In Ch'inan, as we have seen, anyone who hands down land receives a tablet. Although the original settler did not bequeath his land to the Chulun Lims and Ongs, they obtained it as they would have in inheritance, that is, without the need for payment at the time of transfer. It seems likely that this similarity in the way the land was handed down prompted the Ongs to make a tablet for the original settler. Because he was responsible for obtaining the land in the first place, he deserves a reserved seat on it after his death.

Further, the kind of food offered to the original settler reveals the way in which he is regarded by those who worship him. When discussing the difference in the offerings for ancestors and gods, we discovered that similarity between the food offered and that consumed by those offering it reflects a similarity between the beings who offer the food and those who receive it. Because the original settler is not an ancestor or even an acquaintance of those who offer food to him, it is reasonable that he would not receive ordinary food like that offered to the ancestors. The three whole, cooked kinds of food reflect the distance between him and those offering food to him.

Similarly, the times at which the original settler is worshiped indicate his relationship to those who worship him. Among Ch'inan lineage members, worship on the death-day anniversary of the deceased is a duty one owes only to one's direct ascendants. Since the original settler is not an ascendant of the Ongs who worship him, they worship him only on established calendrical holidays along with the gods and ancestors. In this way, the separate parts of ancestor worship—the times and objects of worship—can again be seen to code social relationships between the living and the dead.

Earlier, we saw that the dead have numerous sanctions at their disposal with which to ensure proper attention from the living. The ancestor as he resides in his grave in particular is liable to cause trouble if his dwelling is neglected or his offerings are inadequate. The Chulun original settler also is in a position to ensure that he receives adequate care. Having been buried near the fields he once tilled, he continues in a sense to be present at that location. Some people said that he visits his grave from time to time; others held that one of his souls is resident there at all times. In either case, he would be in the vicinity of the lands now used by the Chulun Ongs—close enough to cause sickness or harm to those obligated to worship him if they neglected their obligation. The go-between said that the settler is just like the ancestors: "If you don't worship them, they turn into hungry ghosts and return to prey on the living."

In Chulun, as in Ch'inan, the cult of the dead expresses not only relationships between the living and the dead but also social relationships among the living. Although the Chulun Ongs do not have an ancestral hall, as the Ch'inan lineages do, the development of such a hall would not be incompatible with their present social organization. The ancestral tablets of the Chulun Ongs are all kept in the central room of their U-shaped compound; there are no tablets in any other place. Although the room has been rebuilt with funds from all members of the agnatic group descended from the founding ancestor, it is used for domestic as well as ritual functions: visitors are usually entertained there, and everyone feels free to store household goods there. In this it is unlike the Ch'inan halls. It is also unlike the Ch'inan halls in that non-Ong tablets can be placed there. The tablet for the original settler is located in the central room on a separate shelf alongside the altar for the Ong ancestors, and the tablets for uxorilocally married men are placed beside the Ong ancestral tablets, separated from them by a wooden board. For all these differences, though, only a few changes would produce a system similar to Ch'inan's. If the group members were to be more concerned with their image before outsiders, they might remove privately owned articles from the central room and perhaps replace the miscellaneous collection of tablets with a more orderly display. If they became concerned that outsiders see only an agnatically "pure" collection of ancestors, they might decide to relegate all non-Ong tablets, such as those for uxorilocally married men, to another place. If, in addition, all future building were in the form of wings attached to the original compound, or at least took the form of nearby houses whose residents continued to use the central room for worship, an early stage of the Ch'inan system would be approximated.

I do not mean to suggest that all this will happen, or is even likely to, in the case of the Chulun Ongs. It is merely one possibility that could come about under the proper circumstances. In fact, this development seems unlikely for at least two reasons. First, there are not enough sources of income to support more than one or two households of Ongs in Chulun. Apart from farming their modest area of rice paddy, picking tea, and mining coal, they have no opportunities for employment in the immediate area. Unlike Ch'inan, Chulun is much too far away from convenient public transportation to factories or businesses in Taipei to make it possible to commute to work. Consequently, young people who want the relatively attractive wages and working conditions of the city are usually forced to take up permanent residence there. Although none have removed ancestral tablets from Chulun yet, it seems probable that the inconvenience of returning to the village to worship will lead them to do so eventually.

The second thing against this development is that it differs markedly from the pattern followed by other groups in Chulun. There, whenever the population of an agnatic group has increased and the original compound has become too crowded, people have elected to build a new, separate compound some distance away from the old one. Since the residents of the new compound remove their ancestral tablets from the original altar, it does not serve as a ritual center for them. In this way, the separate compounds emphasize their territorial and genealogical separation from each other. In Chulun, where settlement was late and piecemeal, scattered up and down a long, narrow section of flat land along the river, agnatic groups did not come to regard one another as competitive units in a single political system. Divisions within the lineage, marked by separate compounds and altars, take precedence over the unity of the lineage, marked in Ch'inan by impressively decorated ancestral halls that serve as the ritual focus for all members of the agnatic group.

The analysis of Chulun shows that the conclusions reached for Ch'inan are applicable in a nearby community. I would like to show now that these conclusions are also relevant to more distant communities, both in Taiwan and in southeast China. In so doing, I hope to demonstrate that in the study of Chinese ancestor worship, as with other aspects of Chinese social life, one can do more than merely list traits in their varying forms in different communities (see Pasternak 1972a for a systematic analysis of local variation in two villages). It is possible to show, as Maurice Freedman once asserted (1966: 168), that variation is not random. We can make a beginning attempt to understand why the cult of the dead takes the form it does in different communities by isolating the factors that influence its form. Four major questions discussed with regard to Ch'inan seem amenable to comparative analysis. How does the organization of the local community affect the ancestral cult? How do the varying debts descendants owe ancestors affect the extent to which ancestors are worshiped? How does jural authority or discipline exercised over young people affect the benevolence or malevolence of the ancestors? And how do people react to the duty of worshiping the ancestors?

The principal difficulty in attempting such an analysis is the lack of appropriate data in the literature. More often than not those who have studied other Chinese communities have not been centrally concerned with ancestor worship, and so their material is frequently thin on the points that are most important to my own study. As a result, I have been forced at times to make much out of very little—and to speculate where there is no information at all to speak of. For that reason, this enterprise must necessarily be regarded as tentative and exploratory.

I have discussed the way the form of the local community has affected the cult of the ancestors in Ch'inan:* the four lineages, sharing the experience of cooperation for survival but competing in other ways, emphasize the ancestral hall that sets each lineage off from the other three. Ritual signs of demarcation within the lineage—domestic altars, kitchen gods, branch halls—are suppressed. I would expect to find a different situation in a community dominated by a single lineage. The parts of the lineage would face one another rather than other groups and would be free to

---

* Here, as I have done implicitly throughout, I take community to mean members of households residing in a given territory who see themselves as belonging to the same group. In most instances, the group concerned is a nucleated settlement tied together by face-to-face contact and commonly organized projects, commonly owned property, or common ritual responsibilities.

mark internal differentiation with ritual signs. The factors that kept Ch'inan lineages whole and undivided would not be present.

One early study of a single-lineage village, Daniel Harrison Kulp's analysis of Phenix Village, Kwangtung (1925), appears on superficial examination to go against this prediction. Some aspects of the ritual performed there seem very similar to ritual objects and acts in Ch'inan that deemphasize internal lineage differentiation. Kulp tells us, for instance, that in Phenix Village ancestral tablets are kept in cabinets in an ancestral hall.

> In the center [of the hall] is the cabinet containing the small *wei* or ancestral tablets. There is one for each of the departed spirits that are supposed after death to reside in the tablets. . . . They are arranged according to rank in an ascending series of small steps; the most recent at the bottom, the most remote at the top. The oldest and most famous ancestor has a special tablet of greater size and more elaborate decoration. The tablets of husbands and wives are placed together. The cabinet is closed with two doors that are opened at the time of worship (p. 154).

There is certainly a strong resemblance here at first glance to the tablet boxes in Ch'inan. However, when we look more closely at the distribution of the ancestral cabinets in Phenix Village, we find that they seem to mark internal differentiation within the lineage, not its unity. There is not just a single ancestral hall in this village, but several—one hall for the oldest ancestors, two large branch halls for ancestors in more recent generations, and several smaller halls for still more recent ancestors (p. 146). The lineage is internally segmented, and this segmentation is expressed in ritual signs in the community. So it is with the tablet cabinets: there is a cabinet in each of the ancestral halls, and, in addition, smaller ones holding tablets for the most recent ancestors in the homes of the living (pp. 270–71). Hence, the contrast between this single-lineage village with internal lineage differentiation and Ch'inan with a lack of internal differentiation is as predicted. In Ch'inan a single box for each lineage reflects the desire of each lineage to seem undivided; in Phenix Village tablet cabinets reflect either one of the many subdivisions in the lineage or an economic-residential division into households.

Another aspect of ritual in Phenix Village also seems at first to be very similar to the cult in Ch'inan. According to Kulp, the people of Phenix Village do not worship a kitchen god in their homes either, but instead worship a kind of equivalent in the village temple, a god and goddess who are patrons of fruit cultivation (p. 295). The fact is, however, that each household does worship a household deity, though Kulp does not identify it as a kitchen god or as even like a kitchen god. There is in each homestead (compound), he says, "a little household image before which the women burn incense on the days indicated by the calendar as days of good fortune, the first and the fifteenth of each month" (p. 154). This homestead altar with its "household image" may serve one household or several economically separate households, according to him, and seems to be the lowest level ritual center (p. 155). Kulp does not tell us why the pair of gods in the village temple rather than this god correspond to the kitchen god, but it is clear that there is ritual demarcation of households through the worship of this image at compound altars. Just as branch halls and domestic altars have proliferated in this community, so have images worshiped by individual households. These developments have been prevented in Ch'inan by the desire of lineage members to present a single face to the rest of the community.

I have chosen to discuss Phenix Village as an example of a single-lineage village because of the unusual nature of the ritual practices Kulp describes. Without going into detail, let me note in passing that one element of the pattern in Phenix Village occurs also in two single-lineage villages in the New Territories—Sheung Shui and Hang Mei. In neither case is there any other surname group or lineage in the community that comes close to the wealth and numbers of the dominant lineage (Baker 1968: 154; Potter 1968: 20). In these communities, as in Phenix Village, there are ritual demarcations of segmentation at many levels below the founding ancestor. In both communities halls and specially set aside lands serve to set off segments of the lineage, and in both there is ritual demarcation at the domestic level by means of ancestral altars in each home (Baker 1968: 62, 99–117; Potter 1968: 28, 1970: 123).*

---

* Neither Baker nor Potter discusses the kitchen god or any deity that might be worshiped at the domestic level.

Whereas in Ch'inan each lineage is regarded as only one part of the community, leading people to suppress signs of division within the lineage so as to emphasize their unity in the face of the other three, in Sheung Shui, Hang Mei, and Phenix the community and the lineage are coterminous, and ritual symbols of division are multiplied quite freely.

We can also imagine a community made up of several lineages, one more powerful than its fellows. Political alignment could vary. The weak lineages might remain separated from one another and subordinate to the strong lineage, or they might combine forces against the strong one. In the first instance, the situation would resemble that found in Phenix; in the second, competition between the allies and the dominant lineage ought to center on something other than ancestral halls, since the allies would be unable to express unity within the ancestral cult. Some community-centered project—a temple, a school, an irrigation system—would probably become the focus of competition instead. To be sure, there would be no reason ancestral halls could not occur in each lineage, but if they did, I would expect them to be less important than in a community like Ch'inan, where lineages of roughly equal strength compete. Alliances among lineages create boundaries that cannot be expressed by halls and the language of the ancestral cult.

There is some evidence of such a pattern in Taitou, Shantung (M. C. Yang 1945). Of the four lineages (or clans, as they are termed) in Taitou, one, the P'ans, is by far the largest, though it had been on the decline for some ten years when the study was made (pp. 6–7). The major lines of conflict in the village seem to be drawn between the P'ans on the one hand and the other three lineages, the Yangs, Ch'ens, and Lius, on the other. The alignment of the smaller lineages against the P'ans became evident in a dispute over the village school, which was originally run and staffed by the P'ans, though children of other lineages could attend. A scholar in one of the three weaker lineages began to agitate to set up another school, fostering "the idea among the families of the Yang, Ch'en, and Liu clans that their children were not treated as well as the P'ans by the teacher in the P'an clan's school. Since all three clans felt subordinate to the P'an clan, indignation was not difficult to arouse" (p. 161). The conflict was complicated by the fact that most of the members of the weaker lineages had converted to Christianity, which led to disputes between the predominantly non-Christian P'ans and the predominantly Christian Yangs and Ch'ens over the annual village opera. The Christians refused to pay for the opera, which they regarded as an idolatrous thanksgiving to the dragon god, but persisted in attending and enjoying the performances. This, of course, incensed the paying groups, primarily the non-Christian P'ans (p. 160). As one might have predicted, conflict in this village, centered on one strong lineage facing several smaller ones, deals with enterprises outside the ancestral cult: a school and an opera performance.

As one might also expect, ancestral halls do not occur in this community (p. 90). This may be because, as I have suggested, they are not appropriate to demarcate the lines of political division within the community. It may also be, as Yang suggests, because two of the lineages "have been members of the Christian church for a long time and since ancestor worship is regarded as unchristian, it has not been practiced by them" (p. 138). If Christian influence is indeed the major reason for the lack of an elaborate hall cult in the Yang and Ch'en lineages, why is it that the P'ans, who are not predominantly Christian, have no hall? The answer, it seems to me, is that in large part the significance of an ancestral hall lies in its use as a means of competition among the various components of a community. If, as in Taitou, one component does not carry on worship of the ancestors in halls, then there is little point in any other component's doing so.*

There may of course be other explanations of why communities like those discussed above take the form they do. Clearly, just because the main factor that has led to suppression of segmentation within Ch'inan is absent in single-lineage communities, one can-

* It seems unlikely that those of the P'ans who have converted would have been able to prevent the other P'ans from building a hall, since "the several P'an families which belong to the Catholic church are poor and of very low social status, and are considered by their kinsmen as a group of outcasts." (M. C. Yang 1945: 158.)

not conclude that this alone is why segmentation occurs within those communities; likewise, one cannot argue that halls do not occur in Taitou simply because they cannot serve the same functions as in Ch'inan. Many other factors would have to be considered to give a complete account of why these villages are different from Ch'inan. An additional test of the model I offered for Ch'inan would be a multilineage village that more closely approximates the situation in Ch'inan. To the extent that the communities are similar, we would expect the form of the cult to be similar. Such a case is Nanching, Kwangtung, studied by C. K. Yang, in which there are two large lineages and three smaller ones (1959: 11). Both of the large lineages have written genealogies, ancestral halls, and corporate land. The main hall in each case is elaborate: "The main ancestral halls of both the Wong and the Lee clans, with their extensive stone foundations, their fine bricks, their elaborate ornaments of carved brick, wood, and plaster, the mural paintings, the great hard-wood timbers of the pillars and roof joists, the spacious stone-paved yards, and the massive effect of the whole structure, were still inspiring sights" (p. 78).

Both lineages are internally segmented, with branch halls in the village; and one is in fact itself but a branch of a lineage whose headquarters is located elsewhere (pp. 41, 79, 81). Since a major reference group for this lineage lies outside the community, the village of Nanching is different in one very important respect from Ch'inan. This in itself makes comparison difficult. Another important difference is that the lineage founders settled in the area centuries ago, as early as 1091 by Yang's estimate. And, unlike the settlers of Ch'inan, they did not arrive at the same time, or even within a generation of each other. The ancestors of the second lineage came some 100 years after the first settlers, and those of the others still later (p. 12).

Yet there are striking similarities to Ch'inan. The lineages are grouped separately in different sections of the village separated from each other by gates (p. 81). The intense rivalry between the two main clans is expressed in the annual opera each presents for its patron god.

On this occasion, there was a traditional practice of firing rocket firecrackers. Each firecracker shot out a core high into the air, and the clansmen raced for it as it dropped to the ground. The winner would have good luck, and he was given a prize. Since all the prizes were displayed in the ancestral hall and their quality and value were taken as criteria of clan prestige, each clan pressed its members to donate as valuable prizes as they could possibly afford (p. 100).

One year, the poorer of the two clans could not afford a celebration that would match the other's, and so gave no celebration at all. This was a matter of deep humiliation for the members of the clan, and accordingly they vowed to surpass the richer clan's celebration as soon as they could afford it. It seems clear that, as in Ch'inan, the separate lineages are competing with each other for prestige and honor. Also as in Ch'inan, the clans manage to cooperate with each other, in this case through the inter-clan council of elders, which meets to handle such projects as road building and village defense (pp. 99–100).

Some elements common to the Ch'inan case are plainly present: elaborate main ancestral halls; competition between the lineages; cooperation among them for projects of mutual interest. But there is a strong point of difference: both the major lineages in Nanching are internally segmented, and the segments are marked by halls in the village. I hesitate to speculate about reasons for this. It may be merely a result of the length of time the lineages have lived there; it may be that, unlike the lineages of Ch'inan, they never formed a cooperating unit in the early period, and thus came to be less concerned with the community as a unit composed of indivisible parts, each part a lineage. Still, Yang notes that the branch halls are comparatively little used and are decaying and neglected (pp. 79, 93). He suggests this is due not to lack of interest but to lack of funds. Even if he is correct in this, it is interesting that when some aspect of the ancestral cult declined in this village, it was the branch hall that was shunted aside, not the main hall. In Phenix Village, where the divisions in the lineage represent the important subdivisions in the community, it is the main halls, not the branch halls, that are seldom used (Kulp 1925: 146). It is perhaps not too farfetched to ascribe the preference for the main hall over the branch halls in Nanching to the rivalry within the community and the desire of the two major clans to show each other up through their main halls. Again, as in Ch'inan, the shape of the community may have affected the form of the ancestral cult.

In yet another community in which several lineages of roughly equivalent strength exist, a similar pattern occurs. In West Town, Yunnan, described by Francis L. K. Hsu, there are three lineages (among several others) that are known as "big clans" because of their size and wealth (1967: 125). As in Ch'inan and Nanching, there is fierce competition among the lineages: they vie with each other in the ceremonies surrounding funerals and marriages, in preparing genealogies, in building graveyards and ancestral temples. "They always desire something unusual which the other clans do not have. In recent years new devices have gone into these traditional usages. The Ye people built a special temple in the graveyard in honor of their recently deceased parents. The Ws and one of the Ys, who are the *nouveaux riches* of the community, built their ancestral temples in the modern style" (p. 126). This is strongly reminiscent of the competition among the four Ch'inan lineages over the decoration of their ancestral halls and the form of their ancestral tablet boxes.

In respect to elaboration within the lineages, West Town also follows the Ch'inan pattern. Each of the three rich lineages has only one main ancestral hall, even though the members could probably afford to build others (pp. 125–26). Contrary to Freedman's suggestion that segmentation occurs when it is economically feasible, in West Town segmentation is financially possible but is suppressed. It may be that, as in Ch'inan, concern over competition among lineages has worked against segmentation. Here, as in Ch'inan, people seem to pour all their energies into defining the boundaries between lineages rather than developing internal differences within the lineage.

Taking the Ch'inan case as a model for other multilineage communities would lead us to expect not only that branch halls would be relatively unimportant (as in Nanching) or nonexistent (as in West Town), but also that ritual demarcation of households would be unstressed. In both Nanching and West Town, however, households are ritually demarcated by the practice of ancestor worship in domestic units.* This practice contrasts with Ch'inan at the present time when most families still worship immediate ancestors in the ancestral halls. But if the number of households that set up domestic altars increases, it is possible there will eventually be ancestral altars in every domestic unit in Ch'inan, too. It is probable, then, that the relative emphasis on main, as opposed to branch halls, is more widely characteristic of multilineage communities than lack of ritual demarcation of households.

In both kinds of multilineage communities discussed so far, competition among the lineages has been an important factor, though it may be tempered by a feeling, as in Ch'inan, that together the lineage-communities make up, and should continue to be part of, the larger community. This does not keep each lineage from striving to outdo the others, chiefly in ritual matters such as the elaboration of the ancestral hall. If, in another community, such competition were missing, if, for some reason, extensive and important connections across lineage lines made lineage ties less important as a mark of prestige in the community, then we might expect the ritual acts and objects important to people to be markedly different from those in villages like Ch'inan. In particular, to the extent that lineage ties are not crucial we might expect the focus for any competition or cooperation within the community to center on something outside of the cult of the ancestors—perhaps, as in Taitou, on a temple, a school, or an irrigation network.

Tatieh, a village in southern Taiwan described by Burton Pasternak (1972a), appears to follow this pattern. In this village, which has five corporate lineages, there is far less emphasis on agnatic affiliation than in Ch'inan. There is little evidence, for example, of agnatic ties playing an important role in renting land, managing irrigation, exchanging labor, and borrowing money (pp. 22, 28, 32,

---

* C. K. Yang mentions ancestor worship performed by families, though he never discusses in detail the distribution of domestic altars (1959: 195); and Hsu says that every household has a domestic altar (1967: 50). But there is too little relevant information in either author's material to comment on the worship of the kitchen god or an analogous deity.

57). Pasternak argues convincingly that it was the need for cooperation among different surname groups in defending their land and building and maintaining irrigation networks that led to the lack of emphasis on agnatic connections in other areas, kinship and ritual. In particular, rituals associated with lineages are unimportant. In this community the ritual focus is not on the ancestral hall; this means of publicly marking distinctions among lineages has never been used by any of the five corporate lineages. Instead, it is on places devoted to the worship of gods in which all, regardless of agnatic affiliation, can participate. "Tatieh's religious life centers in its main temple and around several smaller shrines. Villagers take special pride in these structures, which are virtually the only community resources to which all villagers enjoy equal access. The temple is an imposing edifice, boasting two towers, a nursery, and a small dormitory of lay devotees" (p. 109).

In Ch'inan, though the need for cooperation among lineages for defense was sufficient to tie the four lineages together in a larger community, there was no minimization of agnatic ties of the sort that took place in Tatieh—perhaps because there was no need for cooperation across surname lines to obtain essential resources such as water and land. Fittingly, in Ch'inan, which is at once a multilineage community and four single-lineage communities, two kinds of ritual centers are important: one that stresses agnatic unity and one that stresses the unity of disparate kin groups living in a single territory. Ancestral halls tower over each lineage settlement, but the newly reconstructed earth-god temple sits poised equidistant from them all.

This of course by no means completes the catalogue of all possible types of communities in China. The point I have tried to make is that in order to understand the form of the ancestral cult (or its relative unimportance), one must look at the organization of the community in which it occurs. Ancestor worship, a form of ritual practice closely associated with the family and lineage, is affected by the presence or absence of other groups that are related, not through kinship, but through membership in the same community.

Turning to a different way in which the cult varies, the Ch'inan case shows that how one is indebted to the dead affects how one must worship them. A person may make no tablet for an ancestor who left no land, or may make offerings on a calendrical holiday for someone who is not a direct ascendant. It is evident that similar considerations of reciprocity are important elsewhere. For example, Fei Hsiao-tung (1939) points out that in Kaihsienkung, a village in the Yangtze valley, receiving additional land requires one to perform more services for the dead: in return for an extra share of land, a person holds the head of the corpse when it is placed in the coffin. Likewise, when a person dies without descendants and without property to hand on, no descendant is appointed to serve him and presumably worship either is not carried out or is done perfunctorily in the course of worshiping another ancestor (p. 77).

With data on this precise point sadly lacking, I can do no more than consider in broad outline what the institution of ancestor worship would look like in a community in which people owe very little to their ancestors. We have seen how quite radical change can take place in an existing and otherwise elaborate system of ancestor worship when people come to inherit less from their ancestors. Members of the Li lineage in Ch'inan have probably ceased making tablets for their ancestors because they no longer inherit ancestral land. From this, we might guess that the ancestral cult would be underdeveloped where no one receives major material benefits from his ancestors.

One community in which the ancestral cult is very minimally developed is K'un Shen, a fishing village in southern Taiwan (Diamond 1969). Its lineages engage in none of the functions associated with ancestor worship: they keep no genealogies, have no halls, maintain no corporate lands (p. 68). The founding ancestors are not remembered; instead, the lineages focus their activities on the worship of patron gods in which people who are not lineage members can participate. Pasternak suggests that the lack of developed lineages in this village is the result of people having to form bonds with anyone—not necessarily kinsmen—who can help in cooperative fishing (1972a: 158–59). Presumably, one could then lay the lack of ritual associated with ancestor worship to the lack of elaborate lineages.

Yet this approach, however enlightening, leaves unanswered questions, for the *tsu* (patrilineage) exists in K'un Shen, albeit in an unusual form: it centers on worship of a god, and non-kin are allowed to join. Nevertheless, Diamond finds (1969: 68) that it is "heavily dependent upon kinship lines." Why could these villagers not worship their ancestors in the context of the *tsu* and rely on some other kind of organization to provide ties with non-kin in the community? There is a flourishing temple in the village that seems admirably suited to this purpose (pp. 85–92). One might reply that given an economic situation strongly favoring cooperation with non-relatives, any additional organization that admits non-kin is advantageous. Yet there is the related problem that the people of K'un Shen seem to minimize ancestor worship in other aspects as well. They remember and worship only their parents, grandparents, and in rare instances great-grandparents (p. 72).

In contrast, concern with ancestor worship seems much greater in Kaihsienkung, where there is no evidence of lineage development but where genealogies are kept by priests, and both tablets and graves are worshiped for five generations (Fei 1939: 76, 84). To understand this variation we need another approach, to look, I think, at how the experience of the members of the community is likely to influence their inclination to worship their ancestors. Norma Diamond makes a suggestion of this kind (1969: 72–73):

The ancestors are poor fishermen, laborers, pond cultivators, and small merchants. Filial piety is strong enough so that people look after the needs of deceased parents, grandparents, and, perhaps, great-grandparents. Beyond that, the memory fades, possibly because there is nothing outstanding to remember. They were ordinary people, as are their descendants, and they left behind no land or wealth to support lineage halls and their elaborate rituals.

In a similar vein, the Ch'inan material suggests that the less one inherits from the ancestors, the less elaborated the ancestral cult. Specifically, where no land is forthcoming, no tablet need be made. It seems plausible, then, that the lack of emphasis on ancestor worship beyond immediately preceding generations in K'un Shen is related to the fact that its people simply owe less to their ancestors for having received less. The majority of households there make their living at fishing. In one section of the village with 146 households, 185 males and 146 females listed this as their major source of income (raft fishing at sea for males, net hauling from the beach for females); only 116 adults listed other occupations (Diamond 1969: 11). It is evident that for the large majority of this population of fisherfolk, so far as inheritance is concerned, there is no equivalent to a farmer receiving land from his father. One does not inherit areas of the sea or the right to fish in certain places. Even though movable goods such as rafts and nets may be inherited, unlike land they need frequent replacement. Also, Diamond says that these goods are often handed down to only one son, leaving the others to make their own way as fish traders or hired laborers (p. 64).

A farmer in Ch'inan who has inherited rice land from his ancestors feels that they secured for him the fundamental source and guarantee of his livelihood. He may have to labor hard and depend on the vagaries of the weather, but he feels assured of having food because he owns land, and for this he is indebted to his ancestors. The farmers of Kaihsienkung, who do not belong to lineages but still worship their ancestors for five generations, similarly emphasize the value of land. As one put it, "Land is there. You can see it every day. Robbers cannot take it away. Thieves cannot steal it. Men die but land remains." In another farmer's words, "The best thing to give to one's son is land. It is living property. Money will be used up but land never" (Fei 1939: 182). It is hard to see how a sea fisherman could feel the same sense of indebtedness; he may inherit some tools of his trade, but fish, the source of his income, cannot be guaranteed him by his forebears.

This comparison between how much people owe the ancestors in fishing as opposed to farming villages is especially interesting since there is some indication of a similar pattern in other fishing villages. In the one Wang Sung-hsing studied, for instance, though he does not say how far back ancestors are worshiped, it is clear the people have no halls, genealogies, or corporate property (1967: 67). Likewise, in the fishing community studied by Barbara Ward, families worship only their own ancestors (again there is no information on how long they continue to do so), and once more there are no genealogies, ancestral halls, or corporate property (1965: 127). Finally, E. N. Anderson tells us (1970: 92) that the boat people he studied "formally sever contact with specific ancestors more than three or four generations removed by 'sending them to the Sky,' i.e., burning the images [carvings of individual ancestors worshiped instead of tablets] in a major ceremony and consigning the ashes to the sea."

For all this, one would not want to push the comparison between K'un Shen and Ch'inan too far. It would be more useful to know if there is comparatively more emphasis on ancestor worship in the one segment of the population in K'un Shen that *can* inherit a means of livelihood—those who own ponds for fish cultivation. (It is not clear how extensive pond cultivation is in the village; only 23 men in the section referred to above listed this as their major source of income, and some number of these merely pay rent for the use of ponds that are owned by the village temple, eliminating the factor of inheritance in their case.) What we would want is a systematic comparison of the elaboration of the ancestral cult in pond-owning and sea-fishing families to see if, as in the Li case in Ch'inan, the lack of concern with ancestor worship is most evident among those segments of the population that have the least to thank their ancestors for.

No matter how unimportant ancestor worship is in any given case, as long as ancestors are believed to exist one can then ask what their temperament is and why. It may be that there is as much local variation in this regard as there is in other aspects of the ancestral cult; otherwise why should Freedman see the Chinese ancestors as generally benevolent, whereas I found them in Ch'inan to be quite malevolent, capricious, and jealous of their power over their descendants. So few studies bear on this point, one would be tempted to pass over it were it not of such importance. What we need to do is to relate this apparent variation in people's views of the ancestors to other aspects of social organization that also vary from case to case. It is possible to do this to a limited extent with Hsu's material from West Town, Yunnan. Hsu tells us (1967: 244–45) that the ancestors "are always well disposed and never malicious toward the members of the families to which they are related. In fact, the question does not arise at all. Their goodwill is so taken for granted that any inquiry on that point appeared to my West Town informants as pointless and ridiculous."

Of the two hypotheses I discussed as possible explanations of the character of the ancestors, the inheritance-guilt-fear theory seems even less applicable in West Town than in Ch'inan. Hsu indicates that sons are expected to divide their inheritance and live in separate households after marriage, maintaining only ceremonial functions in common with their father's household (p. 115). This would probably constitute a more complete release from paternal control before the father's death than in Ch'inan, where land is usually not divided until the father dies. From this we might argue that in West Town, where heirs acquire only *some* jural authority and community responsibility on the father's death, their guilt about having somehow brought about his death and fear of his retaliation would be lessened, and that accordingly an heir would be less likely to attribute misfortune to the hostile acts of an ancestor.

Although this argument may have a certain validity, its conclusion clashes with the facts reported by Hsu. According to him, West Town ancestors *never* harm their descendants. Let us see, then, if the other hypothesis we discussed might be more appropriate. There is some reason to think that it is, for by Hsu's account, child training would seem to be less severe in West Town than in Ch'inan. He says (p. 227) that "compared with some parts of China . . . West Town shows mild parental discipline, and is not very consistent—that is, for the same offense a child may get punished at one time, but not at another—depending upon chance or the mood of the parent concerned." Yet this barely scratches the surface. What we need are systematically collected data on the incidence and extent of punishment and its effect on children. The one piece of evidence from Ch'inan that indicates parents there are remembered from the point of view of children—how they are seen in the underworld—is not available for West Town. In that community, people do not travel to the underworld to see their relatives. Rather, when a dead person (or a god) communicates with the living, he does so by writing in sand with a stylus. From the communications Hsu reports (pp. 174–75), there is no way of knowing what stage of life the deceased is regarded as occupying. The final assessment of what factors influence the character of the ancestors must await further and more systematic studies in Chinese villages or wherever people worship their ancestors.

Thus far in this chapter I have attempted to link certain variables to one another in Chinese communities. This enterprise has ignored another kind of question dealt with in the material on Ch'inan: the villagers' own view of things, which is to say their understanding of their experience and of the whole business of ancestor worship and community organization. In a sense, systematic analysis is irrelevant to these questions; certainly, the people concerned, the villagers of Ch'inan, would find such analysis irrelevant to their own explanations of their acts. For example, the discussion in Chapter 5 of the variables that characterize the lineages in Ch'inan would be virtually meaningless to the people who belong to those lineages. Their understanding of variation in lineage form is in terms of *te-li*: the division among the Ongs is related to their ruined *te-li*; the prosperity of the Lous is associated with their dragon *te-li*. To say that a *te-li* merely stands for some social factor like cohesion is to miss the point. Because the *te-li* is believed to be a real entity, its meaning for those who believe in it can never be encompassed by saying merely that it represents something else. Similarly, an explanation of the character of the ancestors based on a correlation between child-training techniques and supernatural malevolence would mean little to the people of Ch'inan. The closest people came, I think, to telling me how they truly feel about carrying out the requirements of caring for their ancestors in perpetuity was in telling the story of the yellow tails. And this tale, though its analysis is in many ways the most difficult task, is at the same time in many ways the most important part of this study. For here we learn at least part of what ancestor worship means to the people who perform it, and come to understand some portion of what makes it live for them.

Yet in another sense systematic analysis of the indigenous view is useful, and indeed necessary, for it is possible that the way people understand their actions may itself vary systematically. For example, it is conceivable that a tale with the import of the story of the yellow tails, which emphasizes the weight with which the cult of the ancestors burdens people, might occur only in a community with certain characteristics. In particular, we might hypothesize that where the most extensive activities in behalf of the ancestors are carried out, we would be most likely to find such a story told. In contrast, where ancestors are not the focus of elaborate activities, we might expect a story with the sentiments of the yellow-tails legend to be absent. In a word, where there are no lineages, where there is no inheritance of major significance, where jural authority of parents is weak and child training relatively mild, we might find the cult of the dead less elaborated, ancestors more benevolent, and people less likely to tell a tale with the import of the story of the yellow tails. If so, we would have strong reason to believe that the institutions involved in worshiping the ancestors and people's attitudes toward the ancestors vary systematically with each other.

Reference Matter

References

Ahern, Emily Martin. "Affines and the Rituals of Kinship," in Arthur P. Wolf, ed., *Religion and Ritual in Chinese Society.* Stanford, Calif.: Stanford University Press. Forthcoming, 1974.

Anderson, E. N. 1970. *The Floating World of Castle Peak Bay.* Washington, D.C.: American Anthropological Association.

Baker, Hugh D. R. 1968. *A Chinese Lineage Village: Sheung Shui.* Stanford, Calif.: Stanford University Press.

Barth, Fredrick. 1966. *Models of Social Organization.* London: Royal Anthropological Institute Occasional Paper, no. 23.

Bloch, Maurice. 1971. *Placing the Dead: Tombs, Ancestral Villages, and Kinship Organization in Madagascar.* New York: Seminar Press.

Bodman, Nicholas C. 1955. *Spoken Amoy Hokkien.* Kuala Lumpur: Grenier and Son.

Burridge, K. O. L. 1967. "Lévi-Strauss and Myth," pp. 91–115 in Edmund Leach, ed., *The Structural Study of Myth and Totemism.* London: Tavistock.

Cohen, Myron L. 1969. "Agnatic Kinship in South Taiwan," *Ethnology,* 8: 167–82.

Davidson, James W. 1903. *The Island of Formosa, Past and Present: The Historical View from 1430 to 1900.* New York: Macmillan.

DeGroot, J. J. M. 1897, 1901. *The Religious System of China: Its Ancient Forms, Evolution, History and Present Aspect,* vols. 3, 4. Leyden: E. J. Brill.

Diamond, Norma. 1969. *K'un Shen: A Taiwan Village.* New York: Holt, Rinehart.

Fei Hsiao-tung. 1939. *Peasant Life in China: A Field Study of Country Life in the Yangtze Valley.* London: Routledge.

Fortes, Meyer. 1949. *The Web of Kinship Among the Tallensi.* London: Oxford University Press.

Freedman, Maurice. 1958. *Lineage Organization in Southeastern China.* London: Athlone.

———. 1966. *Chinese Lineage and Society: Fukien and Kwangtung.* London: Athlone.

———. 1967. "Ancestor Worship: Two Facets of the Chinese Case," pp. 85–103 in Maurice Freedman, ed., *Social Organization: Essays Presented to Raymond Firth*. Chicago: Aldine.

———. 1969. "Geomancy," pp. 5–15 in *Proceedings of the Royal Anthropological Institute of Great Britain and Ireland for 1968*. London.

———. 1970. "Ritual Aspects of Chinese Kinship and Marriage," pp. 163–87 in Maurice Freedman, ed., *Family and Kinship in Chinese Society*. Stanford, Calif.: Stanford University Press.

Goody, Jack. 1962. *Death, Property and the Ancestors: A Study of the Mortuary Customs of the Lodagaa of West Africa*. Stanford, Calif.: Stanford University Press.

Graham, David Crockett. 1961. *Folk Religion in Southwest China*. Washington, D.C.: Smithsonian Institution.

Hsieh Chiao-min. 1964. *Taiwan—Ilha Formosa: A Geography in Perspective*. Washington, D.C.: Butterworth.

Hsu, Francis L. K. 1967. *Under the Ancestors' Shadow: Kinship, Personality and Social Mobility in Village China*. New York: Doubleday.

Hu Hsien-chin. 1948. *The Common Descent Group in China and Its Functions*. New York: The Viking Fund, Inc.

Johnston, R. F. 1910. *Lion and Dragon in Northern China*. New York: Dutton.

Kulp, Daniel Harrison. 1925. *Country Life in South China: The Sociology of Familism*. New York: Teachers College, Columbia University.

Lambert, William W., Leigh Minturn Triandis, and Margery Wolf. 1959. "Some Correlates of Beliefs in the Malevolence and Benevolence of Supernatural Beings: A Cross-Societal Study," *Journal of Abnormal and Social Psychology*, 58: 162–69.

Lévi-Strauss, Claude. 1963. "The Structural Study of Myth," pp. 206–31 in *Structural Anthropology*. New York: Basic Books.

Pasternak, Burton. 1972a. *Kinship and Community in Two Chinese Villages*. Stanford, Calif.: Stanford University Press.

———. 1972b. "The Sociology of Irrigation: Two Taiwanese Villages," pp. 193–213 in W. E. Willmott, ed., *Economic Organization in Chinese Society*. Stanford, Calif.: Stanford University Press.

Potter, Jack M. 1968. *Capitalism and the Chinese Peasant: Social and Economic Change in a Hong Kong Village*. Berkeley: University of California Press.

———. 1970. "Land and Lineage in Traditional China," pp. 121–38 in Maurice Freedman, ed., *Family and Kinship in Chinese Society*. Stanford, Calif.: Stanford University Press.

Report on the Control of the Aborigines in Formosa. 1911. Taihoku, Formosa: Bureau of Aboriginal Affairs.

Taipei Hsien-chih, K'ai-p'i-chih (Taipei Hsien Gazetteer, Settlement Gazetteer). 1959. Taipei: Taipei Hsien Wen-hsien Wei-yuan Hui.

Turner, V. W. 1968. *The Drums of Affliction: A Study of Religious Processes Among the Ndembu of Zambia*. Oxford: Clarendon Press.

[*Wang*] *P'an Shih, Tsu-tsung Tsu-p'u* ([Wang] P'an Shih's Ancestral Genealogy). 1956. Manuscript.

Wang Sung-hsing. 1967. *Kuei-shan Tao: Han-jen Yü-ts'un She-hui Chih Yen-chiu* (Kwei-shan Tao: A Study of a Chinese Fishing Village in Formosa). Taipei: Institute of Ethnology, Academia Sinica, monograph no. 13.

Ward, Barbara. 1965. "Varieties of the Conscious Model: The Fishermen of South China," pp. 113–37 in Michael Banton, ed., *The Relevance of Models for Social Anthropology*. London: Tavistock.

Whiting, John W. M., and Irwin L. Child. 1953. *Child Training and Personality: A Cross-Cultural Study*. New Haven, Conn.: Yale University Press.

Wolf, Arthur P. 1970. "Chinese Kinship and Mourning Dress," pp. 189–207 in Maurice Freedman, ed., *Family and Kinship in Chinese Society*. Stanford, Calif.: Stanford University Press.

———. N.d. "Gods, Ghosts, and Ancestors." Manuscript.

Wolf, Margery. 1970. "Child Training and the Chinese Family," pp. 37–62 in Maurice Freedman, ed., *Family and Kinship in Chinese Society*. Stanford, Calif.: Stanford University Press.

Yang, C. K. 1959. *A Chinese Village in Early Communist Transition*. Cambridge: Massachusetts Institute of Technology.

Yang, Martin C. 1945. *A Chinese Village: Taitou, Shantung Province*. New York: Columbia University Press.

Character List

Āng-kông	翁公	kû	股
bè	尾	kuān-loûq-îm	關落陰
bō-hoû-cē	不好勢	kūaq-tng	割斷
chŭ	厝	kuì	鬼
Ch'inan	溪南	kuī	跪
Chingmei	景美	liēng-hûn	靈魂
Ch'ipei	溪北	lō-cù	爐主
Ch'itung	溪東	muâ:-pò	麻布
Chulun	竹崙	paì-paǐ	拜拜
cô-kông	祖公	Sanhsia	三峽
Cô-sū-kông	祖師公	sīm-pûà	媳婦仔
Hengch'i	橫溪	sū-thiâ:	私廳
hōng-cuì	風怪	tāng-kî	童乩
iāu-kuăi	妖怪	Tanshui	淡水
î-laŭ uı-cí	以老爲止	taù	斗
îm	陰	tě-â:-pò	袋仔布
ióng	陽	tě-lì	地理
kaì-sū-tē	蓋屍	thaú	頭
khiòq-kŭt	拾骨	thî:	天
khuī-mńg	開門	Thī:-kông	天公
kōng-chán	公田	Thô-tě-kông	土地公
kōng-chŭ	公厝	Thô-tě-mà	土地媽
kōng-e	公的	tiêng	丁
kōng-hoū	公號	tiêng-chŭ	頂厝
kōng-tiêk	功德	tuă-páng	大房
kōng-thiâ:	公廳	zĭp-chŭ	進厝

Index